40,000 YEARS OF MUSIC

Da Capo Press Music Reprint Series

40,000 YEARS OF MUSIC

MAN IN SEARCH OF MUSIC

JACQUES CHAILLEY

Translated from the French by Rollo Myers
With a Preface by Virgil Thomson

DA CAPO PRESS • NEW YORK • 1975

Library of Congress Cataloging in Publication Data

Chailley, Jacques, 1910-
   40,000 years of music.

   (Da Capo Press music reprint series)
   Translation of 40,000 [i.e. Quarante mille] ans de
musique.
   Reprint of the ed. published by Farrar, Straus &
Giroux, New York.
   Includes index.
   1. Music—History and criticism. I. Title.
[ML160.C412   1975]   780'.9   74-31227
ISBN 0-306-70661-X

This Da Capo Press edition of *40,000 Years of Music* is an
unabridged republication of the first edition published in
New York in 1964. It is reprinted by special arrangement
with Farrar, Straus & Giroux, Inc.

Published by Da Capo Press, Inc.
A Subsidiary of Plenum Publishing Corporation
227 West 17th Street, New York, N.Y. 10011

40,000 Years of Music

40,000 YEARS OF MUSIC
MAN IN SEARCH OF MUSIC

JACQUES CHAILLEY
Professor of the History of Music at the Sorbonne

Translated from the French by Rollo Myers
With a Preface by Virgil Thomson

FARRAR, STRAUS & GIROUX
NEW YORK

First published in the French language as 40,000 *Ans de Musique*
by Librairie Plon, 8, Rue Garancière, Paris 6ᵉ
© Librairie Plon, 1961
This translation Copyright © 1964 by Macdonald & Co. (Publishers) Ltd.
and Farrar, Straus & Company, Inc.
Library of Congress catalog card number 64-23125
First American Edition
All Rights Reserved

Published simultaneously in Canada by Ambassador Books, Ltd., Toronto
Printed in the United States

Preface

by VIRGIL THOMSON

As can be seen from the title of this book, its author takes a long view of music's history. In the interests of truth, however, he finds himself taking a dim view of almost everything written about that history before the beginning of the nineteenth century.

If the documented study of music's past grew up right along with the Romantic movement itself, so did most of the art's characteristic elements, as we practise or use it today. The instrumental soloist and the conductor, at least in their present relation to music, are a nineteenth-century development. So are the mechanisms of our woodwind instruments and of all our brasses save the trombone. So, too, is the generalized use of the sensitive and powerful Tourte bow for playing on violins, violas, and cellos. Also the full maturity of the pianoforte and of its literature; and the same is true of the saxophone, the harp, and most of our percussion instruments.

As for musical forms, or species, the nineteenth not only perfected the grand opera, both historical and melodramatic, but previewed, in Lalo's *Namouna*, our own century's development of the symphonic ballet by Ravel, Stravinsky, Dukas, and Debussy.

It gave everybody related to music, moreover, his present role, or assignment—that of the composer as prophet, that of the paying public (itself a nineteenth-century growth, though invented in England more than a hundred years before) as taste-giver, and that of the paid critic (also a nineteenth-century invention) as an aid to music's life-cycle (midwife, policeman, gravedigger).

As a result of all these facts, loyally recounted in the text, Mr. Chailley's forty thousand years of music turn out to be, in the proportion of space they occupy in that text, more like two hundred. But since the same two-century span will cover generously the present age of his own profession, which is that of writing documented history, it is ever so proper of him to describe the present and the past in terms of the instrumentalities that have given his profession what little age it has, compared to music itself.

As a scholar, Mr. Chailley believes with Gertrude Stein that "knowledge is what you know" and nothing else. As a modern historian, he assumes that you only know about the past that which you can prove or demonstrate. And as a Frenchman, though he is not afraid of evidence, or of any of the strange conclusions to which evidence may lead, his working hypotheses are all based on a humane and common-sense view. He assumes, for instance, that every time, including our own, has had its foolish aims. He also believes, from straightforward reasoning, that since music is an auditory art, it communicates truly through the ear. Hence his disdain, in olden times and in present ones, for *augenmusik*, *papiermusik*, and for merely arithmetical arrangements of sound.

He assumes further that musicians are men like other men, not priests or magicians (certainly not in the history of civilized man), and that they can be counted on, if civilization prevails, to make sense to other men. As corollaries to this proposition, three more constitute the bases of his examining procedure. They are:

(1) that a clear expressivity, or meaning, in music is preferable to obscurity.

(2) that in spite of all the evolutions already accomplished and all the dead-ends explored, progress in some direction is still possible.

(3) that no matter how firmly entrenched, error, once made clear, evaporates.

It is not my intention to defend or to question these assumptions. I merely wish to note that they are somewhat different from those of his Central European colleagues. Also that they are bound up with a view of twentieth-century musical developments that opposes radically any belief in Germany's being always and automatically right.

He finds Germany in error, for instance, since about 1890 on the theory and practice of the consonance-dissonance relation. Indeed, with no less courage, he questions the primacy of Italian singing style, based on tonal beauty alone, as opposed to the French, which prizes diction and is not ashamed to serve poetry. He also questions the sincerity today of the Catholic Church's attitude toward all music.

In his own profession, he holds little brief for the music or musical writings of the Swiss Jean-Jacques Rousseau, and he is not vastly impressed by German musical scholars, either. He finds, in fact, that the major historical researches, discoveries, and revivals have mostly been the work of English or French investigators.

As for twentieth-century composition, he accepts the French School as mainstream and considers German music as deviationist. Polyharmony he esteems above dodecaphony, and rhythmic research, as practised West of the Rhine, above numerologically governed or chance-governed note durations. Electronic experiment, as practised anywhere, he finds no fault with, nor much to believe in yet, either.

As a matter of fact Mr. Chailley is less worried about history and musicology, as these are practised today, than about music itself. He thinks composers, even in France, have gone batty. Well, the truth is, I suppose, that they have, if only a little bit. But this is not the first time complexity has been practised as a virtue and for itself alone. Look at the French fourteenth century, for example. Music recovered from that and will no doubt recover from today's pseudo-mathematical and pseudo-mystical career boys.

Indeed, if we who write music today may be forgiven an occasional impatience with those who study its past (because we have not their vocation), those who employ the investigation techniques without fear of the consequences may perhaps give us credit for a similar confidence, and even for a certain optimism, about composing methods.

The composers of the world are masters, after all, in the house they have built, and are therefore entitled to destroy it if they wish, or can. Progress, moreover, we have been led to believe, is always possible in some direction. Hence, we must try all the directions. For even error itself, we have also read, when once made clear, evaporates.

If today's composers cannot inspire in Mr. Chailley the same confidence in our ability to survive artistic error that his treatments of musicological error give us toward the discipline of historical research, we can still ask, in all common sense, that he let us do our own worrying about the methodological problems germane to our own discipline. He should either resume composing, an art which he has in the past practised with some skill, or else leave it to us.

A historian of his learning and wisdom, a writer of his wit and liveliness, a scholar of his courageousness (in debunking Palestrina, for instance, and in questioning the influence of the Florentine *camerata* on the origins of opera), all these could be come upon separately perhaps. But to find them in one man, and that man one with a practical relation to music, is indeed a joy. And his own joy of spirit shows through in every paragraph of this amazing and abundant book. If it had reached its closing half way through, we should not have thought to complain, for we should have come to the ending of a book-length book that has had also a beginning and a middle. But when later, after a long and delightful trip through the byways of "who does what to whom and who gets paid", it reaches a final close, one is sorry it could not have gone on for ever. One had got used by this time to its almost overbearing brilliance of mind and phrase and become accustomed, by their light, to viewing music—its creation, its performance, its history, and the writing of its history—in daintier detail than has been our habit and in a grander correlation than is customarily perceived.

Introduction

Forty thousand years: such is the age attributed by archaeologists to that wall-painting in a cave in the Ariège (Fig. 1, p. 61) which, up to now, seems to be the earliest evidence we possess of the beginnings of our musical history. This means, then, that for forty thousand years music has been in existence and developing without interruption to become what it is today. The instrument pictured on the walls of the cave of the *Trois Frères*, a musical bow, is still used by certain African tribes; and from recordings we possess it seems highly probable that our ancestors of the palaeolithic age must have heard very similar sounds to those produced by these tribesmen today. Since the growth of the science of ethnomusicology during the last twenty years or so, the modest 2,500 years separating us from the music of ancient Greece, which in the old text-books was considered to be the earliest known, now seem quite an insignificant period of time. For you or I can put on a record tonight and listen to music dating from the reindeer or stone age, and follow, up to its very latest trends, the uninterrupted development of an art which has never ceased to evolve, without ever having been extinguished at any time or having had to start again from scratch.

This regression in time of our restrospective musical horizon is accompanied by a remarkable extension in space. The music of other civilizations has ceased to appear to us as the product of an uncultured age, or as an oddity with a slight flavour of comic opera. We know how valuable it is as evidence of the results achieved in the course of an evolution proceeding on lines different from, but parallel to, that of our own music, and having a common origin. For it is one of the aims of modern musicology to seek in this continuous graph the bifurcation points which will enable us to reconstruct the network as a whole. Some are near to us, others more distant; and the lines radiating from these points may be either atrophied or excessively long. The line at the end of which our own modern Western music is situated is, no doubt, one of the longest and most complicated; but if the diagram is correctly drawn up, it should be possible to connect any one point with another, if necessary by the addition of further points of intersection.

This new way of looking at our musical history as a whole makes it more and more imperative to adopt a comprehensive comparative method. Gone are the days when every historian, every theoretician and every pedagogue assumed as a matter of course that the music of his day, after going through a period of crude experimentation devoid of interest, had at last reached a definite and unchangeable degree of perfection. No doubt we are still far from having made the fullest use of this new approach, and it may be twenty years or more before our text-books and programmes show any signs of being conscious of this change in outlook. But what, after all, is that—after forty thousand years of music?

While the archaeologist may experience the thrill of having made a key-discovery at a specific moment of time, nothing of this kind is possible in music. We can leave to the cinema the romantic picture of a Berlioz exclaiming at ten o'clock in the evening: "Heavens above! I'm now going to write my greatest work!"—and at six in the morning falling exhausted over the 230 completed pages of the *Symphonie Fantastique*.[1] The history of music is the history of centuries—of millenniums even—with their store of patiently acquired experience.

Is it any the less captivating on that account? Surely not. Every quaver in our scores, every mechanical gesture of a pianist, every emotional reaction on the part of a listener towards his favourite piece, is the final result of hundreds of successive conquests, now for the most part forgotten, but to each of which a story is attached.

When a Karajan raises his baton in front of his eighty attentive players, when a Heifetz in evening dress before an audience of three thousand starts to juggle with the harmonics and double-stops invented by some Paganini, they are, without knowing it, the direct descendants of the man in a mask scraping his musical bow to subjugate a herd of reindeer. But how many tentative efforts, how many failures and successes, how much research must have been required to make such a transformation possible!

A simple text-book exercise, which is presented to harmony students as a sort of inorganic monster, with precise directions as to how to use it as if it were the latest thing in tin-openers, is in itself a living entity; how it came into being and how it had to fight with others of its kind for survival can be studied in history and in books. Sometimes it succeeded in establishing itself triumphantly and engendered others in its turn. Or else, defeated by opposing forces, it faded away and died. There must be hundreds of composers today who are perturbed at the drama now being enacted in twentieth-century music round the deathbed of tonality.

Whichever way he turns, the musician, when he comes to study his art, finds himself

[1] The statistically-minded reader will be interested to know that this cinematographic exploit represents a total of some five thousand staves to be filled in, in a single night. Assuming an average of five bars to each stave, this leaves little more than one second in which to compose and write down one bar. Not bad, considering that the physical effort alone, in the case of a fairly heavily scored bar—e.g., the third bar of the *Witches' Sabbath*—involves no less than 1,615 movements of the hand, including 172 for the first violin part alone. A lot to do in one second, even for the cinema!

confronted by a thousand problems of which the ordinary practitioner, proceeding automatically, knows nothing: these are the problems for whose solution he must turn to the history of music.

This little game of questions and answers cannot be dealt with in a single volume. Our object in this book is to attempt an examination of some, at least, of these problems, without by any means exhausting the list.

*   *   *

This book will be followed by a parallel study of problems of a more technical character which have been intentionally neglected in the present volume. This continuation, now in preparation, will probably appear under the title: *Music in Search of its Sources*. The subjects dealt with will be, provisionally, as follows: *In search of a system of sol-fa; In search of a theory; In search of a syntax; Outline of a history of music without proper names.*

Contents

PART IV: IN SEARCH OF "STARS"

Sources for Figures

Figures 1, 2 and 3 are from 40,000 ans d'rta moderne by J. A. Mauduit, Paris, Plon 1954; 4 from Bibliothèque de l'Arsenal; 5 from *Musick's Monument* (1676) by Thomas Mace; 6 from *Mélanges d'histoire et d'esthétique musicales* (vol. 1, p. 160), Paris, Richard-Masse 1955; 7 from *Musique nouvelle* (p. 154) by Stückenschmidt, Paris, Editions Corréa 1956; 8 from Universal Edition, London; 9 from *Les disques et leur reproduction phonographique* (p. 9) by Marthe Douriau, Paris, Editions L. R. 1954; 10 from the version of Perotinus's *conductus* "*Salvatoris Hodie*" found in the Wolfenbüttel ms 1206 (Helmstad. 1099, known as W2) f° 31; 11 from the Hearst Collection, Metropolitan Museum of Art, New York; 14 from the Metropolitan Museum of Art, New York, cited by Hickmann in *Revue Belge de Musicologie*, X/1-2 (p. 19), 1956; 15 from Elie Salomon's *Scientia Artis musicae* (1274), Milan, Bibloteca Ambrosiana; and 16 from Bibliothèque du Conservatoire, Paris.

List of Plates

(following page 80)

The publishers wish to thank Giraudon for supplying plates VI,
VIII, X, XXVIII(a), XXIX, XXXI and XXXII.

PART I

IN SEARCH OF A PAST

I

Prologue to A History of The History of Music

"I would never have been minded to write a History of Music from the earliest times down to the present day; I would never even have dared to undertake this task had it not been for some curious *Mémoires* on this subject that I found among some manuscripts left by my uncle the Abbé Bourdelot, well-known to learned men both by his works and by his Academy of Science, and also among the papers of my brother, Bonnet Bourdelot, Physician-in-Ordinary to the King and Chief Physician to Madame la Duchesse de Bourgogne. Although more than twelve hundred authors have treated of this Science, not one has ventured to write its history—not in our tongue, at any rate—either because they were doubtful of succeeding, or had never thought of trying."

The Bourdelot who wrote those lines in a preface in 1715 was not a musician, nor was his name Bourdelot. The writer was a Parliamentary Paymaster named Jacques Bonnet, who was so deeply involved in the mysteries of the Cabbala (rendered notorious by the great "Poisons" case in 1676) that when the time came for him to pay the penalty, he stubbornly refused to confess, protesting loudly that all his life he had had a familiar spirit who warned him of future events, and that he was in no danger of dying, since this spirit had not yet come to warn him.

Moreover his uncle, the Abbé Bourdelot, referred to in this preface, was neither a musician nor an Abbé, except in name and as regards the stipend attached thereto. Nor was his real name Bourdelot, but Pierre Michon. Born in 1610 at Sens, he was also a doctor by profession, and in 1642 was appointed to be the King's Physician. He entered on an exceptionally brilliant career when, after being summoned to Stockholm in 1651 to the bedside of Queen Christina, who was dangerously ill, he was fortunate enough to cure her—an exceptional stroke of luck for a doctor in the seventeenth century. Dying at the age of 75 on February 16, 1685, he left a mass of notes which he had accumulated over a long period with a view to writing something which, up till then, no one had ever thought of doing—a history of music.

It was not until thirty years later that these notes were published. Michon-Bourdelot had bequeathed his manuscripts to his nephew and fellow-doctor, Pierre Bonnet, leaving it for him to arrange for their publication. Bonnet, too, now decided to call himself Bourdelot, but published nothing.When he too died, in 1708, these manuscripts, to which he had added some notes of his own, came into the possession of his brother Jacques. Jacques Bonnet in his turn also took the name of Bourdelot, thus continuing the tradition of this curious avuncular dynasty; but he, at least, finally succeeded in publishing in 1715, through the firm of Cochart in Paris, the first history of music in the French language. If his brother had not been so dilatory in carrying out the instructions of his uncle, this work would actually have been the very first of all the innumerable histories of music that have since appeared.

In the meantime, however, the Bourdelot dynasty had allowed themselves to be overtaken; for five years after the death of Michon-Bourdelot, in 1690, a history similar to his own, and equally bad, was published in Dresden under the following high-falutin' title, somewhat in the style of the "patter" commonly used to advertise their wares by the street-hawkers of those days: "Historische Beschreibung der edelen Sing-und Klingkunst, in welcher derselben Ursprung und Erfindung, Fortgang, Verbesserung, unterschiedlicher Gebrauch, wunderbare Würckungen, mancherley Feinde, und zugleich berühmteste Ausüber von Anfang der Welt bis auff unzere Zeit in moeglichster Kürtze erzehelt und vorgestellt werden."[1] The author of this *Historische Beschreibung*, Wolfgang Kaspar Printz, known as von Waldthurn (this being the name of the town in the Palatinate, on the borders of Bohemia where he was born in 1641) also seems to have been a picturesque character. As a youth he had studied both theology and music, and had learned to play the organ, violin and trombone. He began his career as a theologian, and soon got into serious trouble as a result of his preaching in favour of Luther throughout the Palatinate. He was thrown into prison, and only obtained his freedom by promising to give up preaching. Whereupon he took up music again, and entered the service of the Palatine Elector as a tenor in the chapel choir. He was unable, however, to rid himself of his obsession with theology or to steer clear of controversy, with the result that, without waiting for an answer to his arguments, he ran away and took to the road, travelling under a strict incognito. His journey, if we are to believe his

---

[1]"An historical description of the noble art of singing and instrumental playing presenting and relating, in as concise a form as possible, its origin, its invention, its development, its improvements, its various uses and wonderful effects, its numerous enemies as well as its most celebrated practitioners from the earliest times down to the present day." Bourdelot's title is less prolix but no less ambitious: "A History of Music and of its effects from its origin down to our own times." In later editions (of which there were six, published up to 1743 in Paris, Amsterdam, The Hague and Frankfurt) this title was expanded to read: "A History of music from its origin; the progress achieved in this art up to the present, and a comparison between French and Italian music." But this addition to the original title is merely an admission of a plagiarism, the author having incorporated in his original book material "lifted" from a pamphlet by Lecerf de la Viéville (the "comparison" etc.) which had appeared in 1705. . . .

picaresque autobiography, ended in the most romantic circumstances. Finding himself at the end of his resources (so he tells us), he was engaged by a Dutch traveller, whom he had met on the road, as his servant, and visited with him a large part of Germany and Italy. On reaching Mantua, he fell ill and was abandoned by his master. When he had recovered, he went back on foot along the same road, intending to return home through Bavaria. But while passing through Promnitz, he obtained an audition, and was appointed on the spot Kapellmeister to the Count. However, the outbreak of war in 1664 and the death of the Count left him destitute, and once again he took to the road. After that he became Cantor at Triebel, and subsequently at Sorau, where he married, and where, fifty-two years later, in 1717, he died.

*   *   *

Neither Bourdelot nor Printz had written a masterpiece. Although the works of this French doctor and German preacher are not altogether without interest in the parts relating to their own time, what they have to say about earlier periods is nothing but a lot of nonsense. But they were the first men ever to write a history of music. As Jacques Bonnet himself pointed out with justifiable pride: "Although more than twelve hundred authors have dealt with this science, not one had ever ventured to write its history." No doubt because, until a curiously recent date, no one had considered that such an enterprise would be of the slightest interest. Until the middle of the eighteenth century, in fact, there was only one kind of "live" music that aroused any interest, and that was modern music. Talk of being "acclaimed by posterity" and of "the greatest work of my life" were merely romantic inventions for the benefit of disappointed composers. Even in Bach's time music, as Roland Manuel has pertinently pointed out, was still a "seasonal commodity" intended for immediate consumption, which then disappeared without causing anyone any surprise or regrets. Fifty years was the maximum period during which a work remained in circulation. After that, it was forgotten and replaced by something else. What was the good of keeping up old memories? The thing was already dead and of no interest to anybody. Perrault tells the story of the Sleeping Beauty, in which everyone continues doing whatever he or she was doing a hundred years ago: the valet brings the tray which a century ago he had gone to the kitchen to fetch; the horse finishes his century-old nosebag; the orchestra takes up, from the bar where it had stopped, the minuet it was playing when the Princess pricked her finger on the fatal bobbin. And, adds the author: "Although this music was a hundred years old, it nevertheless sounded very pleasing." Can one imagine, asks Roland Manuel, such a remark being made today? Let us imagine a musician waking up in 1957 and playing something composed in 1857. No doubt he would be in the middle of, perhaps, a waltz by Chopin (who would only have been dead eight years when the player fell asleep)—unless his taste was for Liszt or even Wagner (who was then working on the *Ring* and would soon be starting *Tristan*); or maybe he was engaged on an aria from *La Traviata*, or some melody by Schumann who had just died. The same basic repertory, in fact, that forms the staple fare of our operatic and symphonic audiences today—the only alternative to which is music of a still earlier age. No doubt it is only right that we should continue to enjoy this music. But did the music of Rameau seem vital or significant to Schumann? And when Lully was in charge of his "24 violons du Roi" did anyone give a thought to Goudimel or Costeley? And did they, in their turn, take any interest in Binchois or Dufay, any more than the latter were at all concerned with Guillaume de Machaut, for whom Perotinus was already a dead letter? And yet the distance between these different stages is about the same.

Thus it is that throughout the centuries people have been interested only in the music of their own time.

Music's first historians, in fact, were the poets.

2

Antiquity and the History of Music

The poets, then, were the first historians of music. There is scarcely a civilization which does not possess some charming legend describing the origin and creation of this marvellous art. In nearly every case it is a god who discovers it, before passing it on to mankind. This, for example, is how the Chinese describe the invention of the scale. The legend dates from the third century B.C., but it is doubtless an echo of a much earlier tradition:

"The Emperor Hoâng-ti, wishing to endow music with fixed notes, sent his Master of Musick to the confines of his empire—some say to the north, others to the west. This was a kind of Promised Land—a place which had been discovered a thousand years before our era by King Moù, who found such happiness there that he never returned. But Hoâng-ti's minister did go back because he had important news for the Emperor: in the depths of a secluded valley he had seen some marvellous bamboo trees, all the same size. Having cut one of the stems between two knots, he blew into it, and produced a sound. And the sound that emerged was the sound of his own voice when he spoke calmly and without passion. It was also the murmur of the stream called Hoâng-hô which had its source in the same valley. After that, two birds, a male and female Phoenix, came and settled in a tree; first one bird sang six notes, starting from this same sound, and then the other sang six more notes that were different. On hearing this, the minister cut eleven more bamboo tubes which, together with the first one, corresponded to what he had just heard. And he presented to his master these 'sound measures', which were named *liu*, meaning *laws*. He had succeeded in his mission."[1] In all mythologies there are similar legends to explain the origin of music.

According to a Hindu tradition, "music was in the beginning an essentially sacred art, practised in the paradise of Indra by the Gandharvas (spirits) and the Apsaras (nymphs), which Brahma took from the *Vedas* and revealed to mankind through the intermediary of the *Munis*, or members of an ascetic confraternity. The discovery of music is also attributed to Sarasvati, goddess of eloquence and the arts."[2] The Sumerians named the

[1] Cf. Louis Laloy, *La Musique chinoise*, pp. 38–39.
[2] J. Grosset, in Lavignac's *Encyclopaedia*, I, 269.

5

goddess Nina as the patroness of music[1] and the Assyrians called Istar "the harmonious and sweet-toned flute".[2] Greek mythology is so rich in divine attributes that one has the choice between Phoebus-Apollo and Orpheus (whose cults were, in the end, identical)[3] or again Amphion, son of Zeus who, according to Heraclides[4] had evidently learned from his father the art of playing the cithara and writing poetry to be sung to its accompaniment.

The Hebrews were almost alone amongst the peoples of antiquity in crediting music with an historical rather than a supernatural origin. Whether we like it or not, the Bible ascribes the invention of music to the seventh generation in the descendance of Cain; for the eldest son of Adam and Eve, in the Book of Genesis, had a son Enoch; "and unto Enoch was born Irad; and Irad begat Mehujael; and Mehujael begat Methusael; and Methusael begat Lamech. And Lamech took unto him two wives: the name of the one was Adah. . . . and Adah bare Jabal: he was the father of such as dwell in tents, and of such as have cattle. And his brother's name was Jubal: he was the father of all such as handle the harp and organ."[5] This is why Jubal,[6] surrounded by musical instruments, is sometimes represented in mediaeval Christian miniatures or sculpture.

Nevertheless, a Dominican monk of the thirteenth century, Brother Jerome of Moravia, author of an important treatise on music, is unwilling to accept without reservations so regrettable an ancestry. "Moses," he writes, "certainly speaks of this Jubal; but others state that the inventor of music was Linus,[7] Thebeus or Zelus. Others believe it was Amphion[8], while Boethius with good reason credits Pythagoras with the honour."[9]

[1]Ch. Virolleaud and F. Pélagaud, *ibid.*, 1, 38.

[2]*Ibid*, 43.

[3]Cf. W. K. C. Guthrie, *Orpheus and Greek religion*.

[4]Pseudo-Plutarch, *De Musica*. [This work, which was for a long time attributed to Plutarch, is now considered to be apocryphal.   Translator's note.]

[5]Genesis IV, 17-21. In the Vulgate: *Pater canentium cithara et organo*. The word *organum* is evidently a neologism, if meaning "organ".

[6]Not to be confused with his half-brother Tubal or Tubal-Cain, "an instructor of every artificer in brass and iron". It is noteworthy that *Genesis* seems to situate the birth of instrumental music in the iron or bronze age. It is difficult to accept this literally, since we have traces of musical instruments dating from the palaeolithic era.

[7]Son of Apollo and Terpsichore, who received from his father the gift of a lyre with three strings made of linen thread. But because he replaced these with strings made of catgut, which were much more harmonious, the jealous god destroyed his son. (See Fr. Noel. *Dictionnaire de la Fable*, 1815.) Plutarch mentions also a certain Linus of Euboea.

[8]Son of Jupiter and Antiope, wife of Lycus, King of Thebes. Mercury, whose disciple he was, gave him a lyre which helped him to build the walls of Thebes. The beautiful adaptation of this legend by Paul Valéry, with music by Honegger, is well known.

[9]de Coussemaker, *Scriptores*, 1, 6.

The fact that a Dominican friar in the great Age of Faith should thus place Hellenic mythology on the same level as the Scriptures is striking proof of mankind's need to ascribe to music a supernatural origin—and also of the strength with which the traditions of ancient Greece persisted three centuries before the age of Humanism.

*   *   *

It is to this same source that our own traditions can be traced, as regards both the history and theory of the art. At least, that is how it seems to us—perhaps because no Chaldaean, Hittite or Sumerian texts have been preserved. A dialogue, for a long time attributed to Plutarch,[1] the historian and moralist in the first century A.D., contains the first "history of music" known to us. In it the legendary names of Amphion, the centaur Chiron and the satyr Marsyas are juxtaposed with those of historical figures such as Sappho or Archilochus; but it also contains historical facts, an outline of theory and a list of works.

This, in the history of musical literature, is an altogether exceptional case. The Greeks wrote a lot about music but, with the exception of the "psuedo-Plutarch", chiefly as philosophers and theoreticians rather than as historians. The only scraps of historical information we can ever glean are always to be found in some dialogue or pedagogical treatise; and even then, such information is usually based on vague traditions in which an obvious element of legend overlays something more substantial, which may be either factual or symbolic. For legend is not confined to mythology; great men even have their own. One of the best endowed in this respect was the celebrated Pythagoras, the great mathematician of the fourth century B.C., who is not only credited with having demonstrated the *pons asinorum* theorem familiar to every schoolboy, and having invented the multiplication table, but is also considered to have laid the foundations of musical theory. Cicero tells, in the *De consiliis*, how one day when some drunken sailors from the Sicilian port of Taormina, excited by the frenzied sound of Bacchic music, had forced the door of an honest woman, Pythagoras, who happened to be passing just then, calmed them instantly by ordering his flute-player to play a slow, solemn hymn. Boethius, who also relates this story, tells another about a courtesan shut up in a rival house who was trying to set the building on fire. Pythagoras, who was engaged in observing the stars in the vicinity, saw what was happening and concluded that the woman must have been excited by some music in the Phrygian mode. Seeing that the remonstrances of her friends were of no avail, he promptly sent for a musician and ordered him to play something in a different mode, whereupon the woman's anger left

[1]Actually, no doubt, a later compilation dating from the time of the Emperor Hadrian (second century A.D.). Cf. below, p. 10, also François Lasserre, *Plutarque*, p. 104.

her. His disciples looked upon this great man as a kind of super-human personage, almost a demi-god. It was said of him that he could hear the music of the spheres, understand the language of animals, converse with rivers and remember previous existences.[1] Such extravagant claims in fact were made for him that modern critics began to wonder whether the personage himself was not a myth.

Everywhere music was looked upon, not as an art to be enjoyed, but as a powerful means of action in the field of religion, morals and society. Plato made it one of the foundations of his Republic. Boethius recalls that the Spartans lodged an official protest when Timotheus added another string to the lyre.[2] Terpander and Arion cured the Ionians and Lesbians of grave illnesses by their singing, and Hismenias relieved the Boeotians of their gout in the same way. Empedocles used the same method to calm the rage of one of his guests. These legends were still current even after the Middle Ages; and as late as 1641 a priest, Fr. Kircher, actually published the tune required to cure the bite of the tarantula (See Plate 1).[3]

The eighteenth century, so far from throwing doubt upon these stories, tried to give them a new lease of life. Bonnet-Bourdelot, in 1743, records that a famous Court physician told him how he cured "a high-ranking lady who had been driven mad by the fickleness of her lover; he had rigged up an alcove in her bed-chamber where musicians could play without being seen. They played for her three times during the day, and at night sang appropriate airs, some melancholy, others calculated to restore her reason, chosen from the finest passages in the operas of Lully. This went on for six weeks for the purpose of restoring her to her right mind; and the expense was justified since the experiment was crowned with success." In the nineteenth century stories of this kind were scoffed at; but in the twentieth they are no longer treated as a joke, because today we know that among primitive peoples music is used for such purposes; indeed, in some quarters the question is being seriously discussed as to whether it might not be desirable to make use of music's undoubted powers in this direction by applying them to more prosaic ends, such as industrial productivity.[4]

[1]Cf. Carcopino, *La Basilique pythagoricienne de la Porte Majeure*, p. 175.

[2]It is difficult to imagine today an Act of Parliament forbidding composers to resolve the flattened seventh upwards, or to omit the retrograde movement in a serial composition! And yet the example of the U.S.S.R. at the time of the Jdanov decrees in 1948 shows that we can never be certain of anything.

[3]Even today in the south of Italy music is used to cure the bite of this spider and is accompanied by an elaborate ceremony which takes place in church at the altar of St. Paul but in the absence of the clergy. No particular air is required today, but whatever music is performed, according to the initiates, must be played at a faster speed than usual. A film of a ceremony of this kind was made recently by D. Carpitella and shown at the ethno-musicological Congress at Wégimont in 1960.

[4]Cf. W. L. Landowski, *La Musique fonctionnelle*, Paris.

Another characteristic of these "historical" fables of antiquity is to ignore completely the concept of progressive evolution and to present everything in an excessively simplified manner, complete with name of author and patent of invention. For example, in order to explain the "enharmonic mode"[1] the pseudo-Plutarch does not think of observing in actual practice, as we should today, the phenomena which prepare the way for and justify this conception in a way that is universally acceptable.[2] He must needs find an "inventor": "One day, when Olympus was playing a piece in which he often skipped a note, he noticed that this produced a pleasing effect. By bringing together two identical phrases he then obtained a scale which he found admirable and in which he then started to compose."[3] This rather naïve conception of evolution was to become general.[4] An eminent authority on sonata form has hit upon a picturesque formula to define the viewpoint of modern musicology: "It is the old riddle again: how many grains does it take to make a heap of corn?"[5] Until the beginning of the nineteenth century hardly anyone had thought of stating the problem in this way. Musical history was written as if the heap of corn had all come out of the same ear of wheat, neatly wrapped up and labelled with the name of the producer and the exact date of its "invention".

This curious failure to understand the process of evolution has had an unexpected sequel. So long as it was the accepted attitude which everyone took for granted—and perhaps for that very reason—it does not seem to have troubled composers or to have caused them to do anything about it. Until the beginning of this century not one of them ever boasted of having invented a new form or a new chord or a new technique

[1]A form of scale in which two notes out of four are displaced so that there is only a quarter-tone between them and the notes that follow.

[2]Greek music, like many primitive forms of music that flourish today, had "fixed" and "mobile" sounds, which can readily be accounted for by the way in which the intervals were formed. The "mobile" sounds vary in pitch according to whether they are more or less attracted by their neighbouring "fixed" sounds. In our own classical music the same thing can be observed in an attenuated form; e.g., certain degrees of the minor scale vary according to the direction in which the melody moves—i.e., upwards or downwards.

[3]Lasserre: *Plutarque*. We have condensed the quotations and eliminated technicalities which would mean nothing to the lay reader. Whenever necessary, the same procedure will be followed in all quotations throughout this book.

[4]Even in the nineteenth century we are told that the stave was "invented" by Guido d'Arezzo, although it is possible to follow its gradual evolution through various stages on MSS. over a period of three centuries. It is also proclaimed that sonata form was "invented" by Carl Philip Emmanuel Bach, whereas all its different features had made their appearance one by one during the preceding century, and C. P. E. Bach himself was no more committed to this form than many of his contemporaries.

[5]Eugène Borrel, *La Sonate*, p. 57.

of composition.[1] It was just at a time when musical historians were beginning to repudiate the notion of sudden "inventions" and to discover that underneath every step forward there is a continuous process which is beyond the control of the individual creative artist, that the latter, unwittingly taking a backward step, began to show a desire to pose for posterity as "inventors" and to base their researches on premisses which had just been definitely discredited.[2] One composer even got a colleague to draw up a certificate attesting that he had employed a certain procedure on a date which enabled him to claim priority in this field![3] A great deal of contemporary music is, in fact, based on systems that have been "invented", dated and signed. Schoenberg would certainly never have thought of turning to Plutarch to find the psychological bases of his "revolution". Yet he would have found them there.

*   *   *

There may have been other histories of music dating from antiquity. According to the latest scholar [François Lasserre: *Plutarque*] who has studied this text, the *De Musica* by the "pseudo-Plutarch" seems itself to be a *résumé* compiled from an important earlier work, now unfortunately lost, namely a "History of Music" in fifty-six volumes by the younger Denys of Halicarnassus, written during the Emperor Hadrian's reign (second century A.D.) and issued a century later in a shortened version in five volumes by a certain Rufus; to this same source may be traced the biographical notes on musicians and poets attributed to Hesechius of Miletus and preserved by Suidas.

[1]Beethoven or Wagner, for example, who were genuine innovators, took credit for having enlarged the boundaries of music generally, but never for having introduced any technical innovations. Though Wagner christened his work *Zukunftmusik*—"music of the future"—he was referring to his aesthetic theories about the theatre—precisely that part of his work which has been most severely criticized by posterity. In all his copious writings he never so much as mentions any of his inspired harmonic innovations. Again, when César Franck was writing programme notes on works which his master d'Indy had proclaimed to be the prototypes of new, revolutionary forms, he has nothing to say about technical processes which he likened to laboratory prescriptions which, in the opinion of most composers, are of no interest to the public who are only concerned with the result. (Cf. L. Vallas, *La véritable histoire de César Franck*, p. 338.) Debussy, too, in all his witty, picturesque and lively writings about music never even mentions such a thing as a "chord of the ninth" or a "whole-tone scale" which, as everyone knows, are two of his most obvious personal idiosyncrasies.

[2]These "inventions", hailed in specialist circles as "taking one's stand" or as a "clarification of dazzling revelations", are often only comprehensible or clear to initiates. "If, for example," writes H. Stückenschmidt in *New Music*, p. 154, "you take an augmented sixth as the basis of a mobile chord, and go on lowering its intervals by a semitone until you reach a diminished third, you will then get a total of eleven notes and twelve intervals whose upper and lower halves complement each other, being the equivalent of two triple major chords combined with a tritone. . . . This constructivist approach, which liquidates the old ideas of consonance and continuity of sound which we associate with the romantic epoch, and makes a valuable contribution . . . etc." Have you understood all that? I could not, or at least not until I had thought about it for some time, pencil in hand. . . . But see below, p. 113.

[3]N. Obouhow, *Traité d'harmonie tonale, atonale et totale*, Paris, Durand, 1947, p. III.

The *De Musica* abounds in inconsistencies and contradictions; it is nevertheless a valuable and at times irreplaceable source of information. It follows Plato in adopting the traditional form of a "Symposium":—

"On the second day of the feast of Cronos, the worthy Onesicrates invited to a banquet a number of guests well versed in the art of music. These included Soterichos of Alexandria and Lysias, one of his assistants. After the usual rites had been performed, the former spoke as follows: 'My friends, the conclusion of a feast is hardly a propitious moment for discussing the mechanism of the human voice: such a study is better undertaken at a time when our minds are less clouded by the fumes of wine. But since the best grammarians define sound as a disturbance of the air that is perceptible to the ear, and since only yesterday we were discussing grammar . . . let us now consider the second of the sciences devoted to sound—I think this must be music. . . . Therefore it is now your turn to tell your companions who was the first to practise this art: what progress it has made in the course of time; who has obtained distinction in the art of music; and, finally, what is its purpose, and how useful has it proved to be.' Everyone present then spoke in turn, some citing Heraclides, others Alexander, Aristoxenes or Aristophanes, with plentiful references to Homer, Plato and Aristotle. After that, Onesicrates pronounced a thanksgiving, poured out libations in honour of Saturn and his divine offspring and of the Muses, and dismissed the company."

That was to be the last ceremony of this kind for the next thousand years.

3

Histories of Music in the Middle Ages

Works of this nature in the Middle Ages often contain valuable information about their own period, but scarcely ever look backwards to the past. On the rare occasions when it occurs to a theoretician to begin his treatise with a little historical preamble, he seldom does more than refer to Boethius or Guido d'Arezzo, or else regales his readers with a lot of more or less childish legends.

They are interested, among other things, in the origins of music and in the etymology of the word. In the opinion of some, *musica* is derived from the word *moys*, water, because according to the pseudo-Sidrach, it was invented by Japhet when listening to water flowing over the rocks; but Jerome of Moravia refers to a system of hydraulics which *dicitur ab ydor quod est aqua*, while Isidore of Seville adds: *id est a querendo*. Jean Cotton, on the other hand, prefers to invoke the "muse" in the word *cornemuse*, and another theoretician of the thirteenth century speaks of *musicam quasi moduficam, id est a modulatione*. For a history of medieval music we have to rely today on old archives, analyses of works or of practical handbooks and reconstructions of incomplete commentaries; no historical prototype based on first-hand evidence has ever been attempted. One of the most prolix authorities on the subject was an Englishman who would never have guessed that he would one day be known as "de Coussemaker's fourth anonymous writer". Writing at the end of the thirteenth century a treatise principally concerned with notation, he ends a chapter on the rule of "propriety" and "perfection" by pointing out that these rules, now out of date, were in force at the time of . . . and then proceeds to outline in half a dozen paragraphs a historical sketch going back to the beginning of the preceding century. In the same way, he describes the old choir books that were used in an earlier age; and it is entirely owing to this allusion (interspersed with the lecture notes of Johannes de Garlandia) that we first learned the names of the two greatest composers of the twelfth century, Leoninus and Perotinus; had it not been for this lucky find, their works would never have been identified, as they are in manuscript and anonymous. Until the end of the thirteenth century, the biographies and even the names of musicians were of no interest to anyone. We shall never know the names of those responsible for the great burgeoning of Gregorian Plainsong; the only names that crop up in this connection are those of poets, such as Venantius Fortunatus, Theodulf of Orleans, or Hilarius of Poitiers. In the thirteenth century again, St. Thomas Aquinas is cited as the author of the celebrated sequence *Lauda Sion;* but this could only be as far as the words are concerned, because the melody existed long before this time; for example, we find it being used in the twelfth century by Adam de Saint-Victor and a certain Hugues, known as the Primate of Orleans. But who was the author of the melody itself? Was there even an author, in the sense in which we understand the term?[1]

The first composers to emerge from anonymity and to take a definite place in the history of music, no doubt owed this distinction to the fact that they were poets as well as musicians: these were the *trouveurs*—known as troubadours in the south of France, and *trouvères* in the north; and after them came their foreign rivals. But this privileged position was perhaps partly due to the social status of the earliest troubadours, of whom the very first was no less a personage than the Duke of Aquitania, Guillaume IX, Count of Poitiers who at the age of twelve owned territory in comparison with which that of the King of France was no more than a mere province. It is quite possible, even, that before him there were other poet-musicians who, on account of their humble origins, have been forgotten. Experts have often wondered how it was possible for an isolated figure, such as Guillaume, to have attained such perfection in his art, starting from scratch, as it were, if he had had no predecessors; is not the explanation perhaps to be found in this simple difference of social status?

In any case, it was the troubadours who initiated this taste for musical biographies which was to be an essential feature of the musical literature of later ages—especially when one considers the prominent part played in this literature by the fashionable form of *vie romancée.* There are fifteen troubadour manuscripts in which the actual music is preceded by more or less extensive biographical notices. For a long time these were considered to be historical documents, until the day when some authentic, but indiscreet, historians took it into their heads to verify the facts related therein—as many, that is to say, as could be verified—and there were quite a lot. The results were catastrophic. Let us take an example. The biographer of Bertrand de Born tells a pathetic story, which was accepted by all the historians of the last century (e.g., by Henri Martin in his *Histoire de France*), according to which the English King, Henry II, after the siege of Hautefort, had forced the troubadour-owner of the castle to surrender. When the latter came before the king, Henry is reported to have said to him: "So you are the man who has

[1]For information as to what was understood by musical composition in ecclesiastical circles in the Middle Ages, see the remarkable work by S. Corbin: *L'Eglise à la conquête de sa musique* (Gallimard, 1960) which appeared after the present volume had gone to press.

always boasted of his accomplishments?"—"Alas!" replied Bertrand, "there was a time when I could have made such a claim: but ever since I lost your son (that is to say, Richard Cœur de Lion, who was also a *trouvère*) I have lost whatever skill or learning I may have possessed." On hearing his son's name, the King began to weep, and answered: "I can well understand that you have lost your powers, for it was you he loved above all; and so, for love of him, I give you back your freedom, your possessions and your castle."[1]

Unfortunately, it was not Henry II but his son Richard who conquered Bertrand; this one biographical notice alone contains five other historical mistakes of the same order.

These biographies of the troubadours or *razos* as they were called, seem to have been compiled during the thirteenth and up to the beginning of the fourteenth century, for the use of the *jongleurs* (itinerant musicians) who, since they earned their living through these songs, found it to their advantage to accompany them with a few notes about their authors. Several of these *razos* are signed by the same biographer, one Uc de Saint-Circ. Now we know something about this personage; he was, in fact, a *jongleur* who in the years around 1210 was wandering about in Languedoc and neighbouring provinces, and after 1220 travelled through Italy, which seems to have been the source of many of these *razos*. The more fanciful the biography, the more likely it was to please. Modern scholars have discovered the source of many of these stories; more often than not they were inspired by some incident or other in the songs themselves. Peire Vidal had composed his in honour of a lady nicknamed *Loba*, or She-wolf. For this reason "he found it gallant to take the name of 'Wolf' himself, and declared his willingness, no matter how great the risk to play the part of this wild animal":

> Si l'on veut que "Loup" sois nommé
> Ne le tiens pas a déshonneur
> Ni que sur moi crient pasteurs
> Ni que je sois par eux chassé.
>
> . . . .
>
> La "Loba" dit que je suis sien:
> Ce disant parle-t-elle bien.
> (Ed. Anglade, 1923, pp. 106-7)

("If I am to be known as 'Wolf' it is no dishonour to be denounced or hunted by the shepherds. . . . If my 'Loba' says I belong to her, then what she says is right.")

[1]Cf. Jeanroy: *La poésie lyrique des troubadours*, 1934, I, p. 100.

Now let us see what our "biographer" makes out of this: "Not content to have a wolf emblazoned on his coat of arms, the poet puts on a wolf's skin, and thus disguised, takes to the mountains. Shepherds and their dogs give chase, and after being bitten and beaten up, he is carried half dead to his lady's castle, where she and her husband are vastly entertained by this amusing escapade." (Jeanroy, p. 112.) The same "biographer" also relates that Peire Vidal believed he had a claim to the empire of Constantinople, having married a Greek woman who, he had been told, was the niece of the Emperor of that city. Jeanroy explains this as follows: "The adjective *emperial* is sometimes used by the poet in the sense of *reial*, a synonym for splendid, dazzling, incomparable. Since he considered himself superior to all his rivals, in accordance with a tradition which is perhaps not peculiar to those days, it was only natural that he should assume the title of Emperor of the Troubadours, as he had probably done in one of his works which has not survived; in another, which has happily been preserved, in order to explain the esteem in which he was held by the Genoese, he assumed the title of *emperaire dels Genoes*." Hence the attribution.

It is to a work of the same description, the *Récits d'un ménestrel de Reims*, that we owe the legend (which is still current) according to which the *jongleur* Blondel (who has been identified as the troubadour Blondel de Nesles) succeeded in discovering Richard Cœur de Lion in his remote dungeon and in making himself known to him by singing the verses they had composed together. This, as is well known, is the subject of Sedaine's *Richard Cœur de Lion* which Grétry turned into one of the most famous *opéra-comiques* of the late eighteenth century; and, during the Revolution, Sarrette, the Director of the Conservatoire, was thrown into gaol because one of his pupils had been overheard through the window playing on his horn Blondel's famous air: *O Richard, Ô mon roi*. . . .

The most celebrated and the most touching of all these *razos* is undoubtedly the one that gave Edmond Rostand the idea for his play *La Princesse lointaine* (later set as an opera by Witkovsky) after having already inspired Petrarch and Swinburne. It is worth quoting once more in its original text: "Jaufre Rudel de Blaye was a man of noble lineage, Prince of Blaye, and he became enamoured of the Countess of Tripoli without ever having seen her through hearing her praises sung by pilgrims coming from Antioch; and he wrote many poems about her, with good music and poor words" (here the narrator does himself an injustice in expressing an opinion which is by no means shared by modern scholars). "And moved by a desire to see her, he embarked on a crusade and crossed the seas. But on the voyage he fell ill, and was taken to an inn at Tripoli where he lay nigh unto death. When this came to the ears of the Countess, she came to his bedside and took him in her arms. And he knew it was she, and recovered his sight and hearing and sense of smell, and praised God who had preserved his life long enough for him to see her. And so it was in her arms that he died; and she caused him to be buried with pomp and ceremony in the House of the Temple, and on that same day, in sorrow for his death, she became a nun."

When we read this charming story, we feel inclined to curse the musicologists who, as Debussy would have put it, have been poking their historical noses into something that doesn't concern them, by fixing the date of Jaufre's crusade in 1147, hunting up the list of Countesses of Tripoli with reference to this date, and trying to show that Odierne, the widow of Raimon I, the only one who could have been the heroine of this story, died in 1161 at a great age, and had never been a nun. . . .

At the same time, all this goes to show that, even in the thirteenth century, the idea of a history of music which was really historical did not yet exist.

Adam de la Halle, who died between 1285 and 1289, was perhaps the first of the *trouvères*, and consequently the first musician of whom, thanks to the *Jeu de Pèlerin*, we possess anything resembling a serious biographical notice. Even this is in the form of a stage play in verse, evidently written for publicity purposes for some special occasion very similar to the *razos*, whose chief claim to veracity lies in the fact that it was written soon after his death by his own nephew, Jehan Mados. The apparent paradox of its presentation in theatrical form is due to the fact that it was intended as a prologue to a "revival" of the *Jeu de Robin et Marion* at Arras in 1289 (which had had its première at Naples); it was mainly intended to be an encomium in praise of the dead man; of "The magister Adam, handsome and learned scholar, who gave freely of his gifts and was full of every virtue. . . ."

Similarly, the reason why, in spite of numerous *lacunae*, we know quite a lot about the life of Guillaume de Machaut, is firstly because of his political activities, since he was for a long time secretary to the King of Bohemia, Jean de Luxembourg, and secondly because he judged it prudent to write his own biography on various occasions, notably in his *Veoir Dit*, or *True Story*.

These are only exceptional instances, which are not often to be met with, even in the fifteenth century. At the close of the Middle Ages there had never been any history, in the true sense of the word, of its music, nor any objective documentation concerning its musicians. Still less had any attempt been made to carry out researches into the music of the past, although its theory was still taught in the schools, regardless of the fact that it no longer had any bearing whatsoever on the living music of those days.

4

The Renaissance and the Seventeenth Century—
In Search of Antiquity

It was nevertheless due to this somewhat puerile conservatism that, in a curiously roundabout way, the idea of a history of music, abandoned since the days of Denys of Halicarnassus, was taken up once again.

One might have supposed that the normal procedure would have been to start with contemporary music and work backwards gradually to earlier times or, alternatively, to follow the evolution of music from its origins up to the present time, taking care not to omit any link in the chain. But nothing of the kind. Until the beginning of the nineteenth century, as we have already pointed out, all music of a previous age was a dead letter, and of no interest to anyone. One has only to recall the cruel remark— possibly apocryphal—attributed to Bach's sons who used to refer to their father as "an old fogey". From about 1675 and for the next hundred years it was generally understood that music began with Lully. When Lully was dethroned and Bach re-discovered during the early days of the Romantic movement, it was Johann Sebastian who succeeded the Florentine in the unexpected rôle of the "creator of music". It was not until the end of the nineteenth century, as we shall see presently, that this conception was enlarged so as to include the Renaissance. But in this vast cemetery of corpses buried without remorse, a slender trembling flame had continuously been kept alive. The exaggerated conservatism of the musical theorists (which is by no means confined to the past) continued even in the sixteenth century to insist that the student should be familiar not only with the inextricable meanderings of Guido's Hand (see fig. 15, p. 186) but with the four names for every note in the sol-fa system invented in the eleventh century solely for the purpose of being able to use B flat (and therefore completely out-moded and unnecessary ever since B flat ceased to be the only accidental in use, F sharp having made its appearance at the end of the twelfth century, C sharp in the thirteenth, G sharp and D sharp in the fourteenth, and E flat in the fifteenth). He was also expected to know the names of the tetrachords in use at the time of Aristoxenes, and to be familiar with Ptolemy's theory of scales. Treatises which are unable to tell us with any degree of precision whether an F in a contemporary work is to be read as F sharp or F natural, are full of tables relating to the *hypate hypaton* and to the chromatic and enharmonic modes, now long forgotten, which in a rare moment of sincerity, the thirteenth-century theoretician, Jerome of Moravia, admitted were "a matter for speculation"— "*speculatio fiet*". Indeed, speculation in this field was destined to continue for another three centuries and to lead to some quite unexpected developments.

It is impossible to exaggerate the importance of Humanism not only at the time of the Renaissance, but during the next two centuries. The quarrel between the Ancients and the Moderns was not only an episode in literary history, but lay at the root of nearly three centuries of intellectual evolution—and this applies to music as much as to anything else. The reason for a gradually awakening interest in the origins of our art, which finally led to writing its history, is to be sought in the first place exclusively in the context of the boundless enthusiasm manifested at that time for everything Greek or Roman. Since, as far as music was concerned, the Romans had nothing to contribute, the Greeks reigned supreme in this field. One read in the works of the old authors of the marvellous effects of music: of Orpheus taming wild beasts, of Amphion building the walls of Thebes to the strains of the lyre, and of Pythagoras influencing human behaviour by a judicious selection of appropriate "modes". Therefore, argued the devotees of Antiquity, the music of the ancient Greeks must have been incomparable; and if *we* were not capable of building Versailles to the strains of *our* music, this could only be because we had lost the secret of this marvellous art.[1] It was therefore essential to recapture this secret and to find out as much as possible about this Fair Unknown and apply it to our own music so that, in its turn, it could acquire these marvellous powers which it could only have failed to develop through its own inherent weakness.

Early in the sixteenth century this task was begun. Knowledge of Greek music was still based on stale and outmoded theories which had remained more or less unchanged for the last thousand years, in which modes and keys were inextricably mixed up, and the meaning of words had been altered—in some cases lost altogether—so that definitions which had once been intelligible now seemed completely fossilized and bore no relation to any perceptible phenomena.[2] But at least this theory existed, and it was possible to make some use of it. We shall see later on how this veritable "collective madness" produced some surprising and often fruitful results. Though aiming above all at restoring the past, and therefore an essentially conservative and anti-progressive movement, it failed to achieve anything in the field of archaeology; but after being

[1] The story told by Bourdelot (see Chap. 2) of a woman being cured by the music of Lully is an example of our ancestors' desire to emulate the ancients in this field.
[2] Cf. J. Chailley, *L'Imbroglio des modes*, Paris, Leduc, 1959.

intuitively transposed by musicians of genius onto a practical plane, it soon gave rise to an unprecedented wave of modernism—which was, of course, exactly contrary to what the initiators of the movement had intended. We will confine ourselves for the present to what falls strictly within the scope of the present chapter.

The "revolution" of the Humanists did not consist in having discovered the theory of the Ancients, for, as we have seen, this had never ceased to be taught, but rather in the fact that they no longer looked upon it as a useless relic, preserved merely by force of habit (which, in fact, was what it was), but tried to link it up with the living art of the day. With this end in view, instead of confining themselves, as had always been done in the Middle Ages, to copying from their predecessors the formulas and diagrams which the latter had only copied from *their* predecessors, they began to study them seriously and with enthusiasm. This did not, in fact, result in any better understanding of these texts, because, in accordance with a practice which has persisted down to the present day, the approach of those who studied them was conditioned by their exclusive familiarity with the music of their own age. Nevertheless, the interest and curiosity aroused in this way had a stimulating effect and opened up a new era of investigations. For it must not be forgotten that this sudden interest in old music sprang originally from a desire to improve the conditions of modern music, and had no other end in view. Any other results would be supernumerary.

The first of these arose out of a discussion which started at the end of the fifteenth century with regard to the numerical definition of certain intervals. We shall see later that, for historical reasons, the old acoustical system was, precisely at this time, becoming obsolete and was badly in need of reform. Such a reform had already been courageously advocated in 1480 by the Spaniard Ramis de Pareja. As was to be expected, this was immediately opposed by adversaries signing their protests with the Latin names of Burtius, Gafurius and Spatarus. In 1529 a musician from Modena, one Ludovico Fogliani, in defending the new ideas, but forgetting that they were new, cited Ptolemy as an authority, and thus started a "back to antiquity" campaign which was to have wide repercussions. After Ptolemy, it was the turn of Didymus. Were not the Ancients the source of all knowledge and all truth? In any case, theory was soon to be translated into practice. A pupil of Adrian Willaert, the spiritual descendant of Josquin des Prés, Don Nicola, known as "Vicentino" because he was born at Vicenza in 1511, had had an "archicembalo" and an "archiorgano" specially made to prove that the Greek modes, both chromatic and enharmonic, could be realized. In the greatest secrecy he trained six carefully chosen pupils to sing according to the ancient intervals, and began to write motets based on the scale-systems described by the Greek authors, which used to be known as *speculatio*. One day in May, in the year 1551, he met a foreign musician, living like himself in Rome, a certain Vicente, nicknamed "il Lusitano" because he was born at Olivença in Portugal. Soon they were in keen argument about a motet, *Regina coeli*, which had just been performed, and was held by some to show traces of the Greek modes. The discussion ended with a challenge combined with a wager of two gold crowns; and on June 7th of that year, in the Vatican chapel, the man from Vicenza and the Portuguese confronted one another in the presence of the precentors of the Papal chapel and a special jury. The latter finally voted in favour of the Portuguese. However, the argument was carried on in print, and in the next five years each of them published a contradictory treatise on the subject; in 1553 "il Lusitano" entered the lists with his *Introdutione facilissima e novissima*, etc., which was followed in 1555 by Vicentino's *Antica musica ridotta alla moderna pratica*—"Ancient music adopted to modern practice". This last title was symptomatic of the kind of problems with which the age was concerned, and shows clearly the bias with which the sixteenth century had approached the study of ancient texts.

Other pamphlets by both claimants, and also by third parties, soon followed. Then in 1555 a new name appeared in connection with this dispute—that of the Venetian Gioseffo Zarlino—a pupil, like Vicentino, of Adrian Willaert, a Franciscan monk and the future choir-master of St. Mark's at Venice. Zarlino was already a well-known composer; in 1549 he had published a book of five-part motets and was highly thought of. His *Istitutioni Harmoniche* were based on ideas that were current before his time, but never before had they been expressed so clearly and so fully. In future the system he advocated, but did not invent, would be known to posterity as the "Zarlinian system".

He, too, took his stand upon the *diatonon syntonon* of Ptolemy, and questioned Vicentino's claim to be an authority on ancient music. There were subjects in which musical scholars were especially interested, the question of intervals, and the by then defunct chromatic and enharmonic modes—not so much for historical reasons, but because they believed that it was here that they would find the key to the errors which had brought about the degeneracy of modern music and deprived it of the power (see above) to "build the walls of Thebes". They were convinced that if they could rediscover this all-powerful "open Sesame" they would succeed in regenerating the art of music. And year by year they intensified their study of the texts.

The same problems were debated in Florence in the salons of Count Bardi where the main subject of discussion was not, as was thought for a long time, the renaissance of tragedy in music, but the renovation of the madrigal by means of a technique borrowed from the Greeks. The musical member of this circle was an adversary of Zarlino—

Vicenzo Galilei, father of the astonomer. In 1581 Galilei published his *Dialogo della musica antica e della moderna* which dealt at length, once again, with ancient scales and intervals, more briefly with the madrigal, and not at all with the question of the future of opera, to which no one in Bardi's circle had given a thought. (We shall revert to this subject in Chapter 21.)

All these discussions, controversies and conflicting opinions with regard to texts which everyone thought he alone had properly understood, were logically bound to end in the idea of collating the various documents and making a synthesis of them. It was equally logical that all these scattered and haphazard attempts to find therein the foundations of modern music, based as they were on the conviction that these two extremes were really almost identical, if due allowance were made for deformations due to the passage of time, should also have engendered a desire to know how these texts came to be transmitted—a desire which already foreshadowed the notion of a history of music. It was not, however, until the seventeenth century that this intrusion into the sphere of music of an historical approach became a reality, though still only in a very rudimentary and confused form.

The first step in this direction was taken in 1614, not in Italy this time but in Germany, by a musician at the Court of Brunswick, the Thuringian Michael Praetorius. This Latin name, which means a "village Mayor"—the real name is believed to have been Schulz— had belonged for years to an important dynasty of musicians, of whom Michael was the fifth. His great work, *Syntagma musicum*, was published in three volumes at Wittemberg and Wolfenbüttel between 1614 and 1620 (a fourth volume was announced but never appeared). While the last two volumes are treatises of the usual kind, being mainly concerned with organography, or the manufacture of instruments, the first volume, in the form of a Latin Introduction, has the distinction of being the first dissertation in which musical questions, relating mainly, as was to be expected, to ancient Greece, are boldly approached from a purely historical angle.

This set a new fashion. Although during the whole of the seventeenth century no real "history of music" came to be written, more and more historical outlines, in which ancient Greece still figured prominently, began to make their appearance in the musical literature of the period.

One of the most important works of this kind had been prefaced in 1627 by a first extract published under the unknown name of the "Sieur de Sermes" and entitled: "Treatise on universal harmony, on the theory and practice of music in ancient and modern times, together with its causes and effects, with examples drawn from philosophy and music." ("*Traité de l'harmonie universelle où est contenue la musique théorique et pratique des anciens et modernes, avec les causes de ses effets, enrichie de raisons prises de la philosophie et de la musique.*") In this volume of some five hundred pages the author announced the plan of a great work which did not appear for another nine years. Meanwhile, the same mysterious author produced, one after the other, two more works (one anonymous): "Questions relating to harmony including several of particular interest relating to the physical, moral and other sciences" ("*Questions harmoniques dans lesquelles sont contenues plusieurs choses remarquables pour la physique, pour la morale et pour les autres sciences*") and, in the same year, 1634, another entitled: "Introduction to universal harmony, together with some curious questions of special interest to preachers, theologians, astrologers and philosophers" ("*Les préludes de l'harmonie universelle ou questions curieuses, utiles aux prédicateurs, aux théologiens, aux astrologues, aux médecins et aux philosophes*"), signed with the initials L.P.M.M. A title such as this is a whole programme in itself. And so are the following chapter headings, taken from these two works:

> "Whether music is agreeable, whether learned men should take pleasure therein, and what judgment should be passed on those who do not find it pleasing or despise it or detest it."
> "Whether the practice of music or its theory is to be preferred, and whether we should esteem more highly those who know only how to compose or sing, or those who know the theory of music."
> "What relation is there between the foundations of judicial astrology and music?"
> "Whether the perfect musician should be of a sanguine, phlegmatic, bilious or melancholy temperament in order to sing or compose the most beautiful airs conceivable."

Nevertheless it will be seen that some of these headings seem absurd only when judged by modern standards. The second, for example, is only a repetition of an aphorism, derived from Saint Augustine and formulated by Boethius, one of the great authorities of the Middle Ages, to the effect that neither composers nor singers are real musicians, because they are guided by instinct, whereas the true musician is a philosopher who can reason about the nature of music. (Boethius was a philosopher.) Guido d'Arezzo, in his *Musicae regulae metricae*, had even expressed this lofty doctrine in verse (see Chapter 21).

Three new treatises by the same author, one of them in Latin, appeared the following year (1635); and finally, in 1636, came the great work which had been announced nine years earlier: two enormous volumes of some fifteen hundred pages which, under the title of *L'Harmonie universelle*, revealed the real identity of L.P.M.M., alias the "Sieur de Sermes" (an approximate anagram) as Marin Mersenne, a monk of the Order of Minims in Paris.

Although containing a good deal of rubbish, Mersenne's *L'Harmonie universelle*, of which an abridged edition in Latin appeared in 1648, is one of the most important works which have come down to us from the seventeenth century. In spite of numerous digressions on almost every subject under the sun—philosophy, mathematics, occultism, acoustics, organology, theology, cosmogony, etc., the passages relating to the history of music, past and present, are abundant and full of precise and infinitely valuable information. The author stands revealed as one of the great humanists of the seventeenth century, who were in touch with one another all over Europe (he himself corresponded with Descartes, Huyghens, etc.); and it was thanks to him that his convent in the Place Royale (now Place des Vosges) became, as did later that of Padre Martini at Bologna, a spiritual centre to which all foreign *savants* passing through Paris were drawn.

Another priest—this time a German Jesuit—now came on the scene to challenge the supremacy of Père Mersenne. He was a Professor of Natural Science named Athanasius Kircher. After teaching at the University of Wurzburg, he had escaped from a Germany devastated by the Thirty Years War and, in 1633, came to live at Avignon. His first work, which appeared in 1641, was a treatise on the art of magnetism which contained, as we saw in an earlier chapter, a description of the music that was needed to cure the bite of the tarantula—the origin, clearly, of the tarantelle ! His most important work, however, entitled *Musurgia universalis*[1] is largely cribbed from Mersenne, with additions and abridgements. But Kircher was to become famous through a "discovery" of the highest importance. Mersenne in his first book had translated into French two ancient treatises on Greek music, one by Bacchius and the other by the pseudo-Euclid. Kircher wanted to go one better. He claimed to have found on Mt. Cassino, in an unspecified MS., the original melody of one of Pindar's Odes which, after having copied in Greek notation, with a modern transcription, he then offered to the admiration of the world. The enthusiasm aroused by such a discovery as this can well be imagined, especially in view of the fact that the only authentic examples of Greek music in the original notation we possess today were not discovered until the nineteenth century.[2] Scholars of a later age, however, have searched in vain for this famous manuscript; and this Ode by Pindar soon became as celebrated as its "inventor", until early in the twentieth century it was definitely proved to be a complete forgery. Even today it is still often cited in quite serious works.

[1]We will not attempt to give its full title, which occupies fourteen lines and concludes as follows: *tum potissimum in philologia, mathematica, physica, mechanica, medicina, politica, metaphysica, theologia, aperiantur et demonstrantur!*

[2]With the exception of the *Prelude to the Muse* and *Hymn to the Sun* by Mesomedes discovered by V. Galilei, in 1581.

Kircher's "discovery", however, was well timed. For, as we have seen, there was hardly a single serious document on which all this flood of dissertations, controversies, theories and counter-theories which had been let loose over a period of some two hundred years could be based. The ancient authors were known either as part of a scholarly tradition, or in Latin translations; no first-hand text had ever been produced for critical examination. Mersenne had been the first to publish a translation of two such texts. In 1652 the history of ancient music had at last reached the stage from which it ought to have started—i.e., by publishing the ancient texts which formed so much of its subject-matter. As so often happens in undertakings of this kind, it was an amateur, one Marcus Meibomius, who was the first to perform this task. Meibomius (the name with which his works were signed; it is still uncertain whether this should be transcribed as Meibom or Meybaum) was born in Schleswig in 1626, and had spent his life travelling about in search of a publisher for his revision of the Hebrew text of the Bible; he had also tried, without success, to dispose of a nautical machine of some kind which he had invented. In Sweden he met Bourdelot, then Physician to Queen Christine, and quarreled with him over a ludicrous incident arising out of a suggestion which Bourdelot (who was very interested in his work on Greek music) had made to the Queen, inviting her to ask Meibom to sing some ancient music—no doubt, none other than the Ode of Pindar's which Kircher had just published. Meibom, who could not sing in tune, complied against his will, and for the rest of his life never forgave the French doctor for causing him to make a fool of himself on that occasion.

Nevertheless, the fact remains that Meibom was the first—and for two centuries the only—author to have published the original Greek text based on manuscripts, of the leading theoreticians of antiquity; and his edition (1652) of the *Antiquae musicae auctores septem*, accompanied by notes and a Latin translation, is still in use today, in spite of the errors and excessive amount of corrections it contains.

It was thanks to this publication that the history of Greek music was at last able to get out of the rut of more or less fantastic speculation and enter the constructive phase of discussions based on authentic facts. These were soon forthcoming, and in 1657 an English mathematician named John Wallis replied to Meibom in the form of a critical study of his works; this, however, instead of being a mere statement of subjective opinions. was a piece of really scientific criticism. A whole chapter in the history of music—the epoch of prehistorical fantasies—was now closed. In future it would be based on altogether new criteria: the history, instead of the romance, of Greek music was about to be written.

Nevertheless, it was another hundred and fifty years before this new chapter was definitely begun. Adversaries though they were, Meibom and Wallis were pioneers. Inaugurated by them, the musicology of Greek antiquity did not really get under way until 1820, with Boeckh, Bellerman, Westphal, etc. Meanwhile, the old illusions about renovation by means of intervals or melodic *genera* were gradually abandoned, though every now and again they were revived—Rameau himself succumbed to them; but by then they had lost the attraction of novelty. Other aspects of antiquity were now receiving more attention, and we shall see that the treatment they received was no less curious.

5

The Eighteenth and Nineteenth Centuries—
In Search of the Middle Ages

The exploration of antiquity had been the main preoccupation of the sixteenth and seventeenth centuries, and that of the Middle Ages of the eighteenth and nineteenth centuries. The former has only been studied methodically for little more than a hundred years, and the latter for barely fifty; while it is only in the last twenty years or so that the subject has ceased to be confined to a narrow circle of specialists.

Apart from Gregorian Plainsong, the young musicians who were studying at the Conservatoire in the nineteen-thirties had never imagined that there could be any medieval music worth bothering about, and sincerely believed that they had conveyed the whole essence of prehistoric music by writing a few open fifths or omitting some leading-notes in their exercises for the Prix de Rome Cantata. We not only knew nothing at that time of the rare performances of such music given by pioneers in France like Amédée Gastoué or Félix Raugel, but had no idea even that such texts existed.

We must not forget that the nineteenth century was still transcribing the medieval notation into semibreves and deploring the resulting "lack of taste".

If we open the pages of works which until quite recently were considered authoritative, this is the kind of thing we come across:

"The first attempt at harmony(?)[1] was to superimpose two notes—alas! only fourths or fifths. . . . This was known as diaphony or organum; today we should call it cacophony. We can only consider this as an error which for some five centuries retarded the evolution of music." (Lavignac, *La Musique et les musiciens*, 1942, p. 455).

"How strange and harsh, to our ears at least, these two-part exercises from which thirds are almost always excluded, sound . . . The dissonances which were later permitted in the organum did nothing to soften this harshness." (Landormy, *Histoire de la musique*, revised ed., 1946, p. 22.)

"We know with certainty that these bizarre compositions were sung in churches . . . but it is difficult for us to appreciate the musical value of such an art. The pieces published sound to our ears rather like a reading of the famous Strasbourg sermon. All that can

[1]The question mark is in the original text.

26

truthfully be said is that Perotinus had the right ideas about counterpoint, because he seems generally careful to write his parts in contrary motion. But the music itself is strangely harsh!" (Combarieu, *Histoire de la musique*, 1920, pp. 365-366.)

Now let us turn to some recent French works dealing with the same subject:

"The new art of polyphony reached its height at the end of the twelfth century with Leoninus, and at the beginning of the thirteenth, with Perotinus the Great: these were the first big names in the history of music. . . . Perotinus's works show him to have been a prodigious musician, and some of his works, e.g., the great *Viderunt omnes* for four voices, are immensely impressive even today." (Roland de Candé *Ouverture pour une discothèque*, 1956, p. 29.)

"The way in which the melodic lines are interwoven makes this not just an intellectual exercise, but a work of art—creating a pattern of arabesques in which contrary motion is used in such a way as to lighten and balance the sinuous lines of the voices as they come and go." (Emile Vuillermoz, *Histoire de la musique*, 1949, p. 50.)

"*L'Ars Antiqua*, illustrated by Perotinus, had the rough clarity, nobility of outline and abstract nudity which is to be found both in the architecture of the earliest cathedrals and in scholastic theology." (Roland Manuel, *Plaisir de la musique*, II, 1950, p. 101.)

It will be seen how greatly, and also how recently, the attitude towards this subject has changed. This is because it is only quite recently that we have come to look upon the Middle Ages, despite the stupid name bestowed upon them by the eighteenth century, as not only an epoch of transition, but one that was very much alive and extraordinarily fertile and attractive; and still more recently that we have been able to form an opinion about them that is not entirely based on childish fables. For, as we shall see, the history of music has always figured prominently in literature of this sort, of which there is no lack.

The humanists of the sixteenth century—it was the same in the seventeenth—were not in the least interested in whatever music may have existed between antiquity and their own day. We have already observed that until the eighteenth century music was exclusively a "seasonal" product: music of the past was dead music. They made an exception, however, in favour of the music of antiquity, not because of what it was, or might have been, but because of their obsession with the mirage of Perfection associated with anything antique. All the devotees of the vanished golden age studied, or thought they studied, this music, but through modern spectacles. As to the intervening age—*medium aevum*, the "Middle Ages"—that was of no importance.

At the point we have reached in our history, after nearly two centuries of discussion about this "lost" music, a vague sort of historical consciousness was beginning to emerge. We have related the meeting at Stockholm between Meibom and Bourdelot—who was the first to conceive the idea of a general history of music—a history which, in accordance with the fashion of those days, still revolved round the two essential poles: ancient and modern. Nine of the fourteen chapters in his book deal with the music of antiquity, the remainder being devoted to modern music; the tenth is a rather perfunctory transitional chapter entitled: *Music and entertainment in France from the time of the ancient Gauls to the present day*. But the real innovation here is the fact of this transition. It is true that, to judge from what the author saw fit to include in this chapter, we have no reason to regret that he did not make it any fuller. We read, for example, that Charlemagne, "Having laid the first foundations of the famous University of Paris[1] . . . set up a society of musicians, modelled on the ancient Bards, some of whom were called *Trouverres* or *Romanciers* (these were the poets of those days who wrote ballads in verse) while the others were known as *Chanterres* or Minstrels; these were the musicians who wrote the airs to which the ballads were sung. The third category comprised the *Jongleurs* or *Menestriers*, who played on instruments. . . ." Bourdelot then goes on to give the names of some of the *trouvères* which he says he found in Fauchet's *Antiquitez*, among which, along with those of the King of Navarre and Thierry de Soissons, we find, to our surprise, the names of Charles d'Anjou, brother of Louis IX, the Saint, and of Marie de France (who wrote narrative ballads but not *chansons*); while the Vidame de Chartres and the Châtelain de Coucy (these are correct) are mentioned in company with the "*Queus*" of La Marche and Britanny (Bourdelot has mis-read the word *Quens*, meaning Count). "These troupes of musicians," continues Bourdelot, "were governed by the poets who wrote rhymed ballads which were first invented by one Maître Eustache, who was the author of *Brut* in the year 1300."[2] Then, after a casual reference to *la Rioste* [sic][3], Bourdelot concludes with this superb piece of truncated history: "Among the songs and vaudevilles, which were first invented by Olivier Basselin[4], the most highly esteemed are those by the King of Navarre (Thibaut de Champagne, 1201–1253), although their harmonies are extremely harsh; but not one of them is about wine. I believe it was Baïf and Ronsard who first thought of coupling Cupid and Bacchus in their songs, in imitation of Anacreon." After this, without any transition, our "historian" goes on to deal with the *Chanson de Roland*.

Bourdelot had the excuse of writing posthumously; he died in 1685. We can afford

[1]It was in reality founded in 1200 by Philip Augustus, and its statutes date from 1215.

[2]The tale of *Brut* which is by Wace, is dated 1155.

[3]Ludovico Ariosto, known as Ariosto (1474–1533) author of *Orlando Furioso*, was one of the leading poets of the Italian Renaissance.

[4]Basselin lived in the fifteenth century.

to be less indulgent towards Jean-Jacques Rousseau, who completed his *Dictionnaire de Musique* in 1764, and yet is guilty of as many ineptitudes as Bourdelot. This is what he has to say, under the heading *Chanson*, about the troubadours: "This *genre* was handed down to the Romans by the Greeks, and many of the *Odes* of Horace are *chansons* of a 'galant' or Bacchic nature. . . . The moderns also have their *chansons* which vary according to the taste and genius of each nation. The French, however, are supreme in Europe in the art of composition. . . . They take a delight in this pastime in which they have always excelled, as witness the ancient troubadours. They are a happy race, always gay and finding amusement in everything. The women are highly frivolous, the men extremely dissipated, and the country produces excellent wine; it is scarcely surprising, then, that they are much given to song. We still have some old *chansons* by Thibaut de Champagne, the most 'galant' man of his century, set to music by Guillaume de Machault [*sic*]. Marot also wrote many which have come down to us; and thanks to the airs of Orlando (de Lassus) and of Claudin (de Sermisy, or Le Jeune?) we also have several from the time of the Pléiade of Charles IX [*sic*], without counting the more modern *chansons* which have made the reputation of musicians such as Lambert, du Bousset, La Garde and others—although these are not all as famous as the Count of Coulanges and the Abbé de l'Attaignant. . . ."

In 1764, however, though other aspects of medieval music were still neglected, some vague glimmerings of an appreciation of the work of the troubadours begin to be discernible. Thus, in 1742, Levesque de la Ravallière published for the first time some *chansons* by Thibaut de Champagne: "It is not to be expected," he wrote, "that ancient music should sound as pleasing to the ear as modern music. Tastes vary from one century to another; what once seemed charming will appear insipid to modern ears. In truth, the composition of music used not to be as difficult or as erudite as it is today. Good poetry engenders excellent music. . . . And both could claim equal merit at the time of our earliest *chansons*. . . . The music of the Ancients was much less ambitious in this respect than ours today, when great importance is attached to writing for the voice."

This opinion had been preceded by another one, but from the pen this time of an eminent scholar, the Abbé Lebeuf, Canon of Auxerre, who in his *Dissertation sur l'état des sciences en France depuis la mort du roi Robert jusqu' à celle de Philippe le Bel*, which was crowned by the Academy in 1740, has this to say about the *trouvères*: "It will be seen from chants of this kind, transcribed in the thirteenth century in the notation devised by Aretinus[1] that they were far from being melodious, unless, maybe, it was left to the

---

[1]Guido d'Arezzo, who was credited for many centuries with everything the Middle Ages had produced in the way of musical theory and notation.

cantors to supply the ornamentation. One has only to examine the collections of secular canticles or French *chansons* of the twelfth and thirteenth centuries, which are to be found in certain libraries in Paris, to see that they were nothing other than Gregorian Plainsong."

In 1780, in his *Essai sur la musique*, which for a long time was a standard work, Jean-Benjamin de Laborde, who was in charge of the Arsenal song-book (which then belonged to the Marquis de Paulmy), published, in a not very satisfactory transcription into modern notation, about a dozen of these *chansons* of which two were by the Châtelain de Coucy, one by Raoul de Ferrières, and one by Gautier d'Epinal. His comments are curious, and not unlike those of Lebeuf: "Nearly all these poets," he writes, "wrote the music for their songs, but these airs were nothing but Gregorian Plainsong; indeed, they were merely parodies of Church canticles. At the end of many of their songs we find the first words of the hymn, the tune of which is identical with that of the *chanson*."

This strange explanation is based on a twofold blunder: Laborde mistook motets for *chansons*, and thought the reference to the "tenor" meant "the air on which the piece was composed".[1] It was this same Laborde who sincerely believed that the *Chanson de Roland* had been discovered by the Marquis de Paulmy in some fragments which the latter had "assembled and embellished with several couplets which are absolutely similar in spirit in order to make a charming *chanson*" [*sic*]:

> Soldats français, chantons Roland,
> De son pays il fut la gloire, etc.

It was not, however, until about 1760 that the thirteenth century *chanson* ceased to be looked down upon; it was sometimes even sympathetically regarded as the ancestor of the *romances* which, thanks to Jean-Jacques Rousseau, were beginning to be fashionable. Rousseau himself, indeed, in the article *Chanson* in his *Dictionnaire de la Musique*, gives the strange account of it that we have just read above (p. 29), which is a good example of the kind of "erudition" we have already met with in Bourdelot.

Be this as it may, although the ignorance revealed in these judgments is amusing, the tone is no longer sarcastic. What, then, is the explanation of this?

[1] Cf. Th. Gérold, *Le Réveil en France au XVIIIe siècle de l'intérét pour la musique profane du Moyen Age* in *Mélanges, La Laurencie*, Paris, Droz, 1933, pp. 223-224, and J. Chailley, *La Musique du Moyen Age vue par les XVIIIe et XIXe siécles*, in *Mélanges P. M. Masson*, Paris, 1955, pp. 95-107. The present chapter contains several quotations from the last-named article, and the reader is referred to it for detailed references which it was not thought necessary to repeat here.

The explanation is that, in order to keep abreast of the literary movement responsible for the romantic revival of the "troubadour style", which reached its climax in 1774 with the publication of the Abbé Millot's *Histoire des Troubadours* by Sainte-Palaye, a lot of naïvely would-be archaic *romances*, fabricated from beginning to end, began to appear under the title of *Chansons des Trouvères*, with the result that the latter enjoyed a vogue which would have greatly surprised their alleged authors (Cf. Plate II).

These medieval pseudo-*chansons* are nearly always simple forgeries; among their probable authors for both words and music must be counted the following: the Marquis de Paulmy, a celebrated bibliophile who may have employed Laborde; Moncrif, a little-known author (1687-1770), one of whose *romances* was published in 1774 in Baculard d'Arnaud's *Nouvelles Historiques*, and whose forgeries were reproduced in 1765 in Monnet's *Anthologie Françoise;* Papavoine, a violinist in the orchestra of the Comédie Italienne, who in 1780 became first violin and "master of Pantomimes" at The Hague; and possibly Laborde himself, who is credited by Gérold with being the author of a four-part *chanson* alleged to be by Richard Cœur de Lion, and which had originally appeared in a work of fiction in 1705 entitled: *La tour ténébreuse et les jours lumineux, contes anglais accompagnez d'historiettes et tirez d'une ancienne chronique composée par Richard Coeur-de-Lion, roi d'Angleterre*, of which the author was a lady named L'Héritier. It was this compilation, enlarging on the legend to which we have already referred in which Blondel de Nesles appears as Richard I's "Master of Musick", that inspired Sedaine to write his *Richard Coeur de Lion* which has been made famous by Grétry's music.

The part played by Laborde in all this is somewhat strange. Though he may not have thought very highly of them, he knew as much as could be known at the time about the music and the literary style of the *trouvères*. And yet, in spite of this, he had no scruples about joining the ranks of the forgers. Perhaps this was due to his loyalty to the Marquis de Paulmy, who owned the manuscript which is now in the Arsenal Library, and who hoped that this circumstance would earn for him the reputation of being a skilful literary adaptor. Be that as it may, the fact remains that after having, as we have already seen, published the correct literary text of a certain number of *chansons*, including three by Colin Muset, with, moreover, an almost literal translation, he yet did not hesitate to pass off as being the work of this author, translated by the "Marquis de P." (i.e. Paulmy) a Rousseau-esque romance like *Robinet et Mariette*, adding, somewhat cynically: "This is the oldest known example of a *chanson à danser*."

A list of these absurdities could be continued indefinitely. On the following page we find the *"romance chantée par la belle Yseult dans le roman de Tristan de Leonnois"* again translated by the Marquis—although this time Laborde forgets to note, as he had the impudence to do once before (but only once) "We have been unable to discover the original", thus giving the impression that he had been able to do this in other cases. And now, for the reader's edification, here is the final verse:

> L'hiver nous peint l'indifférence,
> Pour nos coeurs il n'existe pas.
> Les seules peines de l'absence
> Sont nos glaces et nos frimas.
> Viens les fondre par ta présence
> Et par l'ardeur du sentiment,
>   Mon beau Tristan, (bis)
>   Mon cher Tristan.

[which can be paraphrased as follows:

> Winter cannot touch our hearts;
> The pains of absence
> Are the only ice and frost we know.
> Come, then, and melt them
> With thy presence
> And the warmth of tender feeling
> O my lovely Tristan (twice)
> O my dear Tristan.]

The most typical example of this multiple and clandestine conspiracy is a song which was to become famous, *Ah, belle blonde*, of which there were no less than four versions, while it was attributed to two different *trouvères*. It was no doubt by Moncrif who, in his *Choix de Chansons*, cites Raoul de Soissons as the author. The original version, if I dare use that expression, having been reproduced by Monnet, was published a second time by Weckerlin in 1855, in the second volume of *Echos du temps passé*. Weckerlin this time exposed the fraud, but nevertheless gives the tune a prominent place, harmonizing it in his own way. Similarly, Laborde repeats it in his *Essai sur la musique*, but being no doubt dissatisfied with Moncrif's music, provides another setting, with trills and roulades which he must have thought added greatly to its appeal. He arranges it for four voices, but so crudely harmonized that it is difficult to believe, as Gérold pretends, that he could have done it himself. After this, fashions in taste changed somewhat, and when we meet it again it is disguised in the purest Empire style as a *romance*, attributed to Thibaut de Champagne, with figured bass; in this form it occurs in several works from the pen of the notorious Castil-Blaze[1], more especially in his "opera-potpourri" *La Forêt de Sénart*, and again as an appendix to the first volume of his deplorable *Dictionnaire de musique moderne* which appeared in 1821 [see Plate III (a) and (b)].[1]

However impudently apocryphal these *chansons* may have been, they sometimes had a literary, if not musical, point of contact with the work of the *trouvères*, dressed up in the fashions of the day. Gérold has drawn attention, in the second stanza of a song by Thibaut, *De nouviau m'estuet chanter*, to two lines which may have given Moncrif the idea for the romance he attributed to the poet: *"Las si j'avais pouvoir d'oublier."* Ah! *belle blonde*, in its turn, could, with a little effort of the imagination, pass as a paraphrase of the fourth stanza of a song by Raoul de Soissons: *Chanson m'estuet et faire et commencer*. Here is the first stanza of Moncrif's romance in which the archaism of the last word no doubt was taken to be a guarantee of its authenticity:

> Ah! belle blonde
> Au corps si gent,
> Perle du monde
> Que j'aime tant,
> D'une chose ai bien grand désir
> C'est d'un doux baiser vous tollir.

The opera and *opéra-comique* were obliged to keep up with these wonderful discoveries. In his opera-ballet *L'Union de l'Amour et des Arts*, in 1773, Etienne Joseph Floquet, a musician from Aix-en-Provence who at one time tried to set himself up as a rival to Gluck, introduced in the third *"entrée"* an "heroic pastoral" entitled *La Cour d'Amour ou les Troubadours*, which represented the romantic love between the Knight Floridan and the beautiful Aglaé, who presided over the Court of Love, against a background of dancing troubadours. The libretto, signed by Devaux, was in reality by the Abbé Lemonnier.[2] With Sedaine and Grétry the pseudo-Middle Ages made their official entry into the world of opera. Even before the celebrated *Richard Coeur de Lion*, Grétry presented, in the presence of Their Majesties, on December 30, 1779 at Versailles, *Aucassin et Nicolette, ou les moeurs du bon vieux temps*. He tells us in his *Mémoires* that his

---

[1]Castil-Blaze was the ex-notary from Cavaillon (Vaucluse) who became music critic of *La Revue de Paris*, *Le Journal des Débats* and *Le Constitutionnel*, and was responsible, among other things, for that travesty of *Freischütz* known as *Robin des Bois*. This was an act of ingratitude towards Weber, because, although unwittingly, the latter had ensured the success of a certain chorus in *La Forêt de Sénart* which Castil-Blaze had had the audacity to introduce as "an extract from an opera by Weber"; performed as such at a Conservatoire concert, it was, as Fétis has recorded, "often asked for and always enthusiastically applauded in the belief that it really was by the author of *Freischütz*".

[2]Marie Briquet has written an excellent thesis, as yet unpublished, on Floquet.

intention was "to set in opposition the ancient and the modern worlds". The Overture to *Aucassin*, he declared, "should transport the audience back a century." It is true that this still does not take us very far, but the intention is plain, and the critics showed that he had succeeded in his aim by grumbling at the archaisms in the score, though these seem to us harmless enough.

As for *Richard Coeur de Lion*, Grétry has this to say about the famous *romance*, the words of which, no doubt, were not by Sedaine, but by the Marquis de Paulmy: "For the same reasons I decided to write this in the 'ancient style', so that it would stand out from the rest. It seems I was successful in this, because I have been asked a hundred times whether I found this air in the old legend which provided me with my subject."

Such was the general level of knowledge among the public in the nineteenth century, when *pastiches* and forgeries continued to flourish, confusing this time troubadours with *trouvères*. One of the most ingenious practitioners in this fraudulent line of business was Fabre d'Olivet. Obsessed by the poems of Ossian, this remarkable Encyclopaedist, who was steeped in occultism, dreamed of becoming a French Macpherson in the language of Gascony ("langue d'oc"). In 1799 he published, one after the other, first a troubadour romance, *Azalaïs et le gentil Aimar*, which he pretended to have translated from an old Provençal manuscript, then in 1804 a hotch-potch of tales, dissertations and poems of his own confection under the title *Le Troubadour, poésies occitaniques du XIIIe. siècle, traduites et publiées par Fabre d'Olivet*. Musicians continued to be influenced by these falsified texts, but soon there were signs of a new approach to this question, largely due to the first studies published by de Coussemaker. This new phase can be said to have originated with Jean-Baptiste Weckerlin. From now on, instead of deliberate fraud, we find honest attempts at what we might call "touched-up documentation".

A mediocre composer, but a keen and conscientious researcher, this Alsatian ex-engineer-apprentice, studied mechanics with Schwilge, the clock-maker who built the astronomical clock in Strasbourg cathedral, then ran away from home in 1843 at the age of twenty-three to study at the Conservatoire with Elwart and Halévy, founded a historical concert society, the *Caecilia*, and became librarian of the Conservatoire. He was one of the first to undertake methodical research into French popular song, to which attention had been opportunely drawn in 1852 by the national research campaign instigated by the minister Ampère, son of the great physicist. He got together an impressive documentation and, as a result of his publications, some of which included contributions by Champfleury, established himself as one of the chief pioneers in the campaign for the preservation of French folk-lore. It was thus from this pseudo-folkloric angle that he approached the music of the *trouvères*, in conjunction with which the use of the word *chanson* merely added to the existing confusion. Himself a composer of *romances*, he was naturally attracted by the *romances* and *brunettes* (pastoral madrigals) of the eighteenth century which he had harmonized correctly, but without originality. After that, he felt a natural but quite innocent inclination to treat much older music in the same style, and in so doing, he destroyed its modal character by introducing inappropriate accidentals and adding an insipid, romance-like accompaniment. Nevertheless, he won for this music a new popularity, based this time on documents which, though distorted, were at least authentic.   Thus, in 1872, he gave at the *Société des compositeurs de musique* the first performance of *Le Jeu de Robin et Marion* which, as Fétis remarked in 1866, was then thought to be the "oldest *opéra-comique* in existence", the author being Adam de la Halle.[1]

Up till now musicians had been concerned solely with the *chansons* of the troubadours and *trouvères*. They had no idea that there could be anything else—such as, for example, a non-Gregorian Latin literature.[2] In 1738, however, Lebeuf in his *Dissertation sur le lieu ou s'est donnée en 841 la bataille de Fontenoy* drew attention to one of the historical sections of MS. 1154 in the Saint Martial Library at Limoges, and so to all the literature that followed therefrom. In 1784 Martin Gerbert, Baron de Hornau, Prince and Abbé of St. Blaise in the Black Forest, after conduting a lengthy scientific correspondence with Padre Martini of Bologna, Mozart's master, published the first collection of documents that could be used for the study of medieval music, i.e., the three volumes of his *Scriptores* which, in spite of the errors they contain, have never been superseded, as well as some ancient documents reproduced in his *De Cantu ecclesiastici*. In addition, local scholars began to rescue from oblivion certain isolated documents which turned up here and there. And in 1852 Edmond de Coussemaker, who had already written in 1841 a rather premature study of Hucbald and his Treatises on music, published what was the first serious work of medieval musicology: *Histoire de l'harmonie au Moyen Age.*

Born at Bailleul, between Lille and Hazebrouck, in 1795, de Coussemaker, after studying the violin, 'cello, singing and harmony, first at Douai and later in Paris where he was a pupil of Reicha and Victor Lefebvre, and becoming successively a lawyer in

---

[1] An opinion which has always been accepted, and which is not entirely unfounded from the point of view of historical evolution; if, however, as in this case, it is taken to mean that the work in question was the unaltered prototype of the Sedaine-type of *opéra-comique*, it is then obviously quite untrue.

[2] A case in point is that of the so-called "La Clayette MS." which was studied and copied by La Curne de Sainte-Palaye about 1773, and then reputed to be lost. The copy only refers to *chansons françaises*, without even mentioning the existence of any music. This MS., however, has recently been re-discovered; it consists of *conducts* and especially Latin, French and mixed motets for 2, 3 and 4 voices. For a description, see Albi Rosenthal, *Le manuscrit de La Clayette retrouvé*, in *Annales musicologiques*, I, pp. 105-130.

Douai, a Justice of the Peace in Bergues, a Judge in Bergues, Hazebrouck and Lille and a high-ranking magistrate in the Nord Department, was also the author of books on law, philology and local history, and an expert in French-Flemish folklore; and although referred to in a recent unfortunate French translation of Paumgartner's *Mozart* as "one de Coussemaker", it is to this man that we are indebted, despite the inevitable errors of detail and confusion inseparable from a too great profusion of new discoveries, for a collection of documents and an example of intuitive methodology which are quite remarkable for the times in which he lived.

De Coussemaker, though a pioneer in this field, had unfortunately trained no one to succeed him, and for a long time his enormously fruitful explorations of virgin territory had no sequel. It was not until around 1900 that the work he had begun was resumed with a pertinacity which has been unbroken ever since.

6

The Nineteenth Century in Search of the Renaissance

After Wallis a hundred and sixty years were to elapse before any attempt was made to follow up his researches into ancient music, and after de Coussemaker there was a gap of half a century before anyone succeeded him in the field of medieval music. One might have supposed that the music of the sixteenth century was sufficiently near to us to render any such discontinuity improbable. But that would be asking too much. The seventeenth century was well under way when the last French masters of the Renaissance disappeared: Costeley in 1606, du Caurroy in 1609, Mauduit in 1627. The latter had worked in connection with Court ballets in collaboration with the "new school" musicians, and had been the friend of Père Mersenne, an important figure, as we have seen, in the history of the music of the *Grand Siècle*. Their style was perpetuated, without any essential modifications, in the work of the English madrigalists, and also in that of the Iberian polyphonic school, and to some extent in Italy—for example, in the case of Lotti, who lived until 1740. And yet, from 1661 onwards, the year in which Lully was appointed Master of the King's Musick under His Majesty Louis XIV, it was well known in France, as the A B C of the history of music, that the latter, after having only just emerged from an infancy shrouded in obscurity, had at last found its final and definitive consummation thanks to the Incomparable Monsieur de Lully, and that there had been nothing before this great man arrived that could possibly be worth remembering. And so they lost no time in forgetting it.

But in music, as elsewhere, *"enfin Malherbe vint"*.[1]

One of the most learned musicians of his day, the Precentor Sébastien de Brossard, who in 1700 was choirmaster at Meaux, while engaged in drawing up a catalogue in 1725 came across some sonnets by Ronsard set to music by one of the most eminent contemporary musicians, Guillaume Boni; whereupon, without turning a hair he sat down to write the following notice: "The verses or words which were considered most excellent in their day seem to us but sorry stuff. Malherbe had not yet shown how

---

[1]Malherbe (1555-1628). Represented the "classical" school of French poetry. The quotation is from Boileau (1636-1711). [Translator's note.]

it was possible to polish up French poetry and render it harmonious.[1] The music to which good Master Boni has set these words is very much of the same order. It is in what the Italians call 'madrigalesco' style but, after the fashion of the old French masters, is in truth harmonious and regular, though little adapted for singing, and lacking a bass *continuo* and bars to mark the time, etc. This might have passed muster in those days, but today scarcely one in ten thousand would look with favour on Ronsard or his musician."

As for the Benedictine Dom Philippe-Joseph Caffiaux of the Congregation of St. Maur, all he could find to say about Palestrina in the monumental *Histoire de la musique* that he had announced (but never published) in 1756 and to which Fétis devotes four columns praising its "careful erudition", is that Kircher mentions a certain "Pierre Aloysius de Préneste whose compositions were so perfect that, according to him, nothing could be added to them." It is true Michel Brenet points out, that on the other hand, Dom Caffiaux "knew all about the 'cats' organ' and gives a detailed description of an admirable mechanical toy representing a skeleton playing the guitar".[2] And so it was universally acknowledged, once and for all, that music began with Lully. The whole of our admirable Franco-Flemish school was effaced from human memory, as all its predecessors had been since Perotinus. Bourdelot, after admitting that he had "passed over the reigns of several kings since there was nothing worth saying about music from Louis XI until François Ier.", finds nothing of interest in the sixteenth century apart from its fêtes and tournaments and the invention of the game of *tric-trac*; while between Robert le Pieux and the violinist du Manoir, who was supreme in 1672, he is unable to find a single musician worth mentioning apart from the *trouvères* we have already cited and, for some reason, it is difficult to say why, Eustache du Caurroy. . . .

---

[1] See, for example, the ridiculous verses he wrote for the composer Pierre Guédron to celebrate the King's marriage to Anne of Austria:

> Cette Anne si belle
> Qu'on vante si fort,
> Pourquoy ne vient-elle?
> Vrayment elle a tort
>
> Son Louys soupire
> Après ses appas, etc. . . .
>
> (This Anne so fair
> Whose praises all men sing
> Why then does she not come?
> It's very wrong of her.
>
> Meanwhile her Louis waits
> While dreaming of her charms, etc. . . .)

[2] *Palestrina*, p. 132.

This music, however, inevitably attracted some attention when the story was told admiringly about Mozart attending a service in the Sistine Chapel and writing down by ear, concealing the paper in his hat, the *Miserere* by Allegri (b. 1582) which the Chapel kept under lock and key, reserving it for its own use exclusively.[1] But because people admired the prowess of the young musician, this did not mean that their interest extended to the music itself, still less to the repertory of which it was an example.

And are we so sure that what Mozart heard was pure sixteenth century? Mendelssohn in 1831 tells in a letter how he in his turn heard the famous *Miserere*: "The best voices are reserved for the *Miserere* which is sung with all kinds of variations, and *crescendos* and *decrescendos* ranging from very soft to very loud. . . . Every piece is ornamented with the same *embellimenti*, a different one for every chord. In the following passage, for example:

instead of singing what I have written, they sing something like this:

In Rome Mendelssohn had met a young inmate of the Villa Medicis who had just arrived there, preceded by a reputation for eccentricity which, one must admit, was fully justified. His name was Hector Berlioz, and he too had heard the Sistine choir—an experience which prompted him, in his *Mémoires*, to ask whether "it is possible to apply the term 'composer' to musicians who spent their lives in compiling chord

[1]This is the somewhat improbable story put about by Leopold Mozart. Wolfgang himself gives a rather more plausible version. On returning home after the service, he tried to write down the piece from memory, after which he went back to hear it again to compare with his version, placing his copy in his hat so as not to attract attention. It was some time before the *Miserere* was sung again, but when at last he heard it a second time he saw that he had only made a few very slight mistakes. There was no question of this exploit being forbidden; on the contrary it was the talk of the town in Rome, and the child was congratulated on every side. What he had actually done was enough to justify this praise, without the unnecessary embroideries added by his showman-father. . . .

sequences like this, from Palestrina's *Improperia*" (here follows an example of a *faux-bourdon*). Thirty years later, in his *Soirées de l'Orchestre*, he numbers among "the worst nightmares one can think of" "the old pedant who finds everywhere mistakes in harmony; the discoverer of ancient manuscripts over which he gloats in ecstacy; the staunch supporter of the rules of Fugue; and those who admire the organ, the *Missa Papae Marcelli*, the Mass on the tune of *L'Homme Armé* and *chansons de geste*." In a review written about the same time (and included in *A travers chants*) of a book on church music by Joseph d'Ortigue, he gives us a specimen of the kind of "knowledge" musicians of those days had of the masterpieces of the Renaissance: "We know to what lengths of cynicism and imbecility the old contrapuntists were willing to go when they chose as themes for their so-called religious compositions popular songs whose frivolous, if not obscene words were known to everyone, and used them as a basis for their musical accompaniment to Divine Service. We all know the mass of *L'Homme Armé*. It was the glory of Palestrina that he did away with this barbarous custom."

Unfortunately this quotation loses all its force when we remember that Palestrina himself, like everyone else, wrote a Mass on *L'Homme Armé*; and only recently it has been revealed that the famous *Missa Papae Marcelli* which, thanks to a persistent legend launched in 1828 by the Abbé Baini, had come to be looked upon as the prototype of a "purified" form of polyphonic music which had miraculously saved sacred music from the fate with which it was threatened by the Council of Trent, was itself in reality, in all save the name, a Mass on *L'Homme Armé*![1] But at any rate, around 1830, the Pontifical chapel was the only one in Italy (as Berlioz pointed out), and probably the only one in Europe, to have preserved both the tradition of *a cappella* singing (hence the expression) and a part of the religious repertory of the Renaissance, even if it did enliven it by the use of *embellimenti* of which we have just given an example. But this repertory had shrunk very noticeably. The Franco-Flemish school which, in the time of Josquin des Prés and even Lassus had been its principal mainstay, had almost disappeared: the only survivor amongst them, and the object of a quasi-mystical cult, was their latest disciple Palestrina who found himself credited with having invented *en bloc* everything it had taken them two centuries to acquire and bring to perfection. And no one else was considered worthy to rank with him, or even to take second place after him except, perhaps, the great Spaniard Victoria (or Vittoria as the Italians called him); and this was perhaps because he had spent most of his life and made his career in Rome. The man who was largely responsible for this legend was one of the choir-masters of the Sistine

[1]Cf. J. Samson, *Palestrina ou la Poésie de l'exactitude*, 1939, p. 177.

Chapel, referred to above, the Abbé Baini—a curious figure who lived in such close communion with Palestrina (whom he had practically canonized in a work of fiction) that he composed his own music as if he had been his contemporary, and was so far from imagining that there could be any other kind of music that he confided one day to a scandalized Berlioz that "he had heard tell of a very promising young man called Mozart".

This would account for the Palestrina legend, still current today. He was undoubtedly one of the great Renaissance composers, but his work was, if anything, rather behind the times in which he lived. Although a contemporary of the first generation of madrigalists, of the Gabrielis, of Cyprien de Rore, of Guerrero and of Claude Le Jeune, he seems by comparison with them rather academic and old-fashioned —especially when we remember that he was acquainted with the early madrigals of Monteverdi, and that the qualities that distinguish him are to be found to at least an equal degree in the masters who preceded him, from Josquin des Prés to Roland de Lassus. Nevertheless, Palestrina is commonly supposed to be not only one of the masters of his particular style, which he was, but its initiator and prototype, which he was not:

> Puissant Palestrina, vieux maître, vieux génie,
> Je vous salue ici, père de l'harmonie . . .
> Car Gluck et Beethoven, rameaux sous qui l'on rêve
> Sont nés de votre souche et faits de votre sève;
> Car Mozart, votre fils, a pris sur vos autels
> Cette nouvelle lyre inconnue aux mortels. . . .
> Née au seizième siècle entre vos doigts sonores!

> (O mighty Palestrina, Master and genius of olden times,
> Father of harmony, I salute you now. . . .
> For Gluck and Beethoven in whose shade we dream
> Were born of your stock whose sap runs in their veins;
> And Mozart, your own offspring, has snatched from your altar
> The lyre which, under your magic fingers, long ago,
> First gave forth sounds till then unheard by mortal ears!)

So sang Victor Hugo in 1837.[1]
Alfred de Musset, in *Lucie*, embroidered on the same theme:

> Fille de la douleur, harmonie! harmonie!
> Langue que pour l'amour inventa le génie!
> Qui nous vins d'Italie, et qui lui vins des cieux. . . .

[1] *Que la musique date du XVIe siècle* (in *Les Rayons et les Ombres*).

(Daughter of suffering, O harmony! harmony!
Invention of genius, the language of love
Which came to us from Italy, and to Italy from heaven. . . .)

This rudimentary distortion of history is particularly regrettable, coming as it does from two compatriots of the old masters who for at least two hundred years had prepared the way for Palestrina.[1] It nevertheless represents a widely held belief, the last vestiges of which are only just beginning to disappear.

The re-discovery of the ancient world had begun with theoretical speculations; that of the Middle Ages with the study of manuscripts purely for reasons of documentation. The Renaissance, however, was brought to light in quite a different way, by means of actual live performances of its music.

One of those responsible for this new approach was the bearer of an historic name—none other than one of the sons of Marshal Ney, Joseph Napoleon, Prince of Moskowa. Born in 1803, Joseph Ney had a passionate love of music and dreamed of becoming a composer and conductor. He came under the influence of a man who was chiefly instrumental in bringing about in France another renaissance for which others were to claim the credit: Alexandre Choron, who founded in 1817 a School of Classical and Religious Music whose place was taken later by the Ecole Niedermeyer. Choron had already organized concerts very different from the ordinary run of those given under official auspices; he had played Bach and Handel and even Palestrina. After being Director of the Opera for one year, he was obliged to resign his post, because the radical reforms he had announced had caused a panic. The Revolution of 1830 had put an end to all his schemes, and Choron died in 1834, apparently without having succeeded in bringing about his own musical revolution. Then in 1843 Joseph Ney founded the *Société de musique vocale religieuse et classique*. His high social standing gave him many advantages, and the pleasure he derived from conducting his concerts acted as a stimulus. His researches brought to light a number of unknown works of the sixteenth, seventeenth and eighteenth centuries; he also financed their publication. There was plenty to choose from, for they were all unknown. It was thus that the names of Josquin, Jannequin and Costeley appeared for the first time. The concerts organized by the

---

[1]The catalogue of the repertory of the Sistine Chapel has never, so far as we know, been published. Félix Raugel, who had occasion to examine this collection, has told of his astonishment on discovering that the great majority, if not all, the composers represented were French, or Flemings from French Flanders. Moreover, we know that Palestrina was a pupil of the Frenchman Firmin le Bel, and that his style is much closer to that of his elder, Roland de Lassus, than to that of madrigalists who were his contemporaries, or even to that of his friend Victoria, heir to a tradition of Spanish romanticism that can be traced back to Cristobal Morales, the contemporary in Madrid of the Fleming Nicolas Gombert.

Prince of Moskowa, intended for a restricted audience consisting of a small number of invited guests, were famous in social rather than in musical circles; musicians were not interested. His editions, judged by the standards of musicology considered indispensable today, were premature, and had to be revised later. Nevertheless, they did at least exist, and gradually musicians began dimly to suspect that there might be something in this music after all.

In Germany a similar movement was started in Ratisbon (Regensburg) by one Karl Proske to whom, by a royal decree of September 9, 1830, King Louis I of Bavaria had granted almost unlimited freedom of action in this field. In 1865 a Belgian organist, named Robert van Maldeghem, undertook the publication of a monumental work, the *Trésor Musical*, of which twenty-nine volumes appeared in 1893. Nearly a thousand pieces of religious and secular music were brought to light in this way, and even today Maldeghem's work, though quite inadequate from a critical point of view, is the only one where certain important compositions of the sixteenth century can still easily be found. In 1892 Charles Bordes, who had been appointed two years earlier choirmaster at Saint-Gervais, founded the *"semaines saintes de Saint-Gervais"* during which music of the sixteenth century was sung for the first time in public in France. Encouraged by the success of this venture, he founded the *Association des Chanteurs de Saint-Gervais*, giving this time concerts of secular music as well; he also published the texts in the form of loose sheets offered at a reasonable price, thanks to the support of the Schola Cantorum of which, together with Guilmant and d'Indy, he had been one of the founders in 1894.[1] Shortly before this event, the man who was to play a decisive rôle in the rebirth of the Renaissance, Henry Expert, began to work in complete obscurity.

Expert at that time was nearly thirty (he was born at Bordeaux on May 12, 1863) and was determined, despite the opposition of his parents, to become a composer. Thanks to Reyer, well known at the time as a composer of post-Wagnerian operas, he was enrolled as a pupil at the Ecole Niedermeyer, which was then situated in the Rue Fontaine-Saint-Georges (today Rue Fromentin), not far from the "fortifications" of Clichy; and there, according to his fellow-pupil Henri Büsser, who came from Toulouse, the young man from Bordeaux became very popular on account of his lively wit and imagination. At the instigation of the Prince of Moskowa, Niedermeyer had, in 1853, started a choral class at which he taught his pupils to sing Bach, Mozart, Handel and even Wagner with piano or organ accompaniment, and Palestrina and Lassus *a cappella*. In the little room, devoid of any comfort, in which he boarded, Expert

[1] 1894 as a Society; 1896 as the existing music school.

got up every morning at 4 a.m. and worked till eleven o'clock at night. This sixteenth century music, which to all but himself and his fellow-pupils was then unknown, exercised a strange fascination over him, and he asked the Director of the school, Gustave Lefèvre, how he could find out more about it. Lefèvre then sent him to Henri Lavoix, Assistant Keeper of the Bibliothèque Nationale, who introduced him to masses by Josquin des Prés and a collection of French songs printed by Attaingnant. "On opening for the first time these precious volumes," he writes, "I was completely be-wildered. Each choral part was published in a different volume, and in a square or diamond-shaped notation, covered with slurs, indications of all kinds—division marks, etc, without bar-lines or time signatures of any kind; the words, too, were full of abbreviations." In vain he sought for an explanation. Bernard Loth has told how, with-out interrupting his composition classes with César Franck and Gigout, Expert spent his time, an obscure and almost unknown figure, working in libraries, poring over bulky tomes and dusty old manuscripts. "At every turn," he wrote, "new obstacles arose. One part of a chorus was in Paris, the rest in Italy or Norway. I had to have volumes sent to me from all over Europe. As soon as I took possession of these works, which were only lent to me for relatively short periods of time—and how obligingly!—I photo-graphed each page and filed it. Eventually I adopted a system which enabled me to photograph four pages at a time and in this way to obtain ninety-six prints per hour."

Musicologists today are familiar with this sort of work; they have international catalogues at their disposal, organisations that specialize in lending manuscripts and well-equipped photographic studios. Nothing of the kind existed in those days,[1] and one can imagine what colossal labour this must have entailed for this indefatigable worker who gave up everything for it, including his dreams of becoming a composer. He also devoted his entire fortune to the task he had set himself, which now involved researches, not only into the texts themselves, but also into theoretical works which would enable him to transcribe them correctly. Finally, in 1895, he started, with the aid of his friends Leduc and Senart, to publish his great collection, which is now a standard work, of the *Maîtres musiciens de la Renaissance française*, embracing every kind of music, secular and sacred—Catholic, Huguenot, Humanist, French and Latin. In 1908 his funds gave out, subscriptions were still inadequate, and the project, to his great grief, had to be abandoned. Then an Egyptian Maecenas came to the rescue, a certain Nicolas Negib

[1]Today microfilms are in current use; they take up little room and give quick results and are not too expensive, and there are also "readers" which can be used for enlargement, thus avoiding the relatively high cost of printing. At the time we are writing about one had to work with glass slides, which were heavy, slow and expensive.

Sursock, and in 1924 a second volume followed the first called this time *Monuments de la musique française au temps de la Renaissance*.[1]

In the meantime Expert, who had been appointed librarian at Sainte-Geneviève, and later at the Conservatoire, gave lectures and organized concerts. He began with a simple vocal quartet, and then gathered round him an ever-growing circle of keen amateurs until, in 1923-4, on the occasion of a Ronsard centenary, he founded his famous *Chanterie de la Renaissance* whose concerts, as they became increasingly popular, played a decisive part in reviving the affection of musicians for this admirable choral music which they had forgotten for three centuries. Those who were privileged to attend these concerts will never forget the exceptional atmosphere which Expert managed to create around them. He would come trotting on to the platform of the Salle Erard[2] or the Conservatoire where his singers were waiting for him in evening dress, with his white hair and bristling moustache, alert and spry, and begin, lisping slightly, to introduce the pieces in the programme, becoming more and more excited as he went on. At the height of his enthusiasm, and overcome by his emotion (which caused him to stammer) he would usually end by saying: "It's . . . it's a marvellous thing . . . just listen now, and you'll see for yourselves. . . ." He would then spring lightly on to the platform and conduct the choir (without a *bâton*)[3] in some magnificent piece by Le Jeune, Févin or Anthoine de Bertrand. Like the Abbé Baini before him, Expert literally lived in the century he loved so well. I remember a conversation with him in the course of which, while telling me about some difficulties he had encountered, he remarked, quite unconsciously (I thought it admirable at the time): "Ah! in our time nothing like that would have happened!" By "our time", he meant the sixteenth century . . . .[4] Since then the movement launched by Expert has never stopped. Other societies have been

---

[1]At his death in 1952 (at the age of 89) Expert left some 2000 transcriptions still unpublished. Thanks to the generosity of Mme. Salabert, these are now in course of publication under the auspices of a *Société des Amis d'Expert*, founded by Bernard Loth, and with the assistance of musicologists responsible for seeing that the publication will be entirely up to date from a musicological point of view. The first volume of this new collection containing the second part of the *Octonaires de la vanité du monde* by Paschal de l'Estocart (the first part was published by Expert) was published in 1960.

[2]The charming little hall in the rue du Mail, so rich in historical memories, now dismantled and dreary, has become the French Radio's "Studio 32".

[3]It would seem that Expert was the first to adopt this method of conducting choirs, which has now become the fashion, and also the first to organize the "lecture-concerts" which are so popular today.

[4]The author of this book in 1937 had the honour to succeed Henry Expert, on his retirement, at the head of the *Chanterie* which was later amalgamated with another similar society, the *Psallette de Notre Dame*, founded a few years previously to do for the music of the Middle Ages what the *Chanterie* had done for the Renaissance. The 1939 war put an end to its activities, despite the efforts which were made until 1941 to keep it alive.

founded, more and more old music is being published in every country, the choral works of the Renaissance are now the basis of the repertory of every choir in the world, and the instrumental works—which Expert had rather neglected—are beginning to be better known. Furthermore, scholars are working everywhere to add to our knowledge with results that are becoming more and more evident every year. . . .

We must not forget that all this has happened because one day a young student at the Ecole Niedermeyer, fascinated by some unusual music used for teaching purposes, asked where he could find the originals, found himself up against a barrier of prejudice and denigrations, and then decided that, even at the cost of losing his fortune and sacrificing his career as a composer, he would learn somehow to decipher this notation so that the living music hidden under these hieroglyphics might be heard again by human ears. . . .

7

The Twentieth Century in Search of——?

To the history we have outlined in the preceding chapters it would not be difficult to add a sequel. When Lully became old-fashioned, no attempt was made to see beyond Gluck. Then it was discovered that among the "old" composers who had been forgotten there was a certain German Kapellmeister called Johann Sebastian Bach who deserved a better reputation than that of a composer of dull exercises—which was how he had always been regarded up till then.[1] Some of the greatest and most famous musicians, such as Mozart, Schumann, Mendelssohn and Chopin had discovered him—in some cases rather late—and declared how much they owed to him. So then it was decided that music began with Bach. When Victor Hugo proclaimed (see above, p. 41) that "music dates from the sixteenth century", this was going back to pre-historical times. A study of the writings and concert-programmes of the nineteenth century shows that Haydn is the oldest of the great classical masters whose reputation has been uninterruptedly maintained up to the present day, and whose music has not had to be "re-discovered". Even so, in his case, as in that of his predecessors, contemporaries and descendants, the list of works that are still well known and regularly performed is

---

[1]Out of his whole vast output, the only works of Bach to be published during his life-time were one cantata, some fifteen harpischord pieces, six organ chorales and the *Musical Offering*. The story of the famous "discovery" of the St. Matthew Passion by Zelter and Mendelssohn in 1829 is well known. But until 1850, when the first volumes of the Bach-Gesellschaft began to appear, Bach, except to a very few, was still known as the author of five-finger exercises—like Czerny—and as a model for students of counterpoint—like Théodore Dubois. My own mother told me how the mother of one of her pupils once remarked in a great state of indignation: "I can understand your wanting my daughter to play exercises by Czerny; but that you should have such a low opinion of her talent as to make her play Bach—that is really too much. . . ."

As to his reputation of being "old-fashioned", which caused his son Johann Christian to speak of him disrespectfully as an "old fogey", it is important to correct a mistake commonly made today in circles known as "advanced" where it is customary to cite the examples of Monteverdi being disparaged by Artusi, and Bach being run down by Scheibe. But Scheibe was born in 1708, twenty-three years after Bach, and happened to be a young avant-garde critic who was not interested in Bach because he was not "up to date". Bach was detested by the partisans of the Weberns and Boulez's of those days, but not by the traditionalists. As for Artusi—his case was rather different, for Artusi was a writer of treatises who was annoyed at the success of works which paid no attention to his theories.

pitifully small.[1] Musicians in general only began to have an inkling of the treasures contained in the music of the remoter past when the repertoire of the gramophone was enlarged, around 1930, by the introduction of electric recordings; the real turning-point, however, was the invention of the L.P. disc in 1952.

The work of the specialists has followed a similar path. We have interrupted our narrative just when the era of modern "musicology" was dawning—and this, as we have seen, was a remarkably recent event. In regard to the various disciplines, it may be said to have occurred somewhere between ten and a hundred years ago. Starting from the point where we left it, its history reveals an entirely changed outlook; it has become a real science, with its own standards of methodology and documentation in no way less severe than those of its literary or scientific sisters. It is organized on an international plane, and its field has become so vast that the sum total of its discoveries and knowledge are more than could be acquired in a lifetime. Already the first history-writers who, following the primitive attempts of Bourdelot and Printz (continued in 1695 by a singer from Perugia, one Giovanni Andrea Angelini, nicknamed Bontempi) had attempted a synthesis, had to give up. In 1757 Padre Martini, famous for his erudition, had embarked on a *Storia della musica*, beginning with the ancient Hebrews; but he scarcely got as far as the Greeks. Laborde in 1780 attempted an *Essai sur la musique ancienne et moderne*, but this was only a collection of scattered notes. A Belgian composer, Fétis, undertook in 1869 a *Histoire générale de la musique;* but in five volumes he got no farther than the fifteenth century, in spite of having revealed in his immense *Biographie universelle des musiciens et bibliographie générale de la musique* (1833-44, 8 vols.) a wealth of knowledge and erudition quite astonishing for those days.[2] In 1788 Forkel embarked on an *Allgemeine Geschichte der Musik*, but had to stop at the sixteenth century, while the Czech from Prague, August Wilhelm Ambros, in 1862-78, only managed in the four volumes of his *Geschichte der Musik*, to get as far as the beginning of the seventeenth

---

[1] A legend, not altogether disinterested, which needs to be contradicted is that of the alleged dislike of the public for any new work of genius. One could even affirm that the opposite is true, namely that until those responsible for it made a bogy of the term "contemporary music", the public was far more interested in novelties than in "resurrections" from the past. The examples so frequently cited of Beethoven, Berlioz or Debussy will not bear examination: the programmes of the first year of the Société des Concerts du Conservatoire in 1828 speak of performances of Beethoven symphonies repeated "by request"; the lamentations of Berlioz go hand in hand with a career which many contemporary composers would have good reason to envy, and Debussy notes that after the organized hostile demonstration at the first night of *Pelléas*, his masterpiece, at the end of the first month, was a great box-office success. The same applies to the "scandal" of the Rite of Spring; when it was performed a year later in a concert version it had a triumphant reception.

[2] In spite of the numerous errors of detail and the necessity of checking every line, the "Fétis" is still a standard work today. Most unjustly, Fétis has come to be discredited on account of the partiality of his judgments and his inability to understand certain kinds of music, both old and new.

century. The English writers Burney, in 1776-89, and Hawkins, in 1776, were the only ones to complete what they set out to do; but Burney was primarily a reporter, whose notes jotted down in the course of his travels are still a source of curious information, while Hawkins was scarcely more than a compiler. The first serious history of music was, in 1801, the *Oxford History of Music* which was a success because its initiators had at last hit upon the only valid formula—that of collective authorship—an example which was followed in Germany by Kretschmar, and in France by Lavignac—and subsequently by all the other publications of this nature, apart from second-hand compilations.

Furthermore, our knowledge grows from day to day as detailed research is being continually extended. Hardly a year goes by without our being apprised that something that has always been sanctioned by tradition and considered certain has been investigated by a research worker and found to be based either on a legend, or on a hasty assertion, or perhaps on an error in transmission. For example, all the histories of music in the world have taught for three hundred years that tragic opera (musical tragedy) was invented in Florence in the *Camerata* of Count Bardi, and that the *Dialogue* by Galileo *père* constituted its birth certificate; it wasn't until 1953 that the truth about this, very different from the legend, was discovered, as will be related in Chapter 21. In April, 1956, in a communication to the *Société française de musicologie*, a professor at the Sorbonne presented a thesis according to which the whole theory of the Greek modes, accepted as gospel for more than a hundred years, taught in thousands of text-books and universally considered to have at last placed the problem in its correct perspective after centuries of misrepresentation (thanks to the work of Westphal, Gevaert, Emmanuel, etc., in the nineteenth century) was in fact based on no authentic evidence whatever; all it did was to apply to ancient Greek music retrospectively ideas which could not have been earlier than the tenth, and in some cases the sixteenth century. In other words, Viollet-le-Duc and not Champollion had been taken as a model. And this thesis—which I have a good reason not to discuss here—might never have been formulated were it not for the fact that in the last ten years or so the progress made in magnetic recording techniques had made it possible to assemble, hear and compare thousands of different pieces of music providing first-hand evidence as to the way in which civilizations not having gone through the same stages of development as our own reacted to the problem of music as they saw it.

This great wave of nostalgia for lost and forgotten music, totally unknown until then, had its origin, together with humanism, in the vast cycle of the myth of the Golden Age, and was at first concerned not so much with music as with the Golden Age itself.

The Renaissance, which had neglected its own music, threw all its energies into re-discovering that of ancient Greece; the Romantics were preoccupied with the music of the Middle Ages, and the late nineteenth century with that of the Renaissance. And what about our own day?

The twentieth century, whose musical debut took place under the symbolic sign of the magical rites of the *Sacre du Printemps*, seems set on going back farther into the past than any of the others. Its hankering after the Primitive in all its forms is revealed in all the arts. Never before have modern works shown such an obsession with incantations, ritual dances, percussion and piccolos simulating a return to primitive sonorities. It is not surprising that in describing the latest researches into Greek music we had to mention those primitive recordings which fifty years ago merely caused people to say that they "sounded all wrong", but which today arouse the enthusiasm and curiosity of musicologists and musicians.

In this way a new branch of musicology—the specialists call it ethnomusicology—has appeared upon the scene, thanks to which innumerable data, consecrated by tradition, have been in recent years subjected to fresh examination. The problem of the origins and development of polyphony, for example, which has hitherto been studied from manuscripts solely in relation to Western history, will from now on have to be examined afresh in the light of entirely new evidence; and after a few more years of study, everything that has been written on this subject in all our histories of music will have to be replaced.

These are only a few examples of what is happening today; there are many others. It was not intended in this chapter to describe the work of our contemporaries, but merely to show how recent and how uncertain is our knowledge in matters of musical history, and to recommend a more humble approach to those who, on the strength of a few hasty historical deductions, imagine that they are in a position to predict the future from what they know of the past. . . .

PART II

IN SEARCH OF SACRED MUSIC

8

What is Music for?

One evening in October 1955 the manager of the Olympia music-hall in Paris telephoned the police. Excited by the saxophone in a celebrated jazzband, the audience, teenagers for the most part, roused to frenzy had smashed all the mirrors and ripped up all the seats. People were injured, and the damage amounted to thousands of pounds.

For the space of an hour music had ceased to be the nodding old lady of the solemn classical concerts and had become again what it used to be in prehistoric times—a redoubtable force whose secret the gods of long ago had revealed and which, if carelessly handled, might expose the State to the gravest dangers, for it gave men power over their fellow-men, and enabled them to dominate the gods themselves.

What we call music today has little in common with that mysterious force which Plato made one of the foundations of his Republic. Rameau defined it as the art of "pleasing and exciting in us various passions": the latter term is now but a faint echo of what it was originally, while the former arouses only distant memories.

Ought we to renounce these memories altogether? There are those who think so nowadays and who have expressed their views in writing, even going so far as to consider the "pleasure" caused by music as a "concession", an "impurity", which they contemptuously dismiss as "hedonism". "I am a musician", writes René Leibowitz who taught so many of our "avant-gardists", in the years round 1945, "and as such a great part of my life is passed in direct contact with sound-patterns which I either endeavour to invent and co-ordinate myself or study in the scores of other. . . . but I can truthfully say that reading or hearing a musical work, no matter what it is, has never been for me a source of pleasure or distraction, or even an indication of any curiosity on my part. If in reading or listening to any music I have ever experienced pleasure or relaxation, or even boredom or irritation, these are qualities which have been superimposed and have nothing to do with what I am studying, the purpose and subject of which are something quite different."[1]

There is therefore a wide gulf between the point where we started and the point at

---

[1] R. Leibowitz, *Schoenberg et son école*, p. 9.

which we have arrived. No doubt the latter only represents the point of view of a small minority, and is still considered by many to be outrageous; nevertheless it has been adopted as a general principle by a whole school of composers. From the domination of cosmic forces to merely playing about with sound patterns, through a period when music was expected to give pleasure or arouse passions—and even then on a purely emotional plane—the downward curve has been continuous. This progressive decline and diminution of its powers make it increasingly imperative to pose the basic question: For whom and for what purpose do we continue to make music?

For primitive man music is not an art; it is a force. Through it the world was created: by the harmony of the vowels, say the Brahmins; by the vibrations of the singing of the gods, say the Bambara; by the Word which was made flesh, said St. John—and in the universal context of this text, we must take this to mean the Sung Word, which existed before the world was created: *in principio erat Verbum*.[1] Music is the only particle of the divine essence which men have been able to capture, and this has enabled them, by means of prescribed rites, to identify themselves with the gods and exercise control over them. Then the process was reversed. After the gods have spoken to men through music, men through music will speak to the gods. Instead of subjugating them, they will now praise and flatter and pray to them. Through music they will have power over fate, and the elements and animals. Sometimes, too, when they are alone they will use for their own purposes some of the marvellous powers of this supernatural language.

A coloured flute-player, when asked what he used his instrument for, replied: "One plays it when one is alone to drive away one's troubles."[2] Though he did not know it, he had just described what had always been for thousands of years, in the eyes of the gods and rulers of this earth, the chief *raison d'être* of the art of music. Guillaume de Machaut in the fourteenth century, had expressed a similar idea in his poem *Veoir Dit*, or *Dit Véridique:*

> Car Musique est une science
> Qui veut qu'on rie et chante et danse.
> Cure n'a de mélancolie . . .
> Partout où elle est, joie y porte:
> Les déconfortés réconforte
> Et n'est seulement de l'ouïr
> Fait-elle les gens réjouir.

[1] Cf. a lecture given by Marius Schneider at the Musicological Institute of Paris in December 1960 on: *Le chant de louange et les cosmogonies d'origine mégalithique.* (Hymns of praise and cosmogonies of megalithic origin.)

[2] This expression "when one is alone" shows how far we have travelled: what would be the reaction of a Conservatoire pupil today if a career of this kind were suggested to him as the goal of his studies?

> (For music is a science
> Which makes men want to laugh and sing and dance.
> There is no place in it for melancholy.
> Where'er it is, there joy goes too:
> It comforts those in need of comforting
> And to hear it is enough to make all men rejoice.)

About a century later a grave and learned theoretician, Brother Jerome of Moravia declared, in sonorous Latin, at the end of his rules for mutations and monochords, that "more than anything a sorrowful heart is an obstacle to the making of fine music; because melancholy persons may have fine voices but cannot really sing well".[1] "*Les plus désespérés sont les chants les plus beaux*", wrote Alfred de Musset. Until then everyone had believed the opposite to be true. The expression of sorrow in music, until the nineteenth century or thereabouts, had been confined to the liturgy (Passion or Penitentiary music) or to the theatre (the lamentations of fictitious characters)—in any case it had nothing to do with the musician himself. In Bach's time, or Mozart's, the fact that the composer was getting married tomorrow or had just buried his father and mother the day before, did not affect his music in any way: he was joyful at Easter and shed tears in the third Act of *Orpheus*. Otherwise nothing of himself, sentimentally speaking, appeared in his music. It has been remarked that only two of Mozart's thirty-two symphonies are in a minor key (both in G minor), and this is cited as a sign of foreknowledge of things to come. Out of the seven thousand eighteenth-century symphonies catalogued by Jan La Rue and Robbins Landon, only 140 are in a minor key (i.e., scarcely one in fifty)[2] and if Haydn one day wrote a sad symphony in the unwonted key of F sharp minor, this was due to exceptional circumstances; and though the story is well known, it is worth telling again: In January 1772 the Prince Esterhazy had forbidden his musicians to receive members of their families at the Esterhazy palace where they accompanied him while he was in residence. Autumn came round, and when there were still no signs of the Prince's departure, the orchestra began to get restive and irritable. One evening when Haydn was conducting his latest symphony in the presence of the Prince's guests, the latter were surprised at the unusual key of the newly composed work: it was in F sharp minor. Then during the last movement, the players

---

[1] Praecipuum autem impedimentum faciendi pulchras notas est cordis tristitia, eo quod nulla nota valet nec valere potest, quae vero procedit ex cordis hilaritate, propter quod melancolici pulchras quidem voces habere possunt, pulchre vero cantare non possunt. (de Coussemaker, *Scriptores*, 1, 94.)

[2] Cf. H. C. Robbins Landon: *The romantic crisis in Austrian music circa 1770*, in *Foreign influences in the works of Mozart.*

were seen one by one to blow out their candles and leave their seats. The orchestra, as it gradually dwindled away, became more and more gloomy until finally there were only two miserable violins left on the platform, and the proceedings came to an end in an atmosphere of embarrassment all round. The Prince understood very well what they were hinting at, and the next day everyone packed their bags and Haydn's symphonies returned to their customary major key.

Even when popular songs are sad—there are some countries where this is the rule rather than the exception—it often seems that the music tends to soften the sadness rather than to heighten it. Georges Duhamel speaks of "music that consoles". And this, minus the suggestion of pity which the term conveys, is essentially the rôle played by music until the dawn of the romantic era. The violence of the conflict which, throughout the nineteenth century separated the superficial brilliance of Franco-Italian music from the "inwardness" of the German *Stimmung* represented in a sense the defensive reaction of an age-old conception which felt itself threatened. At the beginning of the century it looked as if it had been definitely defeated. But can it be said that it really was defeated? Are not we witnessing today a retrospective revaluation of a Bizet or a Chabrier, who used to be looked down upon, while Stravinsky proclaims the superiority of *Rigoletto* over *Parsifal?*

Then came the romantic movement. With Beethoven, Schumann and, above all, Chopin, music learned to express something different: the personal feelings of the musician—his joys and sorrows—and not only the feelings he might occasionally lend to a fictitious personage. Thus Romanticism in the nineteenth century restored to music its primitive mediumistic qualities, but paradoxically in a contrary sense. This time it was no longer the audience which employed the musician to express its collective emotions, but the musician who convened an audience in order to impose upon it his own personal feelings and to cause it to share in his joys and sorrows. The only difference was that, in this new restoration of primitive contacts, the musician himself was, without knowing it, a direct emanation of the collective consciousness, the incarnation, so to speak of the age in which he lived; and because it saw itself reflected in him, his epoch in return, though unconsciously, empowered him to represent it and thus renewed, through him, a far older tradition, the loss of which today appears as the greatest danger which could threaten music.

Jules Combarieu, the first University professor in France since the Revolution to be officially appointed to teach the History of Music (on the occasion of the creation of a Chair thus designated at the Collège de France in 1904), created astonishment in musical circles by the publication in 1909 of a work entitled *La Musique et la Magie* (*Music and*

Magic). He summarized his conclusions by laying down in the first pages of his *Histoire de la Musique* (1913) as an axiom (which in all essentials has been confirmed by recent research) that: "The origins of music can be traced to man's anxiety in the face of the hostility of Nature which he interprets as being due to savage spirits who have to be appeased with incantations, which can be used both as an offensive and a defensive weapon . . .; the development of the primitive incantation into a religious and socially organized lyrical form; and the gradual growth, by a process of abstraction, of an art cultivated for itself purely for recreative purposes—these are the three phases of evolution on which, in every country, a plan for a history of music can be based."

No such history has ever been written, not even by Combarieu, more's the pity. It would be a change from all those anecdotes about composers and their private love affairs which, all too often, pass for "histories of music".

At the origin of music three principal protagonists can be distinguished: the gods; the king; and the musician himself. Under different names and through various vicissitudes these have always been the prime instigators of the extraordinary development of the art of music until quite recent times—indeed, more recent than many people would have believed. The notion of the "public" is quite a recent one, and so is that of the "composer"—that super-man whose infallibility by divine right, the dogma of the twentieth century *avant-garde*, is nothing but an invention of the romantic school which they detest so much. It is only in our own generation that we encounter this chimera of "purity" which condemns the interpreter to be nothing but a faithful reading-machine of that inhuman "tabou": "the text as written" and to replace the old protagonists by a new one: the God of Paper. As for the idea of mortgaging the future on the basis of a convention of language—"serialism", microtonalism or any other 'ism—this is an innovation which we may contemplate with astonishment but not always with conviction.

Yet paradoxically we stupidly continue to multiply barriers and interdictions and inhibitions; and at the same time our nostalgia for music as "active" as it used to be in its primitive state, has never been so strong. It is not by chance that the musical twentieth century was ushered in by the savage incantations of the *Rite of Spring*. Nor that jazz, with its uninhibited abandon, vulgar though it may be, offers a refuge to those who wish to escape from the old-maidishness of a certain kind of "serious" music in search of tiresome "lucidities".

And so the twentieth century in a curious way is closing the circle again. After finally stripping music bare in a most inhuman way, surrounding it with barbed wire and gradually isolating it from life by means of incomprehensible annotations, it suddenly, and no doubt unconsciously, is reverting again to sources which are entirely incompatible with that "purity" which is its ideal—sources which contain not only the mud, but also the gushing spontaneity of music in its infancy. That these two worlds, with few exceptions, ignore one another is of no importance; perhaps a new classicism will emerge from the lessons that can be learnt from both.

One thing is certain—today, as in the past; we can confirm the celebrated saying: "One can live without music, but not so well." And in these days of a mechanized civilization the complaint of Psichari in the silence of the desert seems singularly apt: "What one misses here is music. One longs for it until sometimes it hurts."[1]

[1]*Les Voix qui crient dans le désert*, Chap. IV.

9

Music for the Gods : Magic, Masques and Dancing

Music, viewed as a spontaneous emanation from the human heart, is, in a sense, utilitarian and functional. It has no "public", and does not expect one. Its only public is composed of the mysterious forces to which it is addressed.

The magical power of music is not a fable invented by mythomaniacs. It is with and through music that the African witch-doctor today forms his diagnosis and chases away the evil spirits, and the Indian warrior before a battle has recourse to it to ensure his victory. In our country-side the village "witch", when she casts her spells to bring sickness to her neighbour's cow, often does so in a song; while in the innocent rhyming tags which children sing to decide who's going to be "out", the ethnologists have long ago detected the unconscious survival of the primitive magic by which we were once surrounded: song to begin with, then gradually only the spoken word, as the residual character of customs that are more and more alien to the new social order in which we live becomes more pronounced.

The civilization which has destroyed these powers has never ceased to regret them. We saw in Chapter 2 how rational people like Cicero solemnly recounted the marvellous exploits of the flute-player of Pythagoras; while the humanists of the sixteenth and seventeenth centuries firmly believed that if they could re-discover the intervals of the Greek "chromatic" scale they would be able, like Amphion, to build the walls of Thebes; Bourdelot equally seriously tells us of the wonderful cures effected by Lully's airs. None of them ever gave a thought to the African negro medicine-man who for centuries has been making passes to the sound of the tom-tom or the Ouombi harp over the belly of his patients.

We are much closer to our origins than we think, and we don't have to go and gaze at the skeleton of the Diplodocus in order to approach them again. When we say conventionally "charmed to meet you", or "enchanted to see you", we certainly do not reflect that the "charm" was originally the *carmen* sung by sorcerers or that it was only with the advent of rationalism in the sixteenth century that the term "enchantment" lost its primitive meaning of *in-cantare*, in the sense of casting a spell in song over the chosen victim. Gautier de Coinci, in the thirteenth century, made this a pretext for some pleasing alliterations in the first of his hymns to the Virgin:

> Amour, qui bien sait enchanter
> A plusieurs fait tel chant chanter
> Dont les âmes déchantent.

In nearly all mythologies music was given to man by a god. Primitive musical theory is rarely concerned with technique, nearly always with symbolism. The legend of the Phoenix (see page 5) tells us very little about the ancient Chinese scale, but it does not forget to distinguish between male and female sounds—a notion which we find among the African negroes and also in the works of the Greek theorists as late as the second century A.D.[1] Among the Dogons in the Sudan, the eight kinds of drum correspond to the phases of the creation of the world, from the birth of the great Monitor (the Kunyu drum) to the age when the human race began to increase and multiply (the barba drum);[2] these drums represent the four elements because their parchment, moist at first (water) has been dried by the sun (fire), their frames are of wood (earth) and they contain air which vibrates.[3] These peoples could not analyse the technique of their art, but no one among them could call himself a musician unless he knew everything about its religious symbolism. Christianity itself approached music from the same angle: in the fourth century St. Basil compared the ten strings of the psaltery to the Ten Commandments, and the player of this instrument to the Christian who can see in the Decalogue a perfect consonance; while St. Augustine sees in the tympanum, with its stretched parchment, the body of Christ crucified,[4] just as for the Sudanese Dogon the "harp-lute resembles in its form the body and single leg of the Monitor Nommo when he appears as a musician."[5]

This exaggerated symbolism continued for a long time, and sometimes in the most naïve forms: thus, as late as the seventeenth century "M. Olier", founder of the St. Sulpice Seminary, likened the organ to the Holy Trinity, the organist being God the Father, the blower the Son and the wind the Holy Ghost, while the numerous pipes represented the multitude of angels.[6] The most ancient illustrated document in musical history is a scene of magic: the man with the musical bow wears an animal's mask; he is wrapped in a skin and is playing behind a troop of reindeer which he is no doubt trying

---

[1]E.g., in Quintilian, Ed. Meibom, pp. 101, 134, etc.

[2]Cf. Marcel Griaule, *Symbolisme des tambours soudanais*, *Mélanges P. M. Masson*, 1955, I, p. 84.

[3]Cf. G. Calame-Griaule and B. Calame, *Introduction à l'étude de la musique africaine*, Carnets critiques de la *Revue Musicale*, No. 238, 1957, pp. 17-19.

[4]Cf. Gérold, *Histoire de la musique des Origines au XIVe. siècle*, 1936, p. 140.

[5]Griaule, *op. cit.* p. 85.

[6]Letter 105 "à l'un de ses ecclésiastiques", Ed. Lévesque.

to charm. The mask, the faithful appanage of the musical magic of our remote ancestors, still plays the same part in all the tribes of Africa and Oceania: first it is the mask of an animal, then of a god, then of a legendary hero—the tangible sign of a transfer of personality of which music is a necessary accompaniment—hence the rôle of music in the primitive theatre everywhere. We shall find this same mask again in ancient Greek tragedy, and in the Japanese *No* and the Chinese opera—always accompanied by music.

1. A palaeolithic musical scene from the cave of the Trois-Frères (Ariège). A man wearing an animal's mask is playing a musical bow and dancing behind a troop of reindeer which he is no doubt trying to charm.

Having gradually lost its dignity as a symbol of divinity, it appears again in the comedies and farces of Aristophanes and Plautus, in the frivolities of the *Commedia dell' Arte*, in Court ballets and in the festivities of Carnival. Music is generally present in some form or other; it no longer has the same incantatory powers, but it is always there, a relic of immemorial traditions which no one today understands. Sometimes mask and music together try to find an echo of their former grandeur: in the Court ballets, as a sign of their rank, Louis XIV and the royal princes used to dance in masks. English opera in the seventeenth century had, by analogy, taken the name of "masque", and when in our own day children put on masks for fun on Shrove Tuesday, they little think that they represent the end of a tradition whose origins go back to the very beginnings of a universal religion.

Like the mask, the dance is also a universal sign of the super-human powers of music. Man's first instinct is not to keep still while listening to music. The sight of our modern audience in a concert hall, comfortably ensconced in their velvet *fauteuils*, would astonish anyone who had not been through the five hundred years or so of Western evolution which have brought us to this condition. Music is *ars bene movendi:* it acts on every fibre of our being, body and soul. This no doubt is why dancing is one of its oldest manifestations. It is also the reason why, reduced to its most primitive aspects, dancing is also a religious art *par excellence.*

There is even a theory according to which the instinct to dance is older than the earliest ages of humanity. Naturalists like Carpenter, Koehler or Zuckermann have traced it back to the pre-anthropoid era, and have given us a picture of chimpanzees dancing the equivalent of our children's "rounds", holding hands, under the direction of a "games master", directing the dance by clapping his hands or stamping with his feet on the ground. The gibbon dances after smearing himself with all the colours he can lay hands on. The females collect everything they can that they find attractive—twigs and rags and bits of straw, and decorate their heads and shoulders with these; then they dance, trying not to let them fall off. As Jacques Mauduit, to whom we are indebted for this description, remarks: "For my part I see no difference between this behaviour and that of a certain Moroccan young woman who stole my sock-suspenders to make herself some ear-rings."

Ever since the reindeer age, prehistoric art treats dancing, along with hunting and fighting, as one of the essential activities of man. Our masked musician from the cave of

the *Trois-Frères* dances in order to cast a spell over his reindeer, as does this other figure which is one of the masterpieces of the cave-men's art. Cave paintings frequently represent dancers, sometimes disguised or masked, sometimes naked, like those admirable silhouettes that have been discovered in South Africa (see facing page).

All over the world dancing is a part of religious ritual, and today, especially, in Africa and Asia. In the ancient world, the Old Testament, Greece and Rome all provide well-known examples. The dance of David before the Ark is famous, but there was nothing extraordinary about this; what is really strange is the Christian Church's refusal to recognize this form of worship of which the dance is symbolic. And this brings us to a problem which goes much deeper than musical history.

All forms of religious music, except those to be met with in Western Christianity today,

2. A masked dancer, also from the cave of the Trois-Frères.

are dependent on rhythm and colour. They do not aim at turning the thoughts of the worshipper inwards, but on the contrary are designed to draw him out of himself, to excite him and, in the Greek sense of the word, to put him into a state of "ecstasy". All means are employed for this purpose—dancing and loud cries, percussion instruments and obsessive rhythms. As we shall see in the next chapter, primitive Christianity may have indulged in the same practices.

3. South African cave drawings of prehistoric dancers.

Since music is meant to take possession of a man completely and project him into another world, his body as well as his mind must share this ecstasy which is the foretaste of communion with God. This, together with a desire to sing the praises of the Deity, seems to have been the chief aim and object of music in the Christian as well as all other religions. But soon disputes arose within the Church itself. In opposition to St. Athanasius and St. John Chrysostomos, the abbots Pambon and Silvanus thundered that "music had precipitated many souls, priests and laymen alike, into the depths of hell". St. Augustine himself appears to have "hesitated between an asceticism which caused him to look with suspicion upon liturgical chants, and a quite contrary feeling which made him conscious of their extraordinary power of seduction".[1] As regards dancing, the higher ranking dignitaries of the Church were hostile from the first, but their disapproval was not always unqualified. Many bishops tolerated in private what they had denounced in the Concilium. At Auxerre, for example, in the thirteenth century the cathedral canons used to play a rhythmic ball-game with the "pilotta" (cf. the Basque

[1]Van Den Borren, *Revue Belge de Musicologie*, 1950, p. 151. Cf. J. Chailley, *Histoire musicale du Moyen Age*, 1950, pp. 38 sqq.; Gérold, *Histoire de la Musique*, pp. 145 sqq.

pelota, and see Dom Gougaud, *La Danse dans les églises*); at Limoges they used to dance
in the chapel of St. Leonard singing a refrain which has been preserved:

> Saint Marçau,prega per nos
> Et nos espringarem per vos.
> (Saint Martial, pray for us
> and we will dance for you).

At Sens, in the fifteenth century, the precentor, the highest dignitary after the Bishop,
danced in the nave of the cathedral, wearing his ceremonial ring on his finger and
holding in his left hand his staff of office, resembling an episcopal cross, accompanied
by Gregorian chants.[1]

Then there were the well-known cemetery dances which the medieval episcopal
authorities had such difficulty in suppressing; it was not so much that they objected to
the dances themselves, but rather to their analogy with pagan rites. A crude tenth-
century drawing (Plate IV) represents a scene of adoration in which acrobats, sword-
swallowers and jugglers with knives are all mixed up with the musicians; it is a satirical
representation of paganism representing the worship of Nebuchadnezzar. *Jongleur* was
for a long time the name given to street singers, who as a general rule were forbidden to
enter a church. Sometimes they tried to force an entry, but this aroused the indignation
of the "orthodox" who protested against these *goliards* as they were called (possibly
the origin of the term *gaillard*) who were supposed to be the disciples of a certain
Golias, of whom a thirteenth-century writer remarked that he ought to have been
called Gulias, "*quia gulae et crapulae dedicari dici potest*". And yet the chronicles are full
of stories of processions and religious feasts accompanied by dances, banners and
"attractions" of all kinds which are to be met with today in village church festivities, of
which the most notable example is the famous *Fête-Dieu* at Seville. The margins of a
plain-song missal of the eleventh century are illustrated with drawings of *jongleurs* as
well as musicians (Plate V); and the admirable legend of the *Jongleur de Notre Dame*,
told in the thirteenth-century book of fables and which provided Massenet with
the subject of one of his operas, is a good example of this dualism: A poor juggler,
exhausted by his acrobatics, enters a convent. Unable to sing the psalms or perform the
simple duties of the convent, he despairs of ever being good for anything. One day,
alone in the crypt, he confides his troubles to an image of Our Lady, and an idea comes
into his head:

[1]Cf. J. Chailley, *Un document nouveau sur la danse ecclésiastique, Acta Musicologica*, 1949.

> Je ferai ce que j'ai appris,
> Et servirai de mon métier
> La mère Dieu en son moustier.
> Les autres servent de chanter,
> Et je servirai de tumer . . .
> Douce reine, ma douce dame,
> Ne méprisez ce que je sais.

(I will do what I have learnt to do, and serve with my trade the mother of God in her shrine. The others can serve her with their singing, and I with my acrobatics. Sweet Queen, sweet Lady, do not despise the only thing I know.)

In front of the Virgin he walks on his hands and performs somersaults. Worn out, he falls to the ground exhausted, and begins again the following day. He is seen by a monk, who is scandalized and informs the abbot. Horrified at this sacrilege, the latter rushes to the spot and sees the poor juggler, dripping with sweat, collapsed at the foot of the statue. But bathed in a bright light and surrounded by angels, the Virgin has come down from her pedestal and with a towel tenderly wipes the forehead of her servitor, thus accepting the homage which rules and custom would have forbidden (Plate VI).

The Church's struggle against the dance as an element of worship is only one episode in a controversy of far wider implications which still persists today, and of which we shall now attempt to give some account.

IO

Christian Music: Meditation or Ecstasy?

At the International Congress of Sacred Music held in Paris in July 1957 some speakers expressed some very unconventional opinions.[1] "The view today", said one of them, "is that religious music is meant to create a devotional atmosphere conducive to meditation. Consequently, such music should avoid brilliant effects, violent contrasts, exaggerated expression and any superficial and highly coloured attempts to be descriptive. This is generally believed to be its true, traditional character, authenticated by the masterpieces which conform to this venerable tradition. For my part, I would, until further notice, consider this notion to date from not earlier than ... 1860!"

This is really going beyond the bounds of musical history. Theology next feels called upon to express its own opinions in the matter: "You ask me when do I consider that the mystics first began to turn their thoughts inwards, towards inhibition and contemplation and meditation? Certainly not before the beginning of the seventeenth century"—such was the reply to a similar question of a Catholic University professor; and he added: "A hundred and fifty years is not a very long time for these ideas to have become sufficiently widespread to have affected music, which always lags behind in the great world-current of ideas."

Art history, in its turn, was to express its agreement with these views: apart from a few canvases of Fra Angelico,[2] it argued, we have, broadly speaking, to wait for Murillo, in his pictures of the Virgin, to see the saints represented as lost in inward meditation, with bowed heads and hands crossed upon their breasts. Until then they were always represented as leaning forward in ecstasy, with hands stretched out, their bodies tense, and their eyes turned upwards, it is true, but fixed on some precise point in their vision, and not lost in contemplation of some vague internal image (Plate VII). For we must remember that, in the Middle Ages, hands joined together were not a sign of prayer

---

[1] J. Chailley, *La Révision du critère historique dans les problèmes de la musique d'église*. Proceedings of the Congress 1959, pp. 156-167, and *Revue Musicale, La musique sacrée* 1957, pp. 55-62.

[2] And even here it often depends on the context: for example, the Virgin in the *Annunciation* "receives" the angel's message; her hands are crossed, not in prayer, but to receive the precious gift. Sometimes, too, for the Virgin it is a gesture of humility: *respexit humilitation.*

but of homage—the symbol of the surrender of the vassal to his suzerain (Plate VIII).

We saw in the preceding chapter that in primitive societies, and today also in all religions except Christianity, the object of religious music was exactly the opposite from what it is with us: the words themselves have changed their meaning, so that we now use the term "ecstasy", regardless of its etymology, to express the idea of a devout person turning his thoughts *inwards* in silent meditation, whereas previously it meant an *outward* manifestation, a state of exaltation forcibly expressed in sound and rhythm.

What has happened, therefore, is a complete *reversal* of the idea of spirituality, in which music plays an essential part, since it is now expected to do just the opposite to what it was asked to do before. Instead of exciting, it now has to calm men's spirits. Whereas before its function was to take hold of them and project them violently beyond reality into spheres of divine possession, in its new rôle it has to insinuate itself and become "the music of silence", effacing itself in order to create an atmosphere conducive to meditation and reflection: background music, of which one might almost say, as of the music in certain films, that the less one is conscious of it the better it is.

No doubt this conception is more or less implicit, because to express it so openly would soon invite mediocrity; but who would dare to affirm that this was never the case, in the results at any rate, if not in the intention?

The oldest texts relating to Christian music—and *a fortiori* to that described in the Old Testament—all point to an interpretation similar to that applicable to religious music everywhere. St. Paul in his Epistle to the Corinthians gives his approval to those meetings where, in the general excitement provoked by communal singing, the faithful are carried away by their emotions and start to improvise for themselves (the apostle confines himself to asking them to do it in turn, one after another, in order to avoid confusion). The often passionate discussions which, in the early days of Christianity, divided the partisans and opponents of singing as an element of worship, seem almost incomprehensible if we are to suppose that they referred to the sober and undemonstrative "plainsong", but are intelligible if we assume them to have been concerned with the universal notion of an exalted and inspiring kind of "ecstatic song".

At this point the reader will no doubt seize on the word "plainsong" to refute our thesis in this discussion, pointing out that *planus cantus*, meaning "uniform", moderate and devoid of violent contrasts or sudden changes in mood or style, is the venerable ancestor of our neutral and intimate kind of church music. Unfortunately, this is nothing but a charming misrepresentation of the facts. *Planus cantus* in medieval texts is merely the antithesis of *cantus mensuratus*, or "measured song", commonly used in polyphonic or secular songs. All that it connotes, before the letter, is the absence of implicit bar-lines.[1] In point of fact, fresh evidence is being discovered every day showing the connection between "plainsong" and those Oriental chants, of Yemenite Jewish or Byzantine origin, which, wherever the tradition has remained unbroken, have preserved in their flamboyant *vocalises* an exuberantly lyrical character which is very far removed from the "flatness" associated with "Gregorian" chant.

Quite recently, Herbert Pepper recorded on disc a prayer-meeting on Christmas Eve in a Negro chapel in Harlem. The violent and impassioned address delivered by the pastor, made up of short phrases uttered at an increasingly rapid rate and punctuated by the rhythmic applause of the congregation, almost turns into song as the excitement mounts and the pianist fingers impatiently the keys of his instrument which can hardly bear to remain silent. Soon the whole congregation bursts into song, a kind of syncopated "swing" through which one becomes conscious of all those bodies possessed by the rhythm of music.

These Protestant Harlem Negroes are somewhat similar, from an historical point of view, to the early Christians; Africa has replaced the Orient, but both are equally recent converts to Christianity who have escaped from their ancestral religions. Like the early Christians, the Negroes have made a sort of Christian music for themselves by merging their atavistic culture with the teaching of their pastors. It is quite conceivable that the atmosphere of ecstasy that emanates from this record is similar to that of the first Christian assemblies to which St. Paul spoke; and it may well be that the fervent lyrical and rhythmic appeal of the Negro "spirituals" is nearer in spirit to primitive plainsong than all our learned disquisitions about *ictus* and *incisures*.

This somewhat unorthodox pronouncement is no doubt largely hypothetical. In any case, one thing we can be certain of is that Church music, for the first thousand years at any rate, was an *active* kind of music. The singer did not sing in order to be heard, but for the sake of singing, to offer up his song to God and to surpass himself in singing it. There were no "composers", any more than there were listeners—only participants.

---

[1]Plainsong, as everyone knows, is the name given to the immense musical repertoire, known today as "Gregorian chant", which the Church built up, mainly from the fifth to the ninth centuries. A propos of this term "Gregorian chant", it may be recalled that St. Gregory I was Pope towards the end of the sixth century (he died in 604). His pontifical acts are well known, and have no connection with music. The legend which credits him with being a musician seems to have been current in the eleventh century. A plausible hypothesis is that it originated in England where this great Pope sent a mission, led by St. Augustine, to settle a number of disciplinary details. The English in consequence have tended to attribute to him everything relating to Church discipline, including musical liturgy, and these views may have reached the Continent through Aquitania where England possessed a great deal of landed property. There is chronological evidence to support this theory which, however, is only a hypothesis.

The soloists were not artists performing to an audience, but delegates speaking on behalf of all. Moreover, the soloist's song had to be approved collectively; that is the meaning of the final *Amen* sung by the faithful, and of the primitive refrains forming the "responses".

It is perhaps around 1422, when Pope John XXII launched from Avignon his famous Bull, *Docta Sanctorum*, against the *Ars Nova* movement which was then just beginning, that we shall find for the first time any reference to "discreetness" in connection with liturgical singing, for the Pope here regrets that the abundance of notes in modern music tends to mask the *ascensiones pudicae* and the *descensiones temperatae* of plainsong. In any case, the name only served as a term of comparison between the two arts. For the fact is, that a newcomer, which had surreptitiously appeared some five hundred years earlier, was even then threatening to undermine the whole edifice of the traditional repertory. In the ninth century polyphony had just appeared on the scene, and with it the whole purpose of music was very soon about to change.

II

Polyphonic Music: "More Festivo"

In the first Western treatise to mention polyphony, the *Enchirias* of a certain Ogier in the ninth century,[1] the primary object of polyphony is clearly defined: it is an artifice for ornamenting liturgical melodies on important occasions. This is the reason why it was not until much later that people began to "compose" polyphonic music; at first it was only a new and more solemn aspect, *more festivo*, of traditional liturgical music. The Church is proud, and rightly so, of its repertory of plainsong; perhaps it ought to be still prouder of its polyphonic music, for the origins of plainsong, which are still obscure, are very complex and have their roots in ancient Jewish as well as Eastern sources, whereas the art of polyphony, at any rate in its written forms, belongs exclusively to the Church until, after reaching its maturity, secular music in its turn borrowed it from the Church. This ornamental and "festive" aspect of polyphony makes it possible to explain several centuries of musical history. Until about the twelfth century there was no "composer" of polyphonic music. All the composer did was to "find" the melody. After him came the *descantor* who "organized" the existing melody to make it more solemn.[2] The two persons are as distinct as the two forms of music.

[1]It is amusing to note the nonsensical way in which this title has been misunderstood, so that this treatise is often referred to as *Musica Enchiriadis* and attributed to another author of the same period, Hucbald. *Enchirias* means a "manual"; this (approximately) Greek word was mistaken by a copyist who did not know Greek for an author's name, and the title thus became, elegantly transposed into the genitive, (literally) "music of a Manual", *Musica Enchiriadis*. An eighteenth-century publisher, the Abbé Gerbert, printed it under this title following a treatise by Hucbald and, as had already been done on one of the manuscripts, printed all the other treatises under the same heading—although, through other MSS., the name of the author of the *Enchirias* was known to be Ogier or Otger. Ever since then everyone speaks, without turning a hair, about the *Musica Enchiriadis* of Hucbald de Saint-Amand. . . .

[2]"To find" and "to organize"—"trouver" and "organizer"—are two expressions which our modern speech has borrowed from the medieval musical vocabulary. "*Tropare*" means to "make tropes", i.e., to compose prolongations to liturgical chants, and from there, simply to compose, both words and music. The *tropator* of the ninth century becomes, in the twelfth and thirteenth, the *trouveur* either *trobador* (troubadour) or *troveor* (*trouvère*), according to the region. And so, instead of "finding" a melody, we now speak of "finding" a cauliflower in the market. . . . As for "organize", this means endowing Gregorian chant with a new form and ornamenting it with "organum", i.e., polyphony. Hence the familiar derivation. These are not the only examples. In the notation of the late Middle Ages, for example, a note was blackened, or, in technical terms, "denigrated", to deprive it of a third of its value: today a housewife will "denigrate" her neighbour to deprive her of her good qualities in the eyes of others.

On reflection, it will be seen that this notion persisted for a long time after it was first put into practice; in fact, a great deal of classical religious music (and secular music as well) is really only a more or less amplified extension of the same principle. A motet by Josquin des Prés or Palestrina is hardly ever an original work: it is a polyphonic enlargement of a monodic original, and the same can be said of the first *Credo* in the B minor Mass, of the finale of *King David* or the *Requiem* of Maurice Duruflé. With this difference: the medieval *descantor* ornamented his model without altering it; a single voice maintained it from one end to the other.[1] Josquin or Palestrina develop their model phrase by phrase, section by section, by distributing the fragments among the different voices and developing them there. Bach and the moderns do the same, but on a much more extended scale—that of the work as a whole. The aesthetic principle is none the less the same.

Even before polyphony had been used to build up the most monumental "solemnizations", the ninth century had already invented another artifice for the same purpose. This was the *trope*, which was a method of prolonging the chant by commentaries specially composed for this purpose. There were no cinemas in the Middle Ages and the church services were, in the noblest sense of the term, the people's principal distraction. The more important the occasion, the longer the service; the singing therefore had to go on longer than it would have for an ordinary festive occasion. The *tropes*, banned by the Council of Trent, disappeared in the sixteenth century, but the spirit in which they had been conceived had to be preserved. We have spoken of the increasing importance of polyphonic developments in connection with liturgical chants: there again, we find the same tradition of what might be called the "solemnity of timing". In "figured" Church music (as its polyphony was called at one time) the text used to be prolonged by repetitions which became more and more inept: "*Et incarnatus est, incarnatus est, de Spiritu Sancto, de Spiritu, Spiritu Sancto, et incarnatus est de Spiritu Sancto.*" By the eighteenth century these vain repetitions had attained such proportions that we can understand why Pope Pius X had to issue his *Motu Proprio* forbidding any repetition of the words in sacred music—all the more necessary as this practice had been imitated, not to say caricatured, in Neapolitan opera—and soon after in opera everywhere: in Meyerbeer's *Les Huguenots*, for example, a page vocalizes for three minutes on end, repeating a dozen times "*Nobles seigneurs, salut*"—or in plain English, "Gentlemen, good morning. . . ."

---

[1] This method was preserved until the sixteenth century, in at least one form of Church music, the so-called "tenor" mass and motet, and later in the polyphonic psalms of the Reformation.

But before the *trope*, there existed in the Middle Ages another method of "solemn-izing" a melody, and that was to ornament it with vocalizes. This practice is as old as it is universal, and Roland Manuel gave, in one of his radio talks, an example well-known to French soldiers: on "leave" days in the barracks, the bugler, instead of sounding the regulation:

cheerfully risks his eight days of detention for the pleasure of the "fantasy" variation symbolizing the festive day:

Similarly, on ordinary days the Church sings:

and on feast days:

The polyphonic composers merely carried on the tradition. In the fifteenth century especially the "ornamental garland" (*guirlande ornementale*) became extraordinarily popular, especially as it coincided with the current aesthetic of a flamboyant art, rich in curves and counter-curves. The melody quoted above becomes, in Dufay's hands:

Josquin des Prés is no doubt the greatest master of this undulating line, which, with the growth of humanism in the second half of the sixteenth century, was used more sparingly (it is still to be found in a more desiccated form in Lassus or Palestrina) and with still greater restraint in the classical period of the seventeenth century; eighteenth century baroque,[1] however, restored it to all its former exuberance. Comparable to the decorative exuberance of the altar tables in stucco or gilded wood in Salzburg or Tepotzotlan, ornamental vocalize again becomes a dominant element in the music designed for Church festivals: "scandalous" was the term applied to the trills and runs and coloratura passages which Mozart introduced into the *Et incarnatus est* of his great *Mass in C minor*. (We shall return to this question later.) Yet they are merely the equivalent, in the style of the period, of the *jubili* in the Gregorian *alleluias* of which St. Augustine gave such a charming explanation: "He who is jubilant does not utter words, but expresses his joy in inarticulate sounds. In that state of exaltation he is not content with what can be readily understood, but gives vent to a kind of cry of joy unmixed with words."

The *Et incarnatus est* of the C minor *Mass* is only shocking to those who would refuse to exhibit the Holy Sacrament in a church designed by Bernini, or would accuse themselves in the confessional of not having attended Mass because they heard it celebrated at an altar of gilded wood. This is the religion of J. K. Huysmans. But *En route* appeared in 1895. . . . The foregoing explains the curious predilection of Church music for a form which would seem to be the furthest removed from the religious spirit: the scholastic fugue, the culminating point, historically, of the contrapuntal style in which the musicians of the Renaissance ornamented and developed, in their motets and masses, liturgical themes; Berlioz made fun of this fashion ruthlessly. In his *Damnation of Faust* when Brander, after the song of the rat, proposes to the topers in the tavern:

> Pour l'amen une fugue,
> Une fugue, un choral:
> Improvisons un morceau magistral!

Mephistopheles comments:

> Ecoute bien ceci: nous allons voir, docteur,
> La bestialité dans toute sa candeur!

[1]Contrary to modern fashion, we hesitate to apply this term in music to any period before Haydn and Mozart. Following the example of the German musicologists, the tendency recently has been to apply the "baroque" label not only to J. S. Bach, but even to Lassus and Ockeghem! The grounds evoked for doing so would justify the application of the term "baroque" to the authors of Carolingian *Versus*, and even to more ancient times.

("For the Amen a fugue, a fugue, a chorale: let us improvise a masterly piece!" to which Mephisto answers: "Listen to this carefully, Doctor: we're going to see bestiality naked and unashamed!")

The boon companions take up the challenge, and after a strict fugue full of *A.a.a . . . mens* intended as a mockery of this style, the Spirit of Evil pertinently remarks:

> Vrai Dieu, Messieurs, votre fugue est fort belle
> Et telle
> Qu'à l'entendre on se croit aux saints lieux.
> Le style en est savant, vraiment religieux:
> On ne saurait exprimer mieux
> Les sentiments pieux
> Qu'en terminant ses prières
> L'Eglise en un seul mot résume.

("By God, Gentlemen, that was a fine fugue; to hear it one would think one was in a holy place. The style is learned, truly religious; you couldn't have expressed better the pious sentiments which the Church, at the end of its prayers, sums up in a single word.)"

Alas! to the great discomfiture of Berlioz, it was the fugue which won the unanimous approval of the critics, who thought it the best thing in the whole work!

12

The "Ideal Statue" of Berlioz

"Whoever wishes to write a 'conductus'," according to a thirteenth-century treatise, "must first find a melody, the finest possible. After that, he must use it as a tenor to make a descant on that tenor, as we said above."[1] What was "said above" is what we were saying ourselves in the preceding chapter, namely that polyphony was originally used only to ornament an already existing melody: it was this melody that was called "*la teneur*" (in Latin, *tenor*) because it "supported the descant".[2] This prescription by our thirteenth-century author not only gives us the "recipe" for one of the essential polyphonic styles of his period, and, more than that, a most valuable technical description of the general method of medieval counterpoint; it also shows us the origin of the first notions of composition as we understand the term. For the first time in history a musician did not confine himself to writing a single melodic line, or even to adding a second or third voice to an already existing melody. Wishing to create by himself unaided, a polyphonic composition, he placed himself, as no one before him had ever done, before a blank sheet of paper. But from a technical point of view, the old conception remained unchanged: the musician still began by writing his tune, as if that was all he had to do; then he added the descant, treating his own tune as if it were by someone else. The only difference—an essential one—was that the author and the *descantor* were one and the same person. This was virtually the first appearance of the "composer".

Soon this composer sought quite legitimately to ensure for his work a greater unity. He worked at its overall *ensemble*, tried to make it express images or sentiments contained in the sacred text or his own commentary—because the *conductus* was originally a religious *genre*, and it was only by analogy that later on (towards the middle of the thirteenth century) polyphony in its turn ventured into the secular field. Plainsong itself was aware of these preoccupations: turtle-doves coo over the liquescent strains of the communion service for the third Sunday in Lent; a gust of wind seems to animate the fifths and fourths of the *Factus est repente* of the Whitsun service; the celebrated semi-

[1]Jérôme de Moravie, in Coussemaker, *Scriptores*, I, 132.
[2]Such is the origin of the word tenor, after going through a series of transformations summarized on p. 107, note 1 and p. 154, note 2.

tones of Victoria weep or implore in his masses and motets, just as the chromaticisms of Claude le Jeune strike a wailing note both in his psalms and in his songs.

Until the sixteenth century at least there was no difference in style between religious music and secular music—often it was religious music that was the more progressive. Is it therefore surprising that in the seventeenth and eighteenth centuries Church music and operatic music were both equally concerned with finding more and more expressive ways of setting the words of their respective texts? Bach endorsed the saying of his librettist Neumeister to the effect that "a cantata should be no different from a fragment of an opera", while the fanfares of a Berlioz or a Verdi only shock those who, in the *Requiem Mass*, have forgotten to read first the text of the *Libera me* or the *Dies irae*.

If there was a reaction towards the middle of the nineteenth century, this was because, as always, there had been abuses, and not because the principle itself was wrong. Opinions are unanimous with regard to the sorry state of church choirs a century ago. The wealthy churches turned themselves, both externally and in their repertory, into auxiliary opera-houses, and the "masterpiece" of this school was perhaps that apocryphal *Mass* of Rossini's, fabricated by Castil-Blaze in which the *Kyrie* is sung to the march from *Otello*, and *Cum Sancto Spiritu* to the burlesque *stretto* in the Quintet from *Cenerentola*.[1] As for the poor churches, not being able to afford an organ, they replaced it quite simply by the ophicleide of our brass bands, or by the ancient wooden "serpent", a descendant of the old-time "cornet", as ugly as it was incapable of playing in tune— hence the motto of one of our boldest reformers, Charles Bordes: *Ab antiquo serpente libera nos Domine. . . .*

The force of this reaction lay in the fact that it had two aspects, one sentimental and the other technical. The sentimental aspect we have already noted: since the romantic movement, mysticism had changed its course: it now became an affair of contemplation, silence, and thoughts turned inwards; religious meditation called for low crypts, and dark silent churches: soon the best religious music would be music in which the senses played no part; a little later it would be only logical to treat it as an intruder and purely and simply make silence an ideal—the culmination of a thousand years of a wonderful sacred art envisaged by men of the Church whose good faith cannot be

---

[1]Despite the decadence of this deplorable example, it was the culmination of the whole history of the polyphonic mass, not excluding the great masters of the Renaissance. The "parody mass" made its first appearance in the fourteenth century in the form of the *Besançon Mass* (discovered by the author of this book and identified as a parody by Leo Schrade), and continued in the sixteenth century (Jannequin wrote a Mass on the *Bataille de Marignan*, and fifty per cent of Palestrina's masses are "parody masses", often based on works by his contemporaries). Bach also made short masses out of fragments of cantatas, and introduced, we must not forget, a number of these into his famous *B minor Mass*.

doubted. . . .[1] As for the technical aspect, it links up in a curious way with the other. With the loss of the ancient "modes", musicians had become accustomed to analyse everything in terms of the two classical "modes", major and minor. Insensitive to the tensions and varied attractions of plainsong, all they could see in the latter was a series of conventional notes devoid of any dynamic interest. By a cruel paradox, its first devotees were as much obsessed with this misconception as its adversaries had been, and what they believed they were restoring was not a different means of expression, but music whose principal merit, they thought, lay in its lack of expressiveness, a sign in their eyes of that "catharsis" devoid of passion in which mortification became sanctification, as the very name of "plainsong", so they believed, implied. In 1861 Niedermeyer's representative Joseph d'Ortigue published under the title *La musique à l'Eglise* a manifesto which drew a vigorous reply from Berlioz (*A travers chants*, chap. xix.). Blaming the abuses indicated above (and here Berlioz agrees with him) d'Ortigue preached, in the name of true plainsong, the new ideal which we have just been describing. Let us hear now what Berlioz has to say:

"(These extravagances) are not the fault of music, the 'worldly' art as he calls it, and (d'Ortigue) is mistaken when he allows himself to be persuaded that this noble art is responsible for all the errors committed by musicians, even going so far as to declare that there can be no real religious music outside the ecclesiastical tonality. This would mean that Mozart's *Ave verum*, that sublime expression of ecstatic adoration, which is not at all in the ecclesiastical tonality, cannot be considered as truly religious music. . . . In M. d'Ortigue's opinion, it is precisely the simplicity, vagueness, indeterminate tonality, impersonality and inexpressiveness of plainsong that are its chief merits. It seems to me, if that is so, that a statue reciting liturgical words with cold impassiveness and on a single note, would then represent the ideal of religious music."

This rejoinder was significant. One does not start a campaign of this nature to defend conventional ideas, but to attack them. The attitude of Berlioz is that of someone who is defending tradition against an innovation of which he does not approve. And that

[1]Not only envisaged, but in process of realization. Unless a courageous reaction sets in during the coming years, it seems almost a certainty that sacred music in French catholic churches at any rate, deprived of any possibility of renewing itself owing to the total neglect of modern music, shorn of its prestige by the lack of interest on the part of the clergy who, all too often, are unaware of its value, too seldom used owing to the increasing number of services in which the spoken word predominates, rendered meaningless by the current distaste for the solemnity of the great church services, and deprived of beauty by a mythical belief in the supremacy of the "spontaneous" singing of a crowd wh:ch has no idea how to sing—it seems certain, then, that sacred music, struggling against these odds, will before long be nothing but a glorious and melancholy memory, kept alive only on gramophone records and in concerts devoted to the music of the past.

was precisely the period when for the first time there began to be a demand, as there had never been before, for a plain, unadorned kind of religious music, without colour or brilliance or contrast, abandoning to the theatre all its old fervour and warmth of inspiration.[1]

The disastrous vacuity of what is generally known as "kapellmeister music" at the end of the nineteenth century is only too well known. It even caused authentic geniuses to lose their personalities, and it was in vain that attempts were made to excuse down-right mediocrity by pretending that it was the sign of a new "aesthetic of humility".[2] This sudden deterioration seems to have been the direct result of what we have been trying to describe. Until the middle of the last century Church music was not distinguished by any artificial characteristics; in the vanguard of progress, it had enriched the Church, in all its denominations, with the most splendid masterpieces, such as those, for example, we owe to the anonymous Gregorian masters, Perotinus and Josquin, Bach, Mozart and Berlioz. Suddenly taking refuge in an impersonal conservatism certainly did nothing to add to its prestige. And even though today, in the presence of artists who are undoubtedly building a new renaissance it may be doubted whether the time has come to restore to it its true image, let us not, when discussing it, lose sight of the fact that the "tradition" which is emasculating it is perhaps nothing but a fiction imagined by some ignorant historian of a bygone age. The most obvious result of this is the fact that by the end of the nineteenth century true religious music was no longer to be found in the church, but in the concert hall.

---

[1]Bach, it will be remembered, did not hesitate to introduce a raging storm in the middle of the St. Matthew Passion.

[2]E.g., César Franck's *Messe à trois voix*, and Fauré's *Tu es Petrus* . . . And yet Fauré in his Requiem composed for the church of La Madeleine, was perhaps the only one to elevate the church music of his day to the rank of an admirable work of art.

13

The "Concert Spirituel"

The Dogons from the Niger say that "when a musican sings or plays an instrument he loses some of his vital forces which, through the sound, go to enrich the personality of the listener. . . . In times of mourning especially, the relatives of the dead man, who in their grief refuse to eat, suffer a loss of fats and vital forces which causes them to dry up: the music played at funerals is intended not only to ensure the reincarnation of the dead person's spiritual elements, but also to comfort the living in their sorrow. It is at the expense of the musician that this exchange of forces takes place. That is why they are paid; but they also receive presents of food and drink which should be accompanied by blessings and words of praise. These words replace the water that has been lost and moisten the dried-up fats; beer made from millet seed fortifies the blood, and the food makes up for the loss of fats."

Thus, playing and singing were not artistic activities, but a sacred rite or religious function. When the musician was not alone but was surrounded by people listening to him, the music's magic current did not flow from the musician to his audience, as it does with us today, but just the opposite: it was the musician who received from his hearers the impulse which caused him to reflect their feelings and emotions: he was, in the strict and noble sense of the word, an *interpreter*. The spectators of Greek or Oriental tragedies, like the faithful following a medieval church service, always found in the chanting of a soloist or of the chorus a reflection of their own thoughts. What was originally a collective manifestation, had become a collective manifestation *by proxy*, as it were. Already the idea of a responsible author, of an interpreter and of a public was taking shape; already each of these groups was dimly striving to acquire its individuality. But the first two categories are conscious that they have a mission to fulfil in regard to the third.

It may seem surprising that masterpieces like Bach's *Cantatas* and *Passions* attracted no public notice at the time they were written. The answer is simple: for works such as these there was no public. The worshippers at St. Thomas's went there for the services, and that was all. If the parish choir-master happened to be a genius, that only concerned the church authorities, who were unaware of it, and his colleagues, who probably resented it. In Protestant and Catholic churches alike, the congregation did not hear the music as a work of art, but merely as the reflection of their collective sentiments. The faithful were not interested in the composer, but in what he had to say; and he only said what was dictated by the calendar of Church feasts. The story is told that when Willaert, the creator of the Venetian school in the sixteenth century, arrived in Venice, where he was quite unknown, he happened to hear in a church a motet of his own composition. Feeling very proud, as soon as the service was over he hurried up to the choir ready to be congratulated. "Yes," said the choir-master, "it is a very fine motet— by Josquin des Prés, is it not?" The composer corrected him. "Ah?" replied the other; "we all thought it was by Josquin. However, it's of no importance. . . ." And there he broke off the conversation, leaving the composer somewhat crestfallen.

Such was the rôle of the composer in those days. Like the rest, Bach's music was conceived in these conditions, and there is no reason to be surprised that his master-pieces attracted no critical attention in his lifetime—any more than did Fauré's Requiem when it was first performed at the Madeleine in Paris. When the time came for Zelter and Mendelssohn to make the Saint Matthew Passion famous through the medium of the "concert spirituel", they were able to do this because the Romantics had already arrived, investing the rôle of the composer with a new kind of glory.

Perhaps it was Bach's famous predecessor Buxtehude who, with the *Abendmusiken* which he organized at Lübeck around 1670, was the first to cause music to be listened to for its own sake, and not merely as the accompaniment of the church services. And yet, in principle, these ancestors of the "concert spirituel" were still primarily pious exercises, and only incidentally manifestations of art. Buxtehude's biographer, A. Pirro (*D. Buxtehude*, p. 165) points out that the *Abendmusiken*, like the Hamburg operas, "have much in common with the religious dramas in which Johann Clajus was the only actor, when at Nuremberg (circ. 1644-45) he used to recite, after the service, his edifying tragedies, with interpolated songs . . . in these cases the moral sentiments expressed are the *raison d'être* of the play, which was looked upon as a form of education". And so it was for the purpose of moral edification, and not artistic entertainment, that the Lübeck trade corporations had asked for and encouraged these "concerts spirituels", which were really like church services, but without any definite religious ritual, which enabled the good citizens of Lübeck on Thursdays, before going to their offices, to have a little healthy and edifying distraction. (*Op. cit.* p. 141). So deeply rooted, even as late as the middle of the eighteenth century, was the idea that to listen to music outside the theatre could only be a pious and edifying exercise, that Philidor had to resort to a curious stratagem in order to organize in Paris the first orchestral concerts in history.

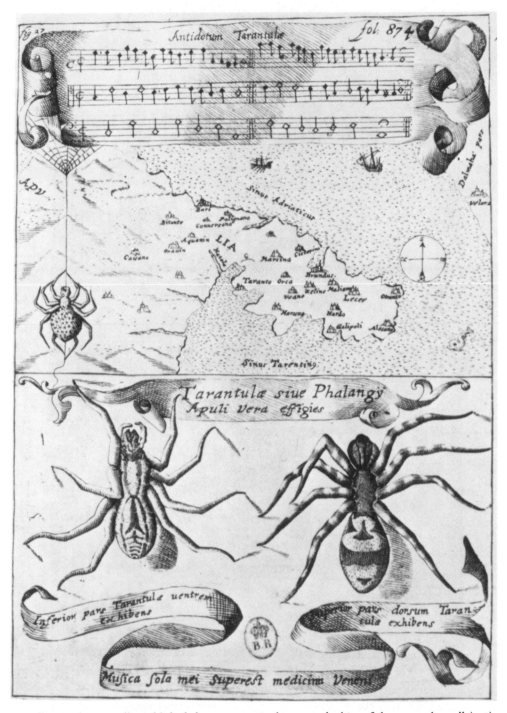

1 "Fr Kircher actually published the tune required to cure the bite of the tarantula . . ." (p. 8). Book plate from *Magnes sive de arte magnetica* by Athanasius Kircher, Rome 1641. *Bibliothèque Nationale.*

11 "A lot of naïvely would-be archaic *romances* began to appear . . . " (p. 31). Second frontispiece from the *Anthologie françoise ou Chansons choises depuis le XIIIe siècle jusqu' à présent* by Jean Monnet, 1765. *Author's collection.*

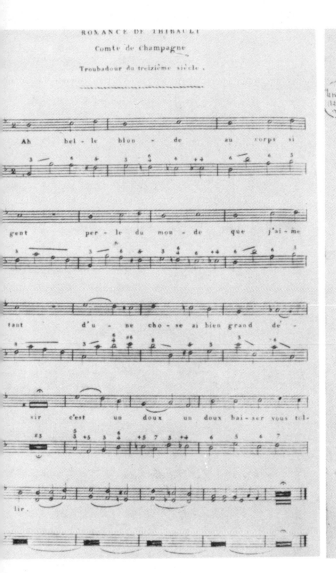

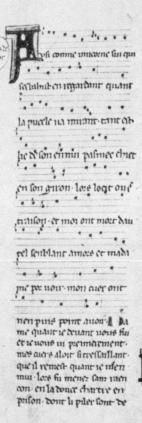

III(a) "The most typical example of this multiple and clandestine conspiracy . . . " (p. 32). The apocryphal song *Ah, belle blonde* in the version published by Castil-Blaze in his *Dictionnaire de musique moderne*, 2nd ed., vol I, Appendix, 1825. *Author's collection.*

III(b) An authentic song of the thirteenth century: *Ausi conme unicorne sui*. *Bibliothèque de l'Arsenal*, ms. 5189, p. 29.

IV "A scene of adoration in which acr
bats, sword-swallowers and jugglers wi
knives are all mixed up with musicians;
is a satirical representation of paganis
representing the worship of Nebucha
nezzar . . ." (p. 64). Illustration from t
Book of Daniel, tenth century. *Bibl. Na*
Latin ms. 6.

VI "The admirable legend of the *Jongl*
de Notre Dame, told in a thirteenth cent
book of fables . . ." (p. 64). *Bibl.*
l'Arsenal, ms. 3516.

V "The margins of a plain-song missal
the eleventh century are illustrated w
drawings of *jongleurs* as well as musici
. . ." (p. 64). *Bibl. Nat.*, Latin ms. 1118

VII "Leaning forward in ecstasy, with hands stretched out, their bodies tense . . . " (p. 66). Detail from a seventeenth century engraving of St. Louis de Gonzague receiving Holy Communion.

VIII "In the Middle Ages, hands joined together were not a sign of prayer but of homage . . ." (p. 67). A thirteenth century carving from Reims cathedral, representing a knight receiving Holy Communion.

IX(a) "A Middle Empire harpist is playing on his knees
before some high official . . . "
(p. 87). After Hickmann, *Le
Métier de musicien au temps des
Pharaons.*

IX(b) "Another harpist who
is playing to a bird-headed
god . . . " (p. 87). *Louvre.*

x "It was in front of Herod's dining table that the medieval sculptors represented the dance of Salome . . ." (p. 89). Thirteenth century carving from Rouen cathedral.

xi "The concerts to accompany banquets have never ceased to exist . . ." (p. 89). The scene is a banquet given by Ferdinand III at the Vienna Hofburg. The orchestra is on the right, opposite the emperor. One can identify the "time-keeper" (marked N). Anonymous engraving (1652), reproduced by Kinsky, *Album musical*, p. 174.

XII "*From one century to another down to the time of our grandparents, the atmosphere among artists was the same: familiar and relaxed . . .*" (*p.93*).

(a) Painting of the sixteenth century by an anonymous artist of the Flemish school. One can make out Notre Dame in the background. *Musée Carnavalet.*

(b) Painting by J. van Loo (1614-1670).

(c) Detail from the Ollivier painting, showing Mozart, aged eleven, playing for the Prince de Conti. *Louvre.*

(d) Moritz von Schwind's drawing of Schubert at the piano (1868). *Schubert-Museum, Vienna.*

(e) The advent of romanticism. Liszt is at the piano. At his feet is Marie d'Agoult; behind him, from left to right, are Alexandre Dumas, Victor Hugo, George Sand, Paganini and Rossini. Painting by Joseph Danhauser (1840).

XIII *"Can the loss of this familiar atmosphere be attributed to the victory of Prussian militarism"?* (p.93).

(a) Frederick II as a young man. Drawing by Adolphe Menzel, taken from *Geschichte Friedrichs des Grossen* by F. Kugler (Leipzig, 1840). Behind the king Quantz and Graun are listening to him.

(b) Frederick as an old man. Painting by P. Haas, reproduced by Kinsky.

XIV "One can see for the first time the position we are accustomed to today in which the artists on the platform are back to back . . . " (p. 93). Joachim and Clara Schumann. Water colour by Adolph Menzel, Berlin, 20 December 1854.

xv "In 1573 the entertainment was shifted from the banqueting hall to the ballroom . . . " (p. 97). Catherine de Medicis's ballet in honour of the Polish Ambassadors. Illustrations from *Magnificentissimi Speculati* by Daurat.

XVI "The year 1581 saw the first Court ballet offered by Henri III to celebrate the marriage of his favourite the Duc de Joyeuse . . . " (p. 97). Illustration from the first edition (1582), *Circé ou le Ballet Comique de la Reine*.

XVII (*above*) "An 'entry of the lute-players' in a Court ballet at the beginning of the seventeenth century . . ." (p. 98). From the *Ballet des Fées des Forests de Saint-Germain*, danced at the Louvre, 11 February 1625. Water-colo ur by Daniel Rabel.   *Louvre.*

XVIII (*below left*) "In France, the first opera, that of Cambert and Perrin, was opened in 1669" (p. 98). Taken from *Les Quinzes salles de l'opéra de Paris* by André Lejeune and Stéphane Wolff (1955).

XIX (*below right*) "Here there are neither barriers, nor seats, nor any arrangements for paying . . ." (p. 98). The Tabarin parade at the Pont-Neuf in 1623.

xx (*above*) "A preview of an embryonic concert-hall . . . " (p. 99). The performance in Vienna in 1666 of Cesti's *Pomo d'Oro*.

xxi(*below*) "The concert halls were at first more like big drawing-rooms, like the Salle Pleyel in the rue Rochechouart, where Chopin so often played . . . " (p. 102). Illustration taken from *Chopin* by Camille Bourniquel.

XXII (*above*) "The Leipzig Gewandhaus . . . arranged after the manner of the Protestant churches . . . " (p. 102).

XXIII (*below*) "Paris was equipped with its first 'big' concert hall, with seating for 2,500 . . ." (p. 103). The new Salle Pleyel (1927).

XXIV (*above*) "The Rondeau is for three voices, but only two are written down along with the text of the first two verses..." (p. 107). *Ma fin est mon commencement* by Guillaume de Machaut. *Bibl. Nat., Fr. ms., 1584.*

XXV (*above right*) "The astonishing cadenza which Pauline Viardot added to the final aria in the first Act..." (p. 153). "*Amour, viens rendre à mon âme*" from Gluck's *Orfeo. Author's collection.*

XXVI (*right*) "It is difficult to realize that it was at the keyboard of one of these old-fashioned instruments that Liszt was portrayed in a print as late as 1824..." (p. 169). *Author's collection.*

XXVII "At first the stage was merely a prolongation of the hall. . ." (p. 177). Engraving by Jacques Callot, representing *La Liberazione di Tirreno*, danced in Florence in 161). *Bibl. Nat., cabinet des Estampes.*

XXVIII "In Lully's days, the men were often in short petticoat-breeches, with ribbons and feathers in their hats, the women in long full, skirts . . ." (p. 180).

(a) Engraving by Lepoutre, after Bérain.

(b) Mlle de Subligny. *Bibl. Nat., cabinet des Estampes*.

XXIX "La Camargo was the first to appear in a short skirt which revealed the calf of the leg . . ." (p. 180). Painting by Schall (circ. 1735).

XXX "At first (the tutu) was long and straight, as worn by Taglioni in *La Sylphide* in 1832 . . ." (p. 180). *Archives F. Nathan.*

XXXI "In the Middle Ages instrumental ensembles were never 'conducted', the players kept an eye on one another, or rather on one of their number who led the rest . . ." (p. 187). Fifteenth century miniature from the Diurnal of René II of Lorraine. *Bibl. Nat.*, Latin ms., L. 10. 491.

XXXII "The miniature is believed to represent Ockeghem 'conducting' the choir at Saint-Martin de Tours . . . " (p. 187). *Bibl. Nat.*, Fr. ms. 1537, f° 58 v°.

XXXIII "Among the alternative and more discreet methods of marking time, the method most commonly adopted was a roll of paper, held firmly in the middle . . . " (p. 188). Frontispiece of the *Musikalisches Lexicon* by Johann Gottfried Walther, Leipzig 1732.

XXXIV (*above*) "A scene from Haydn's *opéra comique, L'Incontro Improviso*, being performed at the Esterhazy château . . ." (p. 189).

XXXV "In the theatre the conductor was often placed facing the stage in front of the orchestra . . ." (p. 190). Caricature sent to the conductor Emile Galle in 1886. *Author's family papers.*

XXXVI "Edouard Colonne conducting, not with a *bâton*, but with a violin bow . . ." (p. 190). *Musée Berlioz* at La Côte-Saint-André.

XXXVII "Habeneck with his handkerchief hanging from his tail-coat, apparently beating time with his feet . . ." (p. 191). Contemporary print after Dantan. *Author's collection.*

Anne Danican-Philidor belonged to the fourth generation of a family of musicians whose ancestor, according to Fétis, had been so baptised because he had won the admiration of Louis XIII. For the latter, at a time when Italian musicians were all the rage, had one day paid his oboist, Michel Danican, the highest compliment he could think of by saying that he had found in him "a second Filidori" (Filidori being an oboist from Siena who had recently played at the French Court). Henceforward all the Danicans—ten of them had been famous as musicians up to the Revolution—added to their family name (in a Gallicized form) that of Philidor. Anne Danican-Philidor, then, had been, along with his uncle Pierre, since 1722 a simple viola player in the King's private orchestra, and since 1697 had been writing dance music for the Court ballets,[1] when in 1725 he conceived the idea of founding a regular series of concerts. There were two necessary conditions that would have to be fulfilled. The first was to ensure the neutrality of Francini, known as Francine, Lully's son-in-law, who would succeed him in his highly privileged position at the *Académie Royale de Musique*, in other words, the Opéra. This he managed to do by undertaking not to allow "any fragment of an opera to be sung, or even any piece in which French words were set". The second condition was that his enterprise should be presented as an edifying entertainment. It was for this reason that the authorization he obtained was limited to thirty-five days in the year, all of which were religious feasts, that is to say days on which, for that reason, there would be no performances at the Opéra. It was also for this reason that the concerts which, although they began with Lalande's *Confitebor*, also included the same composer's Suite of airs for the violin and a *Concerto grosso* by Corelli, were baptised "Les Concerts Spirituels".

Some fifteen years later, but for precisely opposite reasons, there came into being another series of "concerts spirituels", which this time really deserved their name. There had been living in London for the last thirty years one of the most illustrious of operatic composers, George Frederic Handel. Handel was not only a composer; he was also an impresario and theatrical director. Since his departure from Hanover, he had abandoned religious music altogether in order to realize his dream of creating and directing a theatre devoted to opera. But since 1728 there had been considerable competition in this field; his rival Bononcini had the advantage over him on account of a name that ended in "i"—which at the time was quite important; while the resentment of the *castrati* who had been dismissed had led to the disintegration of his company. Another Italian, Porpora, and later his compatriot Hasse, were also among his adversaries. In 1732

[1]Michel Brenet, *Les concerts en France sous l'Ancien Régime*, 1900, p. 117.

Handel was on the verge of bankruptcy, and after 1740 he gave up the struggle. It was then that he conceived the idea of writing his operas on biblical subjects and having them performed in the theatre as "oratorios", or in a concert form which was at once more economical and more manageable. With two exceptions, *Israel in Egypt* and the *Messiah*, Handel's oratorios were all conceived with this end in view. Some of the secular works performed on the concert platform, such as *Acis and Galatea* or the *Ode to Saint Cecilia*, are even described as oratorios, as were later, for example, the *Cris du Monde* of Arthur Honegger.

In Germany, other composers in their turn, more concerned than Bach with their fame and reputation, were well aware that the finest cantatas when performed as part of the church service added little to the fame of their composers. Moreover, the parochial authorities made everything as difficult as possible, both as regards the suitability of the work for liturgical purposes and its interpretation, in which neither women nor *castrati* were allowed to take part.

Although Bach was prepared to bow to these restrictions and have his solos sung by his choir-boys, others refused to conform. Mattheson obtained permission for women to sing in his *Passions* in the church, but only when they were given as performances distinct from church services: Buxtehude's formula of the "concert spirituel" in churches was amplified and became the general practice. As for Telemann, in order to preserve complete freedom of action, he had his *Passions* performed in the theatre, as Handel did for his oratorios. Whether for the theatre in London or Hamburg, or the Tuileries *salon* in Paris, church music was gradually deserting the Church.

And so there gradually came into being the idea, hitherto unthought-of, of giving concerts of religious music. . . . The nineteenth century only added to the confusion. The French Revolution, by brutally abolishing choirs and choir-schools, dealt a terrible blow to religious music which, after the upheaval, the latter tried to palliate by seeking other outlets; and the effects were also felt outside France. Beethoven's *Mass in D* was conceived as a vast oratorio which did not attempt to conform to the requirements of the liturgy. The "Good Friday" music from *Parsifal* began to find a place as "religious" music in the programmes of the "concerts spirituels"; Liszt, conducting in church, mounted a triumphal platform—wearing a cassock it is true, but without a surplice—which showed clearly that he was not officiating at a religious service, but appearing as a concert artist.

The big twentieth-century Psalms, such as those of Roussel, Florent Schmitt and Rivier, are frankly concert settings of biblical texts which made no attempt to avoid the literal descriptions and flamboyant colours which were more and more frowned upon in liturgical music. Honegger's oratorios are modelled on *King David*, which was incidental stage music subsequently adapted for concert performance, and can claim kinship with "secular oratorios" such as *Cris du Monde*. Although Stravinsky's *Symphony of Psalms* reflects the mystical phase the composer was experiencing in the early nineteen-thirties, his more recent religious works, such as the *Canticum Sacrum* commissioned for performance in St. Mark's at the Venice Festival in 1957, seem to be concerned with problems of quite a different nature and to be quite unsuitable for liturgical purposes.[1] Thus we are confronted by the paradoxical situation in which religious music is seen to forsake its normal setting: the Church. And, unless the Church does something about it, this may well mean the end of religious art.[2]

[1]While looking recently at a Review of sacred art, our eyes fell upon a musical quotation (Webern, *Lieder* op. 18, No. 3) which at first sight we took to be a caricature of the "donkey's bray" style from which we are periodically requested not to remove the faded label "Avant-Garde" attached to it nearly half a century ago. To our great surprise we then saw, from the note appended thereto, that, according to the author, this was meant to be a model showing that "it is impossible to keep more closely to (the spirit of) religious inspiration" [*sic*] (Guy Morançon: *Réflexions générales sur la musique d'inspiration religieuse*, *l'Art Sacré*, Nos. 11-12 July-August 1957, p. 16). This is how the example begins:

[2]While this book was printing, a well-documented and serious study by Solange Corbin made its appearance: *L'Eglise à la conquête de sa musique* (Gallimard, 1961) in which the author stresses the utilitarian rôle of church music and the fact that, as has often been said, the Church has always been a protector of the arts. If the ends for which it exists—worship, religious teaching and the sacraments—called for the suppression or negation of all forms of art, there is no doubt but that artists and all their works would immediately disappear from the ecclesiastical horizon. And yet it is impossible to forget how much, in the course of their history, the Church and music owe to one another and how great has been the contribution of music—and still is today—not only to the liturgy, but also to the preservation of religious feeling in a world that is becoming de-Christianized. The Popes have often acknowledged this fact, notably in the recent encyclical *Musicae sacrae disciplina* of Pius XII, in which emphasis was laid on the necessity of a proper musical education for the clergy at the seminary stage. If this advice were to be followed, we should not meet with so many priests who though well-intentioned, know nothing whatever about music and are always ready to minimize its importance, to equate its "pastoral" character with mediocrity and, by a process of "levelling down", deprive their ministry of the most precious of all its allies. As for composers, it would be too much to hope that they will continue to enrich the literature of sacred music if they are to be continually reminded, in Church circles, as everywhere else, of Arthur Honegger's terrible dictum: "The modern composer is a madman who persists in manufacturing an article which nobody wants."

PART III

IN SEARCH OF SECULAR MUSIC

14

Music for Kings

If the first music was for the gods, what came later was for Kings. It changed its name, but still existed. How did it originate? Perhaps through a misunderstanding, almost a dishonest trick. Princes and kings caused themselves to be deified; music was therefore offered to them as gods. But they were men; and when they began to come down to earth again, other men in turn claimed their share in these divine privileges. These false gods in the shape of kings were the first passive audience in history. Under the Old Empire of the Pharaohs, as we learn from inscriptions on their tombstones, there were professional musicians who "came regularly before the king and with their singing made his heart rejoice".[1] They were rewarded with favours and honours of all kinds. A statue reproduced by Hickmann (*op. cit.* fig. iii) is similar to many others in which tribute was paid to various high-ranking officials of the Old Empire. Only from the inscriptions do we learn that the statue represented the flautist at the Court of the Pharaoh Ipi. It is not only by chance that in Plate IX (a) a Middle Empire harpist is playing on his knees before some high official seated at the banqueting table in the same posture as another harpist, in Plate IX (b), who is playing to a bird-headed god.

In spite of the favours showered upon them, musicians were for a long time little more than servants.[2] Mozart was "dismissed" by his master, Archbishop Colloredo, and the terms of the contract by which Joseph Haydn was bound to the Prince Esterhazy, who was nevertheless well-known for his devotion to music, were as follows:

"The said Joseph Haydn will be considered and treated as a member of the household. In consequence, His Serene Highness trusts that he will behave himself in a manner befitting an honourable official in a nobleman's establishment. He must always be good-tempered, and never allow himself to be exasperated by his musicians, but must always be gentle and tolerant, just and of an equable temperament. It is expressly laid down

---

[1] H. Hickmann, *Le métier de musicien au temps des pharaons. Cahiers d'histoire égyptienne*, 1954, p. 261.

[2] Traces of this old tradition still survive here and there. Alfred Cortot, when a young man, was once invited to play at a fashionable soirée. His hostess, so the story goes, offered him a fairly substantial fee, remarking at the same time: "But I must warn you, I would rather you did not mix with my guests." "Oh, in that case, Madame," replied Cortot, "it will be a hundred francs less."

that whenever the orchestra is required to play on social occasions the vice-Kappell-meister and all the musicians in his orchestra will wear livery, and the said Joseph Haydn must see that both he himself and all his musicians will obey the regulations and appear in white stockings, white linen and powdered hair, either tied in a bow or with a wig. . . . The said Joseph Haydn will present himself daily in the anti-chamber before and after noon, to receive instructions from His Highness as to whether or not the or-chestra's services will be required. After receiving his orders, he will communicate them to the other musicians and see that they are punctually carried out. . . . His Serene Highness undertakes to retain Joseph Haydn in his service during this time, and if he gives satisfaction he may entertain hopes of being appointed Kapellmeister. Neverthe-less, His Serene Highness reserves the right to dismiss the said Joseph Haydn at the expiration of this contract should he think fit to do so."[1]

Throughout the fluctuations of history, the position of musicians in the public's esteem has varied enormously. While the moral elevation of their art won for them in Plato's ideal city a place among the élite; while the religious nature of Greek tragedy made it an honour to be allowed to sing in the chorus; and while singers and flute-players, thanks to the grotesque artistic aspirations of a Nero or a Caligula, were appoin-ted to the highest office in the Court; yet the female Roman instrumentalists, *tibicinae* or *ambubaiae*, nevertheless ranked as courtesans in the hierarchy of Roman official enter-tainment. The first fourteen rows of the orchestra were forbidden to artists, musicians or actors; and the latter were destined to suffer for a long time from this affront. Al-though enjoying the patronage of the King, Molière was denied religious burial.

A thirteenth-century miniature throws a curious light upon this hierarchy. It repre-sents the *trouvère* Adenet le Roi, at the feet of Marie de Brabant listening to Blanche, the daughter of Saint Louis, telling him an old Spanish legend. . All three are wearing crowns; but that of the *trouvère* is only a sign of his profession. He had won it in a competition, or "*puys*", in which prizes were awarded to the best professionals; it is also the reason why, although a fully grown adult, he is represented as being very small in comparison with the "great lady" reclining on her couch—about the same size as the little girl who also wears a "real" crown, and the unnamed servant.

Actors, jugglers, musicians—all had the same duties to perform; to pay homage to God and entertain the King. The concert hall was not thought of until very much later. The normal setting for their activities was the *salon* or the banqueting hall. The musician's "turn" alternated with that of the showman with his tame bear, etc. It was in

---

[1]Art. 2, 5, 14 of the contract, H. E. Jacob: *Haydn*, pp. 86-89.

front of Herod's dining table that the medieval sculptors represented the dance of Salome (Plate X). The tradition has not changed since the Egyptian harpist in Plate IX(a), and has persisted even down to our own day. However exceptional they may have been, the concerts to accompany banquets have never ceased to exist (Plate XI). It was at table that Esterhazy, like so many others, "consumed" the music supplied

4. The *trouvère* Adenet le Roi at the feet of Marie de Brabant. Miniature from the thirteenth-century romance of Cleomades.

to him by his servant Joseph Haydn; our own cabaret attractions and restaurant orchestras are a prolongation in an attentuated form of one of the essential forms of the old-time "concert"; and it is a matter for regret that "real" music has disdainfully abandoned this familiar way of maintaining contact with a public from which it is becoming daily more and more estranged.

As long as kings and princes were the backbone of society, an immense proportion of all music was made for them and, in theory at least, exclusively for them. Their entourage and their guests only benefited indirectly and, it might almost be said, by usurpation. Opera itself, as we shall see presently, was no exception.

The friendly dedications which still appear on the title pages of our musical scores are an unconscious relic of the old-time dedications to a noble patron from whom one could expect some pecuniary acknowledgement.[1] For when royalty ceased to receive musical offerings as a divine right, they were able in this way to continue in the rôle of patron or Maecenas.

[1] It was the same in all the arts. The dedication on an eighteenth-century engraving sometimes takes up more room than the picture itself.

Already the *raison d'être* of what had been "music for the King" had changed. For a long time now princes had ceased to be gods. The music offered them was still, to be sure, an act of homage, but another more prosaic and equally imperative reason was now coming to the fore: it was the patron who paid and enabled the musician to earn his living. The expenses in connection with the private musical establishment of innumerable Princes, Electors, Dukes, Counts, Margraves or Landgraves were an important element in State expenditure. The history of music has often been influenced by such things as the financial difficulties which led to a reduction in the number of instrumentalists, wars which restricted festivities, or the piety or libertinage of the musician's patron—or his wife. For example, Bach had to leave Cöthen in 1722 because the Prince had married as his second wife a woman he called an "amusa"—having no taste for music—in consequence whereof the exercise of his art was from now on without aim or object.

But in proportion to the rise of the middle classes and the decline in the prestige of the nobility, the bourgeois, in their turn, began to claim their share in the festivities of the gods. A significant turning-point occurred at the end of the thirteenth century, one of the crucial periods of this social transformation. While the first "*trouveurs*" (troubadours or *trouvères*) were of noble stock, the bourgeois set out to rival them. In a town of rich merchants, such as Arras around 1270, the prince to receive a dedication was no longer, in the eyes of the "*trouveur*", the Lord of the Manor, but the elected "Prince" of the "*puy*"; and everyone aspired to becoming a *trouvère*: we have on record today in this city alone no less than 180 . . . . It is also well known that poets, up to and including Villon and Marot, dedicated to these ephemeral "Princes", real or fictitious, the "Envoi" of their ballades.

It is not certain that this was in the best interests of the art. While Adam de la Halle abandoned Arras and went off to Naples with a real prince, the Comte d'Artois, for whom he composed the *Jeu de Robin et Marion*, his former colleagues, who remained at Arras, competed among themselves in musical debates to decide whether the pleasure of living in luxury was a compensation for having to give up eating pease pudding,[1] or whether it was less trouble to disgrace one's wife at the risk of making her jealous, or of being cuckolded oneself without knowing a thing about it.[2]

And so from the "*puys*" of the thirteenth century to the "academies" of the sixteenth, one can distinguish a public somewhere between that of the Court and the drawing-room; consisting for the most part of educated people forming a close circle, active but

[1] *Jeu-parti* between Gilbert de Berneville and Thomas Hérier.
[2] *Jeu-parti* between Huc d'Arras and Simon d'Athies.

numerically inconsiderable. We shall meet with them again in the chapter devoted to concert-giving. The monied aristocrat, too, seeing himself in the flattering rôle of a Maecenas surrounded by artists, was anxious to play the part traditionally reserved for the aristocracy of blood; and a farmer-general like La Pouplinière, who had at his court Rameau, Stamitz and Gossec, performed the same musical functions in the eighteenth century as the head of one of the German principalities.

Then came the French Revolution. One by one the Courts of Europe disappeared. Happily for music, the *salons* survived, passing progressively from the hands of the nobility to the middle classes. Until quite recently, they were indeed the rightful successors to the royal Courts. We shall see them in action in another chapter. What has become of them today? Two world wars have dissipated too many fortunes and changed too many habits for it to be possible for them, with a few rare exceptions, to exercise the same influence that used to be their privilege. Put into cold storage on records, or relayed by radio, music is now brought into the home; the only people who go out to hear it are the real amateurs who realize how indispensable to a good performance is the human presence of an interpreter, no matter how perfect the actual sound that issues from the apparatus may be. The radio and recording studio have become the new aristocrats, the only patrons for whom the artist know that he can work in the hope of receiving a just reward—for, as everyone knows, except the tax authorities, every public concert, with very few exceptions, results in a heavy financial loss.

A new chapter is now beginning in the sociological history of music. Only the future can tell whether it will be beneficial.

15

Where the Public Appears at first as an Intruder

When I was a child I sang in my school choir. I shall never forget my disappointment when I heard for the first time another choir sing a motet by Victoria which, from my place in the choir, had filled me with enthusiasm: I no longer found in it what had thrilled me when I was taking an active part in it. And my favourite Beethoven symphonies were for a long time the ones I used to play with my teacher in a four-hand arrangement on an old upright piano. Moreover, it was long before I got as much pleasure from listening to the finest performances conducted by a Toscanini or a Bruno Walter.

Contrary to the fashion of today, when a considerable proportion of the music we hear is brought into the home, without any personal participation, by radio, television or recordings, only a relatively small proportion of the music in the world was intended for an audience. Almost the entire repertory of popular music, and notably chamber-music, was written for the benefit of the performers first and foremost, or for those listeners who took an active part in so far as they were confident that they, too, were capable of playing or singing the same music. Until the end of the seventeenth century, nobody ever paid, except at the opera, to listen to music. As we have shown, music was either for the Church, the Court, or for oneself. It accompanied festivities, could be either edifying or entertaining, and enriched family life where everyone could take part in it.

Outside the Church, the theatre or the Court, people made music for themselves and in their homes. What are often labelled "concerts" in picture galleries are more often than not intimate scenes centering round the musician member of the family. What was later to be known as "chamber-music", was not designed to be heard by an "audience", as it is today, but for the pleasure of those taking part. Guests were only there as supernumeraries; the classical string quartet met round a table with a desk at each corner, while the middle was occupied by jars of tobacco and tankards of beer. The scores of string quartets were not published, only the separate parts—which explains to a large extent the suspicion aroused by the late Beethoven quartets: so many works of this kind could be judged from a glance at the first violin part, which "had the tune", as the saying went, that it is not difficult to imagine the bewilderment of those who tried to assess these quartets by the same somewhat simple criteria as they were wont to apply to other works in this form.

"Salon music" has come in for a lot of hostile criticism. And yet this was the setting for all the classical masterpieces; and the free-and-easy atmosphere in which it flourished was perhaps, as experience has taught us, more propitious to its vitality than the concert-platform to which it has now been banished. From one century to another, down to the time of our grandparents, the atmosphere among artists was the same: familiar and relaxed.

To convey this impression engravers and painters invariably introduced some amusing detail: in the sixteenth-century concert portrayed in Plate XII(a), for example, notice the embracing couple on the right, and in the seventeenth-century van Loo (Plate XII(b)), the "galant" conversation being carried on in the background on the extreme right. In the celebrated picture (Plate XII(c)) showing the youthful Mozart playing the harpsichord to the Prince de Conti in 1766, while the ladies in the background are chattering over a cup of tea, we are no doubt reminded of Mozart's strictures on this bad behaviour; but this was a reflection on the lack of education and frivolity of his hostesses, and not on the principle itself of musical receptions of this kind. In the nineteenth century, again, in Moritz von Schwind's picture of Schubert at the piano (Plate XII(d)), the artist does not forget to show, in the left foreground, the two traditional gossiping women, nor on the right, a whispering pair of lovers; it is noticeable, however, that the chairs are better arranged, at any rate for the ladies; from now on the salon is arranged for the purpose of listening to music, while with the advent of romanticism (Plate XII(e)) the female members of the audience are shown in attitudes of langorous ecstasy. Can the loss of this familiar atmosphere be attributed to the victory of Prussian militarism? This is not a mere fancy. Look carefully at the two drawings juxtaposed in Plate XIII; in (a) we see a concert given in his own salon by a distinguished flautist, the Prussian King Frederick II as a young man. The atmosphere is the same as we have seen up to the present. Now turn to (b), we see the same personage now fully mature, but the players are lined up as if on parade, and the royal soloist stands apart like a Colonel taking the salute . . . It is also noticeable that the musicians themselves, when playing together, do not, like actors, sit facing the public, but adopt a less formal and more comfortable and rational attitude, generally facing one another. It is perhaps in a Berlin painting of 1854 (Plate XIV)—Prussia again—representing a violin and piano recital given by Joachim and Clara Schumann, that one can see for the first time the position we are accustomed to today in which the artists on the platform are back to back, the violinist facing the audience. This change of posture is in itself significant.

We have seen how the kings and princes at one time usurped, as it were, the privileges of the gods by making themselves the recipients of a "musical offering". In the same way, to assemble an audience specially to listen to music might also seem to be a transference of what used to be the privilege of the courtiers who were merely the passive recipients of a homage which was not intended for them.

Listening to music was, in point of fact, when we reflect upon its origin, something more than a favour: it was a privilege that was only rarely accorded, and then only for some very good reason. The first concerts, in the accepted sense of the term, were not open to all and sundry. They were real ceremonies for initiates, and they were originally of a religious character. In the sixteenth century one belonged to a musical society in the same way that in the Middle Ages one became a member of a pious confraternity. Take, for example, the statutes of the celebrated Puy d'Evreux, founded in 1570 by Guillaume Costeley "to the honour of God and of the glorious Virgin Mary and all the Saints of Paradise, especially of Madame Saint Cecilia, virgin and martyr, *Amen*".

"The Deed of foundation prescribes in detail the order of the ceremonies which lasted for several days, beginning on the eve of the feast of St. Cecilia at the end of Vespers, and including numerous masses and services 'with music and organ', and ending with a 'Mass for the dead'; the 'prince' of the Puy received his peers at table; in the meantime (according to the foundation Deed) 'a Puy', or concertation of musick, will be given in the local choir school-house, and a whole series of prizes will be awarded for the best compositions submitted. When the judging is finished, the 'Prince', accompanied by the founders and brethren, will march with the precentors, who will then all present themselves at the great West door of Notre Dame to give thanks to God for the happy outcome of their music-making; and there they will sing aloud the prize-winning motets, and when this is done, announce to the assembled public the names of the authors thereof."[1]

These first examples of an organized concert were thus partly religious in character and partly in the nature of a competition and a festive occasion. Soon the pious intentions of the first founders were ignored when, with the advent of humanism, the old religious ideal was replaced by the mythical ideal of antiquity. It was with the ancient Greeks in mind that Baïf, in this same year 1570, founded in his own house, together with his musician Thibaut de Courville, the first Academy (and the first to be so described) "of

[1]Bonnin and Chassant, *Puy de musique*, 1837, pp. 1, 76, 81, etc.

poetry and music". Concerts were given there regularly, but these were rather in the nature of statutory ceremonies, open only to members of the association; the latter were given a medal, to mark the honour conferred upon them, which they had to present in order to gain admittance—the predecessor, in a sense, of our concert ticket. Only this was a ticket awarded for merit and could not be bought for money.

We know that, in memory of these academic occasions, concerts were for a long time called "academies": as late as the nineteenth century people still spoke of "giving an academy"; the word "giving" itself, still used today (we speak of "giving" a concert) has lost its original meaning, but reminds us of a time when anything like a "box office" was inconceivable.

Soon a third conception began to take shape; though more utilitarian than its predecessors, it was none the less a direct consequence. It is now the turn of the virtuosi and musicians themselves who, for the sake of making themselves better known, began to invite their friends and colleagues to listen to them in their own homes. The first to give a concert of this kind was a curious character, one Jean Lemaire, who lived at Toulouse from 1581 to 1650, often visiting Paris in the meantime. Anticipating Ferdinand de Lesseps, Lemaire had conceived the idea of a canal between two seas, and tried unsuccessfully to bring this to fruition. Anticipating Esperanto, he had also advocated the use of a universal language. He was also known as an inventor in the field of architecture and of mnemotechnics. As a musician, Lemaire was no less fruitful in inventions: he had imagined a new system of alphabetic notation; suggested a seventh syllable for the sol-fa series (his *za* being not far removed from the *si* which was eventually adopted); perfected a system of "stops" whereby it would be possible to play on the lute intervals other than those of the diatonic scale, and also added to the lute family a new instrument which he called *almérie*, being an anagram of his own name. The private concerts he organized around 1642 were attended by those who had put into practice his various inventions, and were known in consequence as "*concerts almériques*".

It was also at Lemaire's house that Pierre Chabanceau de la Barre, organist of the King's chapel and harpsichordist to the Queen, Anne of Austria, organized from 1645 to his death in 1656, with the assistance of his children and the best singers of the day, musical receptions attended by his friends. These, together with the above-mentioned "*almériques*", were the first real "concerts" in our sense of the word, as were those gatherings organized under similar conditions about 1655, also in Paris, by a Canon of Embrun, Jacques de Goüy, a composer and a friend of Lemaire's, or again by the celebrated harpsichordist Jacques Champion de Chambonnières.[1]

[1]Cf. Michel Brenet, *Les concerts en France sous l'Ancien Régime*, 1900

But in all these undertakings there was no question of any kind of commercial exploitation. The idea of making the hearer pay for his musical pleasure originated in England, towards the last quarter of the seventeenth century. This opened up an entirely new perspective in the history of music which we shall consider in the following chapter.

16

Where Music becomes a Form of Entertainment

That music could become an entertainment by itself for which a ticket of admittance would be required is an idea which, in its present form, did not exist before the eighteenth century and was the exception rather than the rule until the middle of the nineteenth century. When the ancient Greeks met together to hear virtuoso performers, they tended to look upon these occasions as sporting rather than musical events: the cithara contests were, in their view, on the same level as running or boxing. As for the Romans, their attitude was wholly unambiguous. Athenaeus relates that in 167 B.C. when they saw for the first time a gathering of musicians, they asked what they were there for and then, so as to have their money's worth, insisted that they should all play together and then end up with a boxing match. . . .

The idea that anyone could, at a specified time, pay to go into a hall to listen to music only gained ground after an example had been set by the opera, where this custom had started on account of the element of entertainment inherent in this kind of spectacle.

In its early stages, however, opera, too, was a form of royal entertainment, just as the Greek theatre (and today the Chinese Opera and Japanese *No*) was originally a kind of religious ceremony. Whether we consider it as having originated as an accompaniment to the medieval banquet, or to have sprung from the first Court ballets, its line of descent is the same. Quite simply, in 1573 the entertainment was shifted from the banqueting hall to the ballroom. In that year Catherine de Medicis gave a sumptuous feast for the Polish Ambassadors (Plate XV). The guests of honour were in the front row of the *fauteuils* placed on the floor of the hall. Behind them, in the balcony, sat the other guests. It was an honour for them to be present, because they were only there, one might say, as supernumeraries. The musicians were hidden; they did not form part of the actual spectacle.

The year 1581 saw the first Court ballet offered by Henri III to celebrate the marriage of his favourite the Duc de Joyeuse (Plate XVI). It was to the King, seated almost on a level with the stage, that the actors addressed themselves; and he is even included in the text of the verses as taking a part. The musicians were hidden behind the scenery;

when a little later on they did appear on the stage, as for example in an "entry of the lute-players" (*entrée de luths*) in a Court Ballet at the beginning of the seventeenth century (Plate XVII), they did so as actors, in costume and dancing while they played. Lully, in the *divertissments* he arranged for Molière, still followed this custom, with such indications as: "Entry of the violinists, dancing, . . . " It was also for the Prince and his guests at some great Court ceremony that Peri wrote his *Orfeo*; while the creation of Monteverdi's masterpiece was entirely due to the jealousy of the Duke of Mantua who, stung by the success of the Florentine *Orfeo*, wished to have one of his own and commissioned it from his "musician in ordinary" so that he could offer his distinguished guests something better than his rival had been able to do.

But the real creators of a paying public were no doubt the Princes Barberini, who, inspired by the example of these royal but still only "occasional" entertainments, conceived the idea of opening in Rome, in 1632, a regular theatre for presenting operas which would be open to the public, who would pay for their seats. The example was followed everywhere, and first of all in England, where shows of this kind were known as "Masques"; as early as 1639 Sir William d'Avenant obtained from Charles I a patent authorizing him to build a threatre "to exercise musick and musical presentments". In France the first opera, that of Cambert and Perrin, was opened in 1669; it was of a frankly popular character, as can be seen from the shabby aspect of the hall of the *Jeu de Paune* (Plate XVIII) which was specially adapted for this purpose. The "box office" arrangements, which were in the hands of an unscrupulous businessman, the Marquis de Sourdéac, were conducted, according to the chroniclers, in conditions of indescribable confusion, which encouraged every kind of fraud and eventually landed the trio in jail. The sequel is well known, in which Lully stepped in to deprive Cambert of his privilege, while the latter went off to London where the opera, down to the time of Handel, was to bear for so long the imprint of French influences. As it turned out, Cambert's successor in Paris, Lully, the Court musician, was destined to restore to the French opera its original character of a spectacle for the entertainment of the King; and so the "popular" public, now deprived of the "real" opera it had just begun to appreciate, was forced, in the face of the barriers erected by a system of privileges exploited by a master mind, to put up with parodies and fair-ground shows—which partly explains the success of the French opéra-comique.

The latter, in its turn, had behind it a long tradition of popular entertainment in which music played an important part. Let us take a look, for example, at the Tabarin parade at the Pont-Neuf in 1623 (Plate XIX). Here there are neither barrier, nor seats nor any arrangements for paying; the public apparently consisting of idle spectators walks freely about in front of the platform which is about on a level with their heads. A collection will probably be made at the end.[1]

In the meantime, however, the royal Opera flourished and became more and more magnificent. Consider for example, the performance in Vienna in 1666 of Cesti's *Pomo d'Oro* (Plate XX). The auditorium is sumptuous and the stage well equipped. There is no orchestral pit as yet, but the musicians are hidden by a curtain while seated, as in our theatres today, beneath the stage. There is a vast open space at one end of the hall, as the prince must be seated in the front row, and a certain distance must be observed, as etiquette did not allow anyone to be placed in front of him. A new and noteworthy feature is that the public are seated in *fauteuils* arranged in regular rows; but this may have been a temporary arrangement due, perhaps, more to the majesty of the Court only than a proper respect for the spectacle on the stage. In any case we seem to have a preview of an embryonic concert-hall.

It was in England, at the end of the seventeenth century, that the first "paying" concerts were given, probably on a subscription basis, by John Banister, one of Charles II's violinists. Appointed on his return from France, where he had gone to study, Master of the King's Band, he was dismissed in 1666; according to Fétis, this was because he told the King that the English violinists were inferior to the French; according to Riemann, on the contrary, it was because he had criticized adversely the French musicians who were the King's protégés. . . . Whatever the reason may have been, he found himself without a job, and so it was to the forced unemployment of a London musician that we owe the most sensational development of all time in the social history of music. For being deprived of his livelihood, Banister conceived the idea in 1672 of making some money by giving musical evenings at his house for which admission would be charged. This was an unprecedented innovation. It was so successful that in 1676, Thomas Mace, of Trinity College, Cambridge, published in his *Musick's Monument*, a plan for a most unusual undertaking—namely, a concert room with twelve different galleries for the "severall sorts of Auditors". There was no platform; it was not a theatre, but a "musick room", with a chimney and a table in the middle around which the players and singers would be seated, and in one corner, an organ. The intimate atmosphere,

---

[1]Music in the open air was the Revolution's supreme ideal. "The Republic's god is Liberty; its temple the universe; the proper place of worship is under the celestial vault. In future our public squares will be our concert halls." This was the substance of a petition presented to the Convention on 18th Brumaire of the Year II. Among the signatories were Gossec and Sarette, who was to be the first Director of the Conservatoire. (Constant Pierre, *Le Conservatoire*, p. 90)

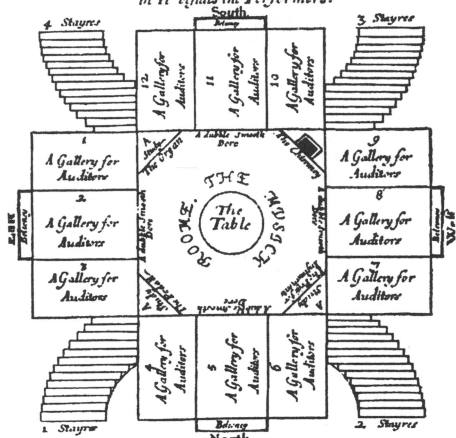

The Description
Of a Musick-Roome. Uniforme.
With Conveniency for Severall Sorts of
Auditors, severally plac'd in 12
Distinct Roomes, besides the Mu=
sick-Roome. w: would haue none
in It besides the Performers.

Supposing the Roome to be Six Yeards Square
The 12 Galleryes would be 3 yeards long, and
Better. The 4 Middle Galleryes Somthing
Broader then the Rest, as Here they are.

5. The oldest known plan of a concert-hall.

indispensable to "chamber music", was thus preserved, in appearance at all events.[1] So it was with the second organizer in the history of "paying" concerts, a rich London amateur, Thomas Britton, a coal merchant by trade. Britton began giving weekly musical parties in his house in 1678; Handel was among his guests. At first they were free; later, following the example of Banister, the coal merchant charged a subscription fee. And in 1690 a musician at the court of William III, Robert King, went into partnership with Johann Wolfgang Franck, a German who had come from Hamburg after having, in a fit of jealousy, stabbed a musician at the court of Ansbach and wounded his own wife; together they founded a real business under the name of "Concerts of vocal and instrumental music".

These London concerts were a kind of commercialization of the private type of chamber music hitherto in vogue. It was left to France to extend the system to orchestral and choral concerts. Already under Charles IX, Baïf and Courville's "Academy of poetry and music" gave regular concerts for its members. The *Académie du Palais* (so called because it held its meetings at the Louvre) which succeeded it under Henri III gave alternate shows of ballet and music unadorned. Other "academies" which provided their members with regular "concerts" were founded in Rouen (1662), Orleans (1670), and Lyons (1713), and later at Marseilles, Pau, Carpentras, Dijon and Tours. London, from 1710 to 1792, had its "Academy of Ancient Music", founded by Pepusch and specializing in old music—i.e., music of the previous century. We have seen how, in 1725, Anne Danican-Philidor became aware that on religious feast days, when the opera was closed, music lovers were deprived of their favourite distraction. They paid for the opera, so there was no reason why they should not pay for concerts. The title *"Concert spirituel"* saved the face of the moralists, although the repertory was by no means confined to masses and oratorios. These were the first public orchestral concerts; in 1762 they employed some ninety-three musicians. The provincial "academies" followed suit, and inspired by their success, in 1775 a rival company was set up, the *"Concert des Amateurs"*, later known (after 1780) as the *"Concert de la loge Olympique"*, (the name of the new premises). This was followed by the *"Concert de la rue de Cléry"*[2] and, after 15th Brumaire, in the Year IX (November 6, 1800) by the public performances given by the students at the Conservatoire which led in 1802 to the foundation of the *"Concert français"* in the Rue de la Victoire, and in 1828 to that of the *"Société des*

---

[1] A similar arrangement can still be seen in the Holywell Music Room at Oxford, built in 1748 and believed to be the oldest concert room in Europe. It was restored in 1959.

[2] Cf. Michel Brenet, *Les concerts en France sous l'Ancien Régime*, op cit.

Concerts du Conservatoire". The rest is now common knowledge. All these concerts were run on a subscription basis: they aimed at creating a faithful public of their own and hardly catered at all to the casual listener. The "occasional" concert is a still more recent invention. Until the end of the eighteenth century no one "gave" concerts. The virtuoso could be heard in the churches or at Court, or in the drawing-rooms of wealthy patrons before an invited audience. The composer wrote for the regular *ensembles* for which he was responsible, or with which he was associated. Music, as we have seen, was a "seasonal product" for immediate consumption. Only the theatres invited audiences to hear a specific work. When Telemann or Handel gave public performances of their works—generally in a theatre—they treated them rather as if they were operas, paying as much attention to the visual presentation as to the music itself.

The concert halls which began to multiply in the nineteenth century were at first more like big drawing-rooms, like the Salle Pleyel in the rue Rochechouart, where Chopin so often played and which survived until 1927 (Plate XXI); or else, like the Leipzig Gewandhaus (Plate XXII shows it as it was in 1840) they were arranged after the manner of the Protestant churches where religious music was given, with rows of seats facing one another. The Paris Conservatoire[1] which, until it was moved to the rue de Madrid in 1909, was sited between the rue Bergère, the rue du Conservatoire, the rue Sainte-Cécile and the rue du Faubourg-Poissonnière, had had its own concert hall since 1811. Its original name is significant: according to the *Courrier de l'Europe* of July 9th of that year, in its account of the inauguration ceremony, it used to be known as the pupils' "new practice room". Among its peculiarities, the chronicler observed with surprise that "the orchestra is placed at the back of the hall, like the actors in a theatre, although in all theatres the orchestra is placed in the centre, between the actors and the spectators". But, the report continued, "since a concert-hall is something new for Paris, everything has to be tried out". Moreover, the Conservatoire was not only intended for music; it was also for "declamation"; and this was no doubt the reason why the architect Delannoy decided to place the musicians "as if they were actors in a theatre".

All through the nineteenth century this hall preserved its very individual character: the Salle Gaveau was not built until 1907. In Paris, chamber music concerts around 1920 were generally given in the Salle des Agriculteurs—now a cinema. The big orchestral

[1]The word *Conservatoire* does *not* mean what Ambroise Thomas is said to have replied one day to someone who came to speak to him about reforms: "Au Conservatoire, Monsieur, on conserve." *Conservare* in Italian means to "preserve"; e.g., the Curator of a museum. A *conservatorio* in the sixteenth century in Naples, Venice or Palermo, was a hospice where orphan or abandoned children were educated and cared for. As musical instruction was a particular feature of these places, the term has come to mean any kind of musical school.

societies, other than the Conservatoire (which used its own hall until the 1939 war) were housed in various theatres (Colonne was first at the Odéon in 1873 and afterwards at the Châtelet), or even circuses (Pasdeloup was in 1861 at the Cirque d'Hiver).

In 1927 the house of Pleyel left the rue Rochechouart for the Faubourg Saint-Honoré. When the little red hall was demolished, the souvenirs of Chopin and so many others disappeared with it, and Paris was equipped with its first "big" concert hall, with seating for 2,500 (Plate XXIII). The director of the firm, Gustave Lyon, a well-known engineer, had been working for many years on a plan which would embody all the latest acoustic discoveries. A year later the hall was burned down. When rebuilt on exactly the same lines as before, the acoustics were marred by inexplicable echoes, and it was not until 1957 that a remedy was found for this defect. The hall had none the less served as a proto-type. In Brussels the Palais des Beaux Arts was built according to the same principles. In America these were again applied on a gigantic scale, and as I write an enormous "block", the Lincoln Centre, a veritable citadel of music, is being erected, which will include the successor to the old and out-of-date Metropolitan Opera House. London has also possessed since 1951 its own Royal Festival Hall. Today every self-respecting big town possesses its own large concert hall; music by itself is now an attraction.

17

Paper Music

"I never go to concerts any more," André Pirro, my master and eminent predecessor at the Sorbonne told me one day. "Why listen to music? To read it is enough."

Deformation of musicology? Perhaps, and I pray the gods that I may be spared this in my old age. It is also a striking symptom of the end of an evolution as manifested in a once sensitive and enthusiastic man, who was an organist and choir-master, but who had become so saturated with music at the end of his career that intellectual desiccation had taken the place of sensuous enjoyment. Spread over the centuries, this also represents the ultimate stage in the evolution of our too-ancient Western musical civilization.

When a civilization is young, its music is never written down—we shall have occasion to refer to this later. All ancient civilizations and, to some extent, medieval, depend on oral tradition. Notation, when it exists, is used as a kind of *aide-mémoire a posteriori*, referring to tunes that are already well known, and not as a means of learning them, still less of composing them. This system still prevails in the East, in the Islamic countries, etc. When the pseudo-Plutarch speaks about "ancient composers", he shows them to us with a cithara in their hands, or an *aulos* at their lips, but not with a scroll of paper in their hands. For example, the first funeral dirge, in honour of the serpent Python, was, he tells us, "played on the *aulos*" and not "composed" by Olympos.[1] Similarly, in the Middle Ages the chronicler[2] writes, quite naturally, that Tutilon "dictated" the melodies he composed: there is no paper-work until the act of composition is finished. On another plane altogether, this was also Mozart's method.

Surprise is often expressed that from the thirteenth to the end of the sixteenth century, when the complexity of the contrapuntal combinations obliged the composer to calibrate most carefully his simultaneous melodic lines, which would have been impossible without writing them down, no synoptic "scores", like those in use today, have come

---

[1] The following detail clearly shows our constant tendency to attribute to the Ancients our own modern prejudices: the latest editor of this text interpolates precisely this word in his translation, in order to make the meaning "clearer": "Olympos, having composed. . . . . played it on the flute" (Lasserre, *Plutarque, de la Musique*, Lausanne, 1954, p. 139). There is no word in the Greek text to justify this addition.

[2] Ekkehard IV, *De Casibus Sancti Galli*, Chap. III.

down to us. Manuscripts and old editions always provide us with the "component parts" of the polyphony: each part, or voice, is presented complete, in isolation from its companions, whether they follow one another on the same page, or are copied or printed under separate covers. Clearly, each part was intended to be read only by the performers: the total effect would be revealed in performance, and nobody found it necessary to examine the work visually.[1]

An explanation for this singular state of affairs was discovered recently in curious circumstances. In 1953 the archaeological services of the Belgian Royal Art and History Museums brought to light, near the church of Saint-Feuillien de Fosse, a well that had been blocked up since 1723. All sorts of heterogeneous objects were taken from it

6. The "composing slate" found at Saint-Feuillien.

which, on examination, showed that the well had been used for the disposal of rubbish from the fourteenth to the seventeenth century. Among these objects was a slate of about 30 × 15 cm. on which were engraved, lengthwise, six musical staves, each of five lines. The director of the operations, M. Mertens, fortunately decided to send the slate for examination to Mme. Clercx-Lejeune, professor of musicology at the University of Liège. This lady then remembered the existence of some sixteenth-century texts which

[1]Until quite recently, this practice was common in the case of string quartets; the parts were published separately, but not the score. Down to about the middle of the thirteenth century polyphonic writing usually ensured the concordance of the voices. Later this practice was discontinued, except in the case of the *conductus* and its derivatives. From 1250 to approximately 1600, apart from tablatures intended for a single executant, there were practically no synoptic scores in existence.

had never been explained, notably a treatise by a certain Lampadius, a cantor of Lune-
bourg, in which reference was made to *tabulae compositoriae* said to have been used by
contemporaries of Josquin and Isaac, and of which "no verbal or written record remained".   Continuing her comparative study of the texts on the one hand and the
slate that had issued so miraculously from the earth on the other, Mme. Clercx arrived
at the conclusion that composers used to work on a sort of perishable rough foundation, of which the slate was a specimen example.   When the work was finished,
each part was copied out for the performers on some durable material, and the score
was considered to be of no further use.[1] The notes were rubbed out, and the slate was
ready to be used again.[2] Music and literature thus follow the same path, for the earliest
literature was oral—and often sung. Paper came into use later to assist the memory of
the *jongleurs* (the MS. of *La Chanson de Roland* at Oxford is thought to be a *jongleur's* text);
or, again, as a curiosity intended as a present for a nobleman. In any case, the written
score came afterwards, and was not used as an aid to composition. And this evolution
continued down to the "typographical" poetry of Mallarmé's *Coup de Dés* or certain
pre-1920 Cocteau poems.

It was the same with music. The finest contrapuntal *tours de force* filled the composer
with pride, but apart from the performers or the pupils to whom the master showed his
work as an example, the final arbiter was the ear and the ear alone. There was no score
available for dissection; no piece was definitive until it had been "tested", i.e., tried out
in actual performance.

The first offensive of Paper versus Ear seems to have occurred towards the end of the
fourteenth century, during the decadent period of the Ars Nova. But Guillaume de
Machaut was already so fond of verbal rebuses that he used to insert them in his music.

> Dix et sept cinq trese quatorse et quinze
> M'a doucement de bien amer espris
>
> Ten, seven, five, thirteen, fourteen and fifteen
> Have gently advised me to love well.

he sings in one of his Rondeaux. Count the letters in alphabetical order (making no
distinction between I and J) and you will find the numbers 17, 5, 13, 14 and 15 corre-

---

[1]This would explain the term "partition". *Partire* means to divide; and so to arrange a "partition", or
"score" as we say, meant to separate the written notes by bars to facilitate their concordance—the precursor
of our modern bar-lines. These bars, however, disappeared in the final copies of the individual parts.

[2]Suzanne Clercx, *D'une ardoise aux partitions du XVIe. siècle*; *Mélanges*, Paul-Marie Masson, 1955, I, 157-170.

spond to the letters R E N O P, an anagram of the first part of the name of his girl friend, Péronne. He introduces a similar kind of puzzle in another Rondeau:

> Ma fin est mon commencement
> Et mon commencement ma fin,
> Est teneüre vraiement.
> Ma fin est mon commencement.—
> Mes tiers chant trois fois seulement
> Se retrograde et einsi fin.
> Ma fin est mon commencement
> Et mon commencement ma fin.

> My end is my beginning
> And my beginning is my end.
> It is in truth the tenor too.
> My end is my beginning
> My third part three times only
> Goes back, and so it ends.
> My end is my beginning
> And my beginning is my end.

The Rondeau is for three voices, but only two are written down along with the text of the first two verses: the "triple" and the "contre-teneur".[1] The words were written upside-down, and only in the "triple" part; to read them the paper has to be turned round (Plate XXIV). It was a real "parlour-game", the key to which, however, was discovered long ago.

There was no written "teneur"; we have to guess it from reading the "*triple*" upside-down, beginning with the last note. Then join it to the "*triple*" and the "*contre-teneur*" as they are written, and we get our three voices. But in the middle of the "*triple*" indicated by a vertical bar-line, we find that the written "*contre-teneur*" has come to an end; and so for the second part we must read it, in its turn, upside-down, while continuing to follow the written "*triple*". As the "*triple*" we are now reading is the part that has already been retrograded by the "*teneur*", while the "*teneur*" is now about to retrograde the part that has just ended, the two "*triple-teneur*" voices are now symmetrically in inverse relation to one another. In other words, the text only provides for one "*triple*" in two

---

[1]The *teneur* (later *tenor*) was the lower part, unless there was a "*contre-teneur*". The "*triple*" was the highest of three voices, and by extension the top line of any number of voices. It was sometimes called *treble* or, later, *trouble*. Arnoul Greban, in his *Passion*, introduces an amusing pun by making one of his devils in the discordant infernal concert sing "trouble". All these terms were familiar to Machaut's readers.

parts, A and B, and one *"contre-teneur"* C. The game consists in developing AB and C in accordance with both the rules of this form of composition and the conventions imposed. If we indicate the retrogradation by a comma, the three real parts will follow one another in this way, while respecting the traditional repetitions of rondo-form (AB -aA -ab -AB):

       Triple: A B A A A B A B

     Teneur: B,A,B,B,B,A,B,A,

Contre-teneur: C C,C C C C,C C,

so that we get in the *"teneur"* the three retrogradations A, of the *"tierschant"* ["third-part"], as stated.

Amusements of this kind, which are only interesting because of their complexity, have no auditive significance whatever, because not even the most practised musician could possibly, by listening to the piece, have any idea of the *tour de force* involved, or, even if he knew about it, be able to grasp it by ear. But it is easy to imagine the satisfaction of the composer who, having set himself a difficult problem for fun, realizes that he has been successful and is thus convinced of its great technical value, anticipating in advance the admiring comments of those who will later be known as "the critics"! All the more so, in that he will not have failed to warn them about it beforehand: in the *rondeau* just quoted it is actually the "canon" in the game that provides the text for singing![1] At the end of the fourteenth century this kind of aesthetic puzzle, as attractive as it was deceptive, which is also to be found in the literature of the great Rhetoricians, became all the rage. It was practised especially in the sphere of rhythm, which in those days was a particularly suitable field for such exercises. In the absence of any definite notation, the thirteenth century had to make do with relatively elementary rhythms. Recently a method of varying these rhythms in writing to an almost unlimited extent had been discovered, and this was being taken up with ever-increasing zeal.

Imagine at a Conservatoire examination or elsewhere a candidate being asked to read at sight a piano piece with two bars in common time in the left hand, and in the right something like this:

---

[1] A word here in passing on the meaning of the term "canon": why is this name given to a tune that keeps on recurring and is taken up by several voices in succession, e.g., *Frère Jacques?* In the Middle Ages (the procedure made its appearance at the end of the thirteenth century) it was called, more logically, *rotundellus*, a tune that goes round; the English have kept the word *round*. It was found, no doubt, that the term was apt to be confused with *rondeau*, itself a derivative of *rotundellus*. But for a tune of this kind it was unnecessary to write out all the parts, so it was only written down once, with a note added explaining how it could be transformed into a piece for several voices. It was this note, or "rule" called after the Greek word *canon*, which eventually gave its name to this type of piece.

The above example[1] is the exact equivalent in modern notation of the "Chinese puzzles" which gave so much pleasure to the successors of Machaut and Philippe de Vitry in the name of an *Ars Nova* which despised the "old works" of the time of Perotinus and was convinced that it was building up the language of the future.

There was thus a danger of music becoming a kind of complicated and abstruse algebra, although its complexities were only apparent on paper and to the eye; in actual performance nothing much remained of all these tricks. It is not surprising that posterity allowed this aesthetic system to die a natural death, or that it was succeeded at the beginning of the fifteenth century by a "reactionary" return to simplicity. This period was not by any means sterile, since in two hundred years of an uninterrupted evolution, and without any set-backs, it established, from Dunstable to Palestrina, through Dufay, Ockeghem, Josquin des Prés, Janequin, Lassus and many others the extraordinary succession of masterpieces of the so-called Franco-Flemish Renaissance.

Composers nevertheless had acquired a taste for the pleasures of overcoming difficulties. As counterpoint, the art of combining different melodic lines[2] developed, all kinds of audacious experiments became possible. For example: Thomas Tallis in 1540 wrote a forty-voice motet for eight five-part choirs; Pierre de la Rue treated in simultaneous counterpoint the *Vexilla regis* and the psalmody of the Passion. Josquin des Prés, the master of masters, performed the most astounding feats. But here the god Paper is domesticated and in the service of music: one can listen quite innocently to the song *Petite Camusette* and admire its simple and expressive harmonization without being aware of the fact that the main theme carries at the same time one canon at the octave and two at the fifth, while the two remaining voices form, for most of the time, a complementary canon which uses all the germ cells of the theme.

---

[1] It might appear stupid—although examiners too often take pleasure in puzzles of this kind—but it is perfectly correct: count first the number of quavers at 6/8, and then the number of semiquavers at 2/4; each of these calculations will give a total of two bars of 2/4 time mixed up. This used to be done with binary and ternary divisions and major or minor prolongations. Many examples will be found in W. Apel's *French secular music of the late fourteenth century*. The published transcriptions on staves attempts, by syncopation, to simplify the concordances; in order to get an idea of the old notation it is necessary to consider the original rhythms indicated above the stave-lines.

[2] *Punctum contra punctum:* phrase against phrase, and not, as commonly interpreted, note against note See for example, the meaning of "function" in the treatise by Jean de Grouchy (thirteenth century)

Nevertheless, despite prodigious feats of this kind, with the advent of humanism at the end of the sixteenth century people began to tire of all this virtuosity. Hypnotized by the simplicity of Greek music, despite the fact that they knew next to nothing about it, the collaborators of Baïf in France, or Bardi in Florence, declared war on counterpoint, and declared that it should be possible to hear everything a composer put on paper. When the vogue set in for old-style music, Court arias, new-style madrigals, and eventually opera, paper music fell into such disfavour that even the notation soon became a sort of simplified shorthand; whole operas were written on two staves—one for the melody and one for the bass, and Vivaldi noted with satisfaction that he wrote one of his in five days. The vocal line was often jotted down in an extremely simplified form; it was left to the interpreter to add whatever embroidery he or she liked to the bare bones of the tune. There is a very striking example of this in Monteverdi's *Orfeo*. In Orpheus's big aria, in which he lulls the suspicions of Charon and thus succeeds in crossing the Styx, Monteverdi, exceptionally, has written this melody twice over: once unadorned as in the rest of the score, and then, instead of allowing the singer to ornament it according to his fancy, the composer has himself written out the version to be sung as he wished it. In comparing the two texts, one cannot help wondering how it is possible to know what the music of this period was really intended to sound like since, when we have read what is written in the top line in the following example, the music in actual performance would have sounded as we see it in the bottom line:

And so operatic conventions and the continuo had between them robbed Paper music of its former prestige. It was to find it again in Germany at the beginning of the eighteenth century.

The greatest musical genius of all time, Johann Sebastian Bach, was perhaps the only true heir to that other great genius, Josquin des Prés. As with the latter, the least important of his ensembles not only sounds impeccable, but is also an architectural construction whose too-rich complexity the ear alone is unable to grasp. Bach was conscious of his virtuosity in composition, and sometimes took pleasure in underlining it visually.

Let us, for example, take a look at the *Musical Offering* dedicated to Frederick II of

Prussia on a memorable occasion when the King had supplied Bach with a theme to develop. Here we have, in addition to the royal theme, three fugues, two trios and a long series of unresolved canons of mysterious appearance. Some of these have two clefs juxtaposed; in one the second clef is upside-down (to solve it you have to turn the paper round and read it in a looking-glass) and the composer has added mischievously: *Quaerendo invenietis* (seek and you will find). The manuscript is covered with acrostics and puzzles worthy of *Ars Nova*, and the language of the Court is turned into a musicological commentary: *notulis crescentibus crescat fortuna regis* (in other words, it is a canon "in augmentation").

But this was not done just as a gratuitous joke for amusement. The fact is that the object of the *Offering*, the development of a theme proposed by an illustrious patron, was specifically to demonstrate in a flattering manner the essential richness of the royal theme and, at the same time, the science and skill of the musician who accepted the challenge. The object of the *Art of Fugue* was very similar; it was a demonstration by a teacher of genius, a regular examination piece conceived in the abstract, on paper only, simply to show his pupils everything that a skilled contrapuntist should be able to do with a theme. One can but smile at certain panegyrics loaded with expressions such as the "purity" of a "sublimated" art "transcending" all mortal contingencies under the imperious urge of an "inner necessity", etc. etc.

There has been a great deal of discussion about the "esotericism" of Bach, and some of the speculations on this subject, surprising though they may seem at first, gradually become more convincing in proportion to the number and variety of instances adduced. For example, according to Geiringer[1] "the figure 14 symbolizes Bach because B is the second letter of the alphabet, A the first, C the third and H the eighth, and this adds up to 14. In reverse, 14 becomes 41 which represents the name J. S. Bach, since J is the ninth and S the eighteenth letter, and 9 plus 18 plus 14 make 41. In Bach's very last composition, *Vor deinen Tron tret'ich*, the first line contains 14 notes and the complete aria 41—as if the dying composer wished to announce to the world that he, Bach, J.S. Bach, was entering the choir of eternity."

One can, according to one's disposition, pronounce such speculations to be either puerile or inspired. The fact remains that, whether or not they have any foundation in reality—and Bach himself never confirmed this—they are only an additional aspect of one of the loftiest forms of inspiration to be met with in any composer. There is no need to count the number of notes in order to experience the beauty of the *Erbarme dich* in the

[1]*Bach and his family*, p. 232.

St. Matthew Passion, or of the adagio in the E major violin concerto. But is there not a danger that this illustrious example may tempt some epigones to replace inspiration by speculation, instead of controlling and enriching it? One would like to be sure, in view of certain pronouncements made by our modern dodecaphonists, that this great example has not been distorted and reduced to the level of a mere accessory.

Atonal music, in Schoenberg's conception of the term, frankly rules out one of the two above-mentioned criteria; for one could seek in vain in such treatises on serial composition as those of Jelinek or H. Eimert a single sentence referring to the judgment of the ear as a means of controlling or justifying the arrangements of notes, the numerical recipes for which are submitted for our consideration.

If the following example is found so captivating by Maurice Le Roux that he quotes it no less than three times in his book *Introduction à la musique contemporaine*, this is not

because he finds it beautiful, but because "using at once all the twelve notes of the chromatic scale, thereby constituting a 'series', the accompaniment is formed of chords, the first of which sounds simultaneously the two notes of the interval constituting the melody; the second is a major sixth, i.e. the inversion of the minor third in the melody; while the third again is made out of the minor second heard horizontally in the melodic line." Similarly, Stückenschmidt asks us to admire "a massive chord of eleven intervals and twelve notes" which Klein calls "the mother chord" because it is in liaison with a

7. Klein's "mother-chord".

series which uses "not only the twelve notes, but eleven different intervals",[1] and points out that Nicolas Slonimsky, not content with having realized chords of twelve notes and eleven intervals, has compiled a "grandmother chord" of eleven notes comprising twelve intervals, the upper and lower halves of which complement one another. Furthermore, he has "reduced the bitonal interval of F sharp and C to a purely mathematical function: if, for example, we construct out of a chord of the augmented sixth, G—E, a mobile chord whose intervals will steadily decrease by a semitone until they reach a diminished third, we shall then arrive at the total sum mentioned above, equivalent to two triple major chords and the interval of a tritone".[2]

By means of a series of experiments carried out with the strictest scientific objectivity,[3] R. Francès has endeavoured to discover to what extent the criteria approved by the serial school are capable of being transferred from the sphere of verbal commentary or compositional procedure to that of pure perception divorced from any preconceived suggestions. The results were catastrophic. For even the serial specialists—composers of this school, pianists, even Conservatoire professors—were incapable of distinguishing between two different series employed in the simplest fashion according to the strict rules of a "compositional technique" whereby the unity of a work is made to depend entirely on the unity of the series.

Another experiment was a still more cruel exposure of certain aspects of professional musical education today: in the presence of three groups of listeners of different categories (professional, amateur and non-musicians) a tune was played accompanied in two different styles. The first was banal, but classical and correct. The second was of the "wrong note" type, deliberately eccentric and puerile. In the "professional" group not a single person (and I mean zero per cent) dared to express an opinion either favourable to the correct but banal style, or critical of the "wrong note" version; whereas the "non-professional" responded with exactly the same percentage, but in the opposite sense: not one of them (zero per cent) blamed the correct-banal version, and not one attempted to defend the "wrong note" version. The "cultivated amateurs" reacted in a less uniform manner, but the majority favoured the "classical" harmony (75 per cent), while expressing with a slightly smaller majority (66.6 per cent) their disapproval of the "wrong

---

[1]H. H. Stückenschmidt, *Musique nouvelle*, Editions Corréa, 1956, pp. 153-154.

[2]Op. cit. p. 154. This statement, already quoted in a earlier chapter (footnote p. 10) is not only obscure; it contains several absurdities due, no doubt, to a faulty translation from the German. For "augmented" sixth we should read, obviously, "major" sixth (*grosse sext*); for "diminished" third, "minor" third (*kléne Terz*) and for "triple" chords, chords of three notes. It is obvious that even the book's translator has given up trying to understand.

[3]*La perception de la musique*, Paris, Vrin 1958; see especially pp. 140 and 372.

note" harmony. Nothing could reveal more clearly the dangers of a certain kind of undigested musical "education".[1]

By comparing his experiences with regard to this aspect of a certain type of modern music with what is written about it by some of its most enthusiastic supporters, the author arrived at the conclusion that serial music was based on the rejection of any criteria of a perceptual order in favour of a purely conceptual approach in which perception plays no part.

It follows, then, that composers who belong to this school are more interested in abstract combinations of notes than in conveying any musical sensation to their hearers; it is therefore not surprising that they have practically ceased to have any communication with a public unable to share their interest in these combinations, although this same public is blamed for not recognizing in this music qualities which the composer has not attempted to put into it.

Yet this is the path being followed today by more and more composers, who find the serial procedure, devised by Schoenberg and perfected by his successors, an easy and convenient method to work by.

We shall now, by way of example, invite you to join in composing together a strictly multi-serial work that obeys all the latest rules. Do not be alarmed: no abstruse knowledge is called for, as you will be able to see for yourselves; everything on the mathematical side is of an elementary nature, and on the musical, well within the reach of a first-year harmony pupil.

(1) Write down the 12 notes of the chromatic scale in any irregular order. For example:

1	2	3	4	5	6	7	8	9	10	11	12
E flat	D	A	A flat	G	F sharp	E	C sharp	C	B flat	F	B

Your "inventive" work is now finished. The rest can be left to the copyist, or even an electronic machine.

(2) Now work out the *inversion:* i.e., starting with No. 1 write the same intervals, but in contrary motion up instead of down, or vice-versa. Keeping the same number for each note in the series, we then get the following:

1	7	3	10	12	9	2	11	6	4	8	5
E flat	E	A	B flat	B	C	D	F	F sharp	A flat	C sharp	G

[1] An electric-encephalographic recording was taken during the experiment which showed that the disapproval of the various groups took the form of boredom or inattention in regard to the series considered uninteresting, rather than irritation or positive displeasure.

(3) Now, keeping the same correspondence between notes and figures, write down the numbers of a *chromatic scale*: C, C sharp, D, etc., which gives us:

9. 8. 2. 1. 7. 11. 6. 5. 4. 3. 10. 12.

These three series will give you your foundation, but you must now have the patience to copy out 48 lines of figures.

A: *straight series.*
Write horizontally the figures 1 to 12; then, starting from each figure complete the chromatic series in vertical columns in a circular direction:

A 1:	1 –	2 –	3 –	4 –	5 –	6 –	7 –	8 –	9 –	10 –	11 –	12
A 2:	7	1	10	3	4	5	11	2	8	12	6	9
A 3:	11	7	12	10	3	4	6	1	2	9	5	8
A 4:	6	11	9	12	10	3	5	7	1	8	4	2
A 5:	5	6	8	9	12	10	4	11	7	2	3	1
A 6:	4	5	2	8	9	12	3	6	11	1	10	7
A 7:	3	4	1	2	8	9	10	5	6	7	12	11
A 8:	10	3	7	1	2	8	12	4	5	11	9	6
A 9:	12	10	11	7	1	2	9	3	4	6	8	5
A 10:	9	12	6	11	7	1	8	10	3	5	2	4
A 11:	8	9	5	6	11	7	2	12	10	4	1	3
A 12:	2	8	4	5	6	11	1	9	12	3	7	10

Chromatic series

B: *recurrence of the straight series:*
Read the *A* lines in the above table horizontally backwards:

B 1:	12 –	11 –	10 –	9 –	8 –	7 –	6 –	5 –	4 –	3 –	2 –	1
B 2:	9	6	12	8	2	11	5	4	3	10	1	7

etc. (down to B 12)

C: *inversion of series:*
Write the inversion horizontally, and complete vertically with the chromatic series, as in A:

C 1:	1	–	7	–	3	–	10	–	12	–	9	–	2	–	11	–	6	–	4	–	8	–	5
C 2:	7		11		10		12		9		8		1		6		5		3		2		4
C 3:	11		6		12		9		8		2		7		5		4		10		1		3
C 4:	6		5		9		8		2		1		11		4		3		12		7		10
C 5:	5		4		8		2		1		7		6		3		10		9		11		12
C 6:	4		3		2		1		7		11		5		10		12		8		6		9
C 7:	3		10		1		7		11		6		4		12		9		2		5		8
C 8:	10		12		7		11		6		5		3		9		8		1		4		2
C 9:	12		9		11		6		5		4		10		8		2		7		3		1
C 10:	9		8		6		5		4		3		12		2		1		11		10		7
C 11:	8		2		5		4		3		10		9		1		7		6		12		11
C 12:	2		1		4		3		10		12		8		7		11		5		9		6

Chromatic series.

D: *recurrence of inversion:*
Read the C lines backwards:

| D 1: | 5 | 8 | 4 | 6 | 11 | 2 | 9 | 12 | 10 | 3 | 7 | 1 |
| D 2: | 4 | 2 | 3 | 5 | 6 | 1 | 8 | 9 | 12 | 10 | 11 | 7 |

etc. (down to D 12)

Thus we get, reading horizontally, 48 lines of figures which give us, not only the notes to be used, but their time-values [this is an "improvement" invented by P. Boulez]. All that is necessary is to draw up a table of equivalences, e.g.:

$$1 = 1 \text{ demi-semi-quaver}$$
$$2 = 2 \quad \text{,,} \quad \text{,,} \quad \text{,,} \quad \longrightarrow = 1 \text{ semiquaver}$$
$$3 = 3 \quad \text{,,} \quad \text{,,} \quad \text{,,} \quad \longrightarrow = 1 \text{ dotted semiquaver}$$
$$\text{etc. . . .}$$

Let us take, for example, the figures of *A*1 for the notes, and those of *D* 5 for their duration; then at the same time give to a second piano the notes of *C* 1 with the time-values of *B* 9. With dynamic nuances added, we now have obtained the first sequence of *Structures* for two pianos by P. Boulez. By changing the combinations at every sequence, it would now be possible, provided we knew the number of lines used

STRUCTURES

Pierre **BOULEZ**

1 a

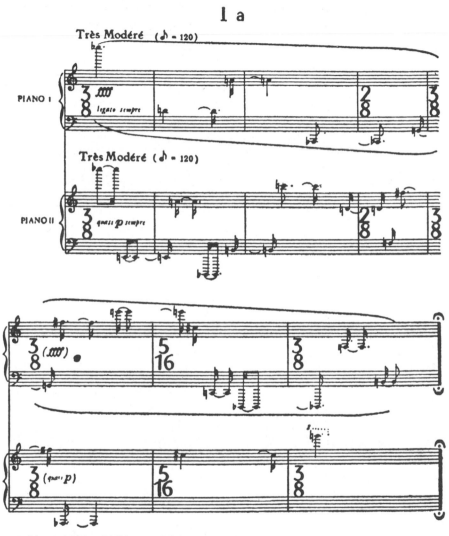

Universal Edition Nr. 12267

8. The first page of "Structures" for two pianos by Pierre Boulez.

by the composer and his choice of marks of expression, to reconstitute the whole of his ninety page score.[1]

I can only hope that my readers will experience, when listening to works of this nature, the pure satisfaction promised them so confidently in the abundant literature in praise of this music. It is also to be hoped, however, that in the contrary event they will be frank enough not to imitate the spectators in Florian's fable, full of admiration for the pictures projected by a magic lantern whose operator:

> . . . . n'avait oublié qu'un point,
> C'était d'éclairer sa lanterne.

> (. . . . had only forgotten one thing,
> And that was to light his lantern.)

---

[1]Except for the bar-lines, mere points of reference arbitrarily fixed, and the choice of the pitch of each note: according to Antoine Golea (*Rençontres avec P. Boulez*, p. 167) the composer declares that the latter is also extracted from the initial series, but I have been unable to discover how this is done. The formula supplied by the composer (cf. *Eventuellement*, in the special number of *La Revue Musicale: Oeuvre du XXe siècle*, p. 134) is incomprehensible, unless it applies to *musique concrète* on a magnetophone.

18

Twentieth Century Twelve-Note (Serial) Composition

We have now to consider a very special aspect of an important part of so-called *avant-garde* music which is described, perhaps too schematically, by the none too euphonious term "dodecaphony".

What, then, is dodecaphony?[1] Everything that can be said on this subject is coloured very much by the attitude of the writer, according to whether he is a partisan or an opponent of this system, which by some is looked upon as the only music of the present or future, almost as a religion, having its own dogmas and saints and heretics, and by others as an arbitrary and unattractive sort of game based on postulates which defy common sense. The very words have a different meaning, according to the writer who uses them, which makes it very difficult for the best-intentioned uninitiated reader to discover what it is all about.

The dodecaphonic system is the development of a series of propositions, logical and ineluctable according to some, and merely arbitrary according to others, propounded by its founder Arnold Schoenberg some fifty years ago with the object of *replacing an intuitive and analytic perception of the elements of music by a synthetic and rationalized system* based on a predetermined logical relationship between sounds in which the intuitive element of perception is deliberately discounted.

Schoenberg's "reform" was not, as is commonly believed, intended to reinforce the ascendancy of dissonance as an aesthetic ingredient as Stravinsky, for example, attempted to do in the *Rite of Spring*.[2] It was quite independent of this movement, though chrono-

---

[1] This chapter in all essentials is based on a study published in 1958-9 in the *Guide du Concert* and in the *Education Musicale*. The *Feuilles Musicales* of Lausanne also published it in an abridged form, and then invited contradictory opinions from some of the leading Swiss musicians. Far from constituting a refutation of the author's arguments, this enquiry (fourteen replies were published between October 1960 and March 1961) merely confirmed, in varying degrees, the general agreement of the musicians consulted, of whom Frank Martin was one of the most outspoken. The only real opposition was based on such a distortion of the sense of the original study that it could not be considered as a contribution to the discussion.

[2] The word dissonance is not to be understood here in the arbitrary and inexact sense attached to it in treatises on harmony which apply this term to any chord other than a perfect triad, but in its real sense of being an aggregation incapable of being perceived as any kind of consonance—a term which is itself extensible and varies according to the evolution of the musical language. I may perhaps be permitted to refer the reader here to my *Traité Historique d'Analyse Musicale* which studies in detail the bases and evolution of this term.

logically contemporary and even slightly earlier, and was the result of certain historical contingencies. At the beginning of the twentieth century, the musical evolution of Germany and central Europe was in a desperately static situation. Through Brahms, Mahler and Strauss it had followed for half a century, without any essential modifications, the impulse given by Beethoven and Schumann. Schoenberg himself, until about 1905, had followed this post-romantic tradition which he had enriched by his great talents, but without showing any signs of a reforming spirit.[1] There is therefore nothing surprising in the violence of a reaction as sudden as it was far-reaching (the more so since it had been long delayed), nor in the fact that, until 1945, it aroused little interest in countries which had not experienced the same need.[2] And in order to understand the later evolution of the movement it is necessary to reconstitute the state of mind which led Schoenberg to effect so complete a rupture with the past, including his own.[3]

The point of departure seems to have been a conscious effort, which his disciples describe as "heroic", to force himself against his instinct, and based on pure speculation, to write aggregations of notes which could not be justified by perception alone.[4] His reasoning appears to have been as follows: "Since chords are formed by the superposition of triads, they could also be formed by superposing other intervals."[5] Schoenberg began by superposing fourths, at first in a tentative manner (*Pelléas et Mélisande*, 1902), later investing them with a reinforced structural rôle (*Chamber Symphony*, 1906)

---

[1]The only real innovation introduced by Schoenberg until then had nothing to do with harmonic structure; it was a new method of musical declamation, a stylization of a highly modulated kind of literary declamation which he super-imposed on a different plane over traditional harmonies (cf. the last section of the *Gurrelieder*). He reverted to this procedure later, calling it *Sprechgesang*, literally "spoken singing".

[2]A refusal to adhere to the system did not mean that it had no influence. Ravel, for example, on several occasions profited by some of Schoenberg's pre-serial experiments, but assimilated them to his own individual style (e.g., the *Chansons Madécasses*), and he was not the only one to do so.

[3]Schoenberg was always irritated by any reference to this absence of transition. He defended himself against the accusation (notably in *Mon évolution*, in the *Revue Internationale de Musique*, No. 13, 1952) and was defended by his disciples (cf. Leibowitz, *Schoenberg et son école*, p. 68 sqq.), citing as revolutionary, details in his works of that period which were no more advanced than anything to be found in all the post-romantics, not excepting Liszt or Wagner. It is impossible to take seriously some of his wilder statements on this subject (cf. my *Traité Historique d'Analyse Musicale*, p. 10). On the other hand, we can see already his predilection for wide intervals, which he inherited from Wagner and later integrated into his system, as well as his original orchestral effects, such as the *glissando* for trombone which he seems to have been the first to make use of in his *Pelléas et Mélisande* (1902): Ravel copied this in 1909 (in *L'Heure Espagnole*) and Stravinsky in 1910 (*The Fire-Bird*).

[4]This important point is established by Schoenberg himself: cf. Leibowitz, *op. cit.*, p. 75.

[5]That normal chords are formed by the superposition of triads is absolutely false (cf. my *Traité Historique*); but a belief that it is so, resulting from a mistaken judgment of Rameau's, is still firmly entrenched today.

and finally proceeding to use "any kind of vertical aggregation, which was what he called the emancipation of dissonance".[1]

This desire to escape from too well-known and hackneyed harmonic combinations was, moreover, typical of the period almost everywhere. It was first manifested in France, where the problem was virtually solved, in their own way, first by Fauré, and then by Debussy and Ravel. But the Germanic school, with few exceptions, remained deaf to these experiments. Later, around 1905, it began to experiment in its own way, starting exclusively from its own repertoire.

Schoenberg was not the only pioneer. Quite independently, Scriabin in 1908 invented his "mystic chord" (C, F sharp, B flat, E, A, D) which was the basis of his *Prometheus* and *Seventh Piano Sonata*. In 1906, in his *Neuer Aesthetik der Tonkunst*, another post-Romantic, of half-Italian, half-German origin, Ferruccio Busoni, also called for an extension of the musical vocabulary. He advocated the use of quarter-tones and sixteenths of a tone, as well as model scales of seven notes "which would conform neither to the ecclesiastical modes, nor to the ordinary major and minor modes".[2] In point of fact, such modes have always existed, but they were not formed arbitrarily, and obeyed very precise structural laws, which were certainly not a feature of the researches carried on at that time.

Edgar Varèse, a French musician, now a naturalized American, who met Busoni in Berlin in 1907, also abandoned the post-Romantic style about this time and devoted himself to researches in this field.

We can see now what the situation was during these ten years in which music found herself at the parting of the ways. The desire for new sonorities, the logical outcome of a static condition which had gone on too long, was absolutely universal. It was normal and legitimate. *Grosso modo*, two different solutions, independent of each other, were proposed.

The first was the French solution, which conformed to an age-old procedure which consisted in enlarging the general conception of consonance (Debussy introduced the chord of the eleventh which Ravel finally stabilized: cf. *Daphnis*) and in establishing and individualizing the sonorities produced by new chords formed from notes which at first were alien, but later gradually assimilated. The development of the chord of the eleventh led logically to bi-tonality, which in its turn became individualized, and finally resulted in the sometimes aggressive and arbitrary poly-tonality which was the

[1]Quoted textually from R. Leibowitz, *op. cit.*, p. 83.
[2]Stückenschmidt, *op. cit.*, p. 23.

aesthetic fashion in 1925. Classical tonality, a temporary architectural principle scarcely two hundred years old and already seriously undermined by romanticism, lost its structural value and dissonance, which up till then had provided a temporary tension to be swiftly followed by its "resolution", became an aesthetic element in itself for the purpose of creating shock and contrast. But—and this is important—*dissonance was still perceived as dissonance*, and consonance as consonance. Misunderstandings arose from the fact that the extension of consonance may at first hearing have seemed like dissonance to listeners who were not yet sufficiently accustomed to the new sonorities. These misunderstandings, which are traditional, were only temporary, like those which had preceded them; in themselves they exercised no real influence. Of a very different nature is the obstinate refusal, which still persists after fifty years, on the part of an immense section of the public, not exclusively consisting of ignoramuses or old fossils, to accept the second solution based on very different principles.

The French solution, which began to take shape about 1895, was countered by the Central European solution proposed by Schoenberg between 1906 and 1910. Instead of seeking new consonances, it consisted in *eliminating the whole concept of a consonance* and in treating as consonances any chance juxtaposition of sounds, provided that the presence of these sounds could be justified on some other grounds, while avoiding as far as possible any combination resembling a normal consonance which would tend to re-establish the hierarchy of sounds which the system desired to abolish.

It was no longer a question of the public being slow to assimilate an innovation which, as had always happened in the past, it would soon catch up with, but of a complete change in what had for centuries been the ultimate criterion of the ear. It was indeed, as the Schoenbergians are never tired of proclaiming, a "radical attitude" which, if it was ever to be understood, called for an equally radical abandonment on the part of the hearer of his ancestral reflexes. Unless this can be done, this music cannot live, and that is the real crux of the problem.

We must now consider how this attitude of "resolute liquidation" led to the appearance of a new phenomenon, namely dodecaphony as we now know it.

*   *   *

We have just been examining the line of thought which led Schoenberg, around 1910, to make a complete break with the tradition which had always assumed that the ear was the ultimate criterion by which music could be judged, and to envisage, under the name of "the emancipation of dissonance", a combination of lines and sounds which would exclude any kind of perception relating to a consonance ("classified" chords) or to a hierarchy based on the interdependence between one note and another (i.e., tonal relationship in the widest sense of the term). This explains the works of this period, of which *Pierrot Lunaire* (1912) is the most perfect example—an example which we shall find again in a great deal of the composite *Wozzeck* (1918-1922) by his disciple Alban Berg. In this important work, one of the finest and most significant in modern operatic repertory, there are lines which perpetually cross one another, and although there is no harmonic relationship either between them or between the notes of which each line is composed, their intermingling, thanks to the linear design and especially the rhythmic combinations, produces a continual pattern of lines and timbres of quite remarkable suppleness and mobility. Monotony, which is always the chief danger of any mono-chromatic procedure, is avoided, sometimes only narrowly, by the absence of any rigidity in the use of this new colour, and by a lively feeling for the theatre, relying on effects which owe something to this technique and could have been obtained equally well by using traditional musical language. Schoenberg, for his part, obtained the same results by the brevity of his pieces and by his use of strongly contrasted instrumental combinations.

It should be explained at this point that up to now we have been dealing with what is wrongly termed "atonal music",[1] and not "dodecaphony", or "serial music".

The principle of dodecaphony, or "composition with twelve notes"[2] is not, as is commonly supposed, the invention of Schoenberg, but of another Viennese, his junior by some nine years, Josef Matthias Hauer, a school-teacher and self-taught musician who died in 1959. Hauer also aimed at atonality, but within a relatively consonant context. To achieve this, he had the idea of fixing in advance the order of appearance of the twelve notes in the tempered scale, and of basing his composition on that order of appearance. Once a note was sounded, he prolonged or repeated it until it was cancelled by another number; and with this end in view, he often grouped several notes together in a cell which he called a "Trope", sometimes inverting the order of the notes within one cell, but not the order in which the cells were used. Hauer wrote in this way several pieces for piano or harmonium, and then in 1920 published his theory under the title

[1] It would be better to speak of "non-consonant music". Atonality is only one of its aspects, and is found in other kinds of music quite unconnected with this.

[2] And not "twelve tones", as it is sometimes called in a literal transcription of the German "*Zwölfton*". The name itself is not strictly correct: it could be said that a chromatic study by Czerny is also written "with twelve notes". One ought to say "twelve notes harmonically independent of one another". But some abbreviation is legitimate. . . . The completely correct expression is: *Zwölftonreihe*, "a row of twelve notes" the word *Reihe* implies the idea of notes arranged in a definite order, which the word "series" fails to convey.

Vom Wesen des Musikalischen: ein Lehrbuch der Zwölftonmusik, to which, however, he added some rather vague symbolist speculations.[1]

At this time Schoenberg himself was seeking for a system of composition which would fit in with his new aesthetic. He realized that all his previous "acquisitions" had been purely negative, and he felt the need of some positive rule, Music until then had always been based on a *relationship* between one note and another. He repudiated this principle. Hauer suggested another to him—that of a definite *succession* without any particular relationship. He adopted this idea, introducing two essential modifications: he did away with the "tropes"—and consequently the internal inversions of the notes in a cell—and also abolished the system of prolonging sounds by repetitions, laying down the rule that "no note in a series must be repeated before all the other eleven have been exhausted". Thus, the order of the twelve notes, baptised *Reihe* (row), must remain unaltered from beginning to end. To vary their presentation, however, it was permissible to transport or invert or play the series backwards, and to mix the different combinations obtained in this way.

Two other postulates were also laid down: one was that the melodic succession of the notes and their simultaneous sounding together (in a chord) are equally admissible: for example, a melody consisting of notes 1-2-3-4 can be replaced by 1-4 accompanied by 2-3. The other principle, known as "disjunction", lays down that a note keeps its number in the series no matter what its pitch may be; this ensures that no melodic relationship may inadvertently occur in the series by the transference of a note from one octave to another—hence the characteristic zig-zag aspect of all serial music.

We saw in the preceding chapter how, by arranging the figures 1-12 in a given order, it is possible to get forty-eight lines of figures.

To avoid making fresh calculations, let us keep to the series given as an example and write down the numbers of the rows *A* 1 and *C* 4 one above the other, like this (order chosen at random):

```
2     4 6 7     11 12  5        4 3 7
1  3     5 8 9 10     6  9 8  2  1 11 12 10
```

[1]It was Hauer, no doubt, whom Thomas Mann took as a model for the episodic character of Beissel in his *roman à clef, Doktor Faustus*, in which the hero, Leverkuhn is a mixture of Nietzsche and Schoenberg. In *Doktor Faustus* Beissel is depicted as a kind of "illuminé" who advocated, before Leverkuhn, an obviously arbitrary alternation of "mistress" and "servant" notes. Leverkuhn's reaction to him is exactly that of Schoenberg's towards Hauer. Cf. our *résumé* of this book in the *Revue Internationale de Musique*, No. 11, 1951. Stückenschmidt informs us that Hauer also served as a model for a character in another musical novel, *Verdi, the Story of an Opera*, by Franz Werfel.

Translating this into notes, we get the following:

All we have to do now is to put in time-values and space out the octaves in order to obtain the beginning of a piece in two parts which will continue along the same lines:

The author of the example given here pledges his word that he has placed the figures strictly at random, according to the plan agreed, and that he has not touched up the result in any way.

Already in 1921 in his *Suite* for piano Op. 25, Schoenberg tried his new method of composition which is the only and exclusive criterion for "serial music".[1]

---

[1]"Serial" and "dodecaphonic" are not necessarily the same. *Serial* refers to the use of a series, and *dodecaphonic* to the use of all twelve notes in the chromatic scale. Thus it is possible to be "serial" without being "dodecaphonic", if, for example, one uses a series of less than twelve notes, as is sometimes done.

He never abandoned it—except on a few occasions when he reverted to "tonal" music unconnected with his theory—for which he was bitterly rebuked by his disciples. For some twenty years there were never more than two or three of these: Alban Berg adopted the series round about 1925, and Anton Webern never departed from it after his Op. 17 (1924). When Schoenberg, to escape persecution as a Jew under the Nazi régime, settled in Hollywood—not far from Stravinsky—the number of his disciples began to increase considerably; the movement began to be "fashionable", and the courage which the original "trinity" had needed to pursue their theories in opposition to the general attitude at that time was now the distinguishing mark of those who dared to resist what had now become the new fashion.

Schoenberg frequently protested that he had not intended to create a system,[1] but it is not certain that his disciples always respected his repeated warnings on this point.

Whereas Berg endeavoured to obtain through the series (or in spite of it) a means of expression to which traditional reflexes were still able to respond[2] and sometimes succeeded in doing this (for which he was blamed by the "ultras"), Webern relied entirely on the numerical sequences in his series to replace any other melodic or harmonic conceptions. He thus carried Schoenberg's postulates to their extreme logical conclusion, with consequences before which the latter seems in the last resort to have recoiled since what they amounted to was, in effect, to cut music completely away from its former foundations and to view it henceforward as merely a rational arrangement (or supposedly so) of numbered sounds, isolated from one another with no connection between them, theoretically, apart from the order resulting from their numerical sequence.[3]

In order to emphasize the fact that each sound[4] thus becomes an "abstraction"

[1]"I did not create a system, but only a method, which means a way of applying a pre-conceived formula according to regular rules" (*Polyphonie*, IV, 1949, p. 14). Schoenberg also, in the same article, declared that "the method of composing with twelve notes is something more than a mere technical process, and must be considered no less important than a scientific theory."

[2]Cf. for example the "dodges" he employs in the *Violin Concerto* whereby the series is manipulated in such a way that the serial numbers do not prevent the occurrence of classical chords.

[3]Theoretically—for in point of fact Webern was careful, when notes were in conjunction, not to ensure a normal relationship between them but, on the contrary, to eliminate any such relationship, according to his master's teaching (cf. article quoted above: "Even a faint reminiscence of the old harmony would be undesirable, since it would inevitably raise false hopes with regard to its consequences and continuations"). But as the evolution of music up till then had increased the number of "normal" relationships, he was forced to seek almost exclusively those rare combinations which were still considered "unharmonious" (in the old sense of the Greek word *ekmeles*) being based almost always on the tritone, or on derivatives of the minor second (major seventh, minor ninth, etc.) which did not make for diversity.

[4]The neo-dodecaphonist vocabulary prefers the word "sound" to "note", the latter being too reminiscent of the past. Stockhausen even speaks of a "sinusoidal sound", thus virtually reducing a musical note to the rank of one particular undulatory line among other noises; here is an implicit reference to electronic music.

Webern isolates it in every possible way: he likes to surround it with rests, to separate it from its neighbours by a systematic process of disjunction and, in orchestral music, to give almost every note a different *timbre;* the succession of these various *timbres* (which, incidentally, he combines with the greatest ingenuity) constitutes, in his eyes, a melody in itself, which he calls *Klangfarbenmelodie,* i.e., a "melody of colours in sound" (more commonly referred to as a "melody of tone-colour").

Apart from the Viennese "trinity", to which the history of dodecaphony was practically confined until about 1945, the pre-serial experiments carried out by Schoenberg had had a temporary, but real influence on a number of composers who had borrowed from him, principally, a linear style of writing independent of chords, even though these were implicit, and an ever-increasing tolerance of dissonance and tonal relationships, without, however, doing violence to their own individuality or becoming mere slavish imitators. Of these could be cited, among many others, Ravel, Honegger, Bartok, Jolivet or Messiaen. Serialism, on the contrary, was scarcely ever spoken about until after the second world war except as an oddity which had borne only somewhat bitter fruits.

But from then on the situation changed. The legitimate desire for renovation, inherent in any abrupt change of period, failing to discover any really new path to pursue, took the form of a general move backwards to continue experiments which were already twenty years old and which, until then, rightly or wrongly, had for the most part been judged disappointing in their results.

The neo-dodecaphony which has been developed since 1945, and is still flourishing in certain well-publicized and specialized musical *milieux* (and practised, it must be admitted, by some genuine musicians), seems to owe more to the element of rupture and intellectualism of which Webern, rather than Schoenberg, is the outstanding example. Under cover of a provocative vocabulary in which pleasure is dubbed "hedonism", aridity "purity", intellectualism "strictness" and sensibility "compromise", he devoted his energies to creating a formula of musical composition based on what he called "the organization of an integral awareness"—that is to say a condition in which every detail, regardless of how it may sound (this is what is called "total liberation") is exclusively determined by a pre-conceived plan of rationalization.

Webern, in his conception of serialism, now generally adopted, divided the act of composition into two distinct parts: one, purely rationalistic, deduced the notes to be used from speculations with the figures connected with the manipulation of the series; the other, non-codified, allowed him to group the notes, so far as rhythm and line were concerned, according to the prompting of instinct and sensibility. The efforts of the neo-dodecaphonists, however, seem to have been mainly concerned with the elimination of this last remaining, though restricted zone in which personal expression is still tolerated. For example, during a public discussion in which the present writer took part in 1953 at Cologne, one of the most prominent leaders of the German twelve-note school, Karlheinz Stockhausen, deplored the fact that, after the successful elimination of the subjective personality in composition, one should still have to put up with entrusting one's work to an interpreter; and he reaffirmed his confidence in the machine (electronic music) as a means of eliminating in the future this last remaining element of impurity. By a curious paradox, the instigator of this last offensive was not a "serial" composer, but on the contrary a musician who both in his works and in his writings had never ceased to extol the "auditive perception of voluptuously refined pleasures" in highly spiced and colourful music very far removed from the Webernian ideal—Olivier Messiaen.[1]

Messiaen's experiments with rhythm seem at first to have been inspired by a desire to note in the minutest detail, and therefore by observing a strict isochronism from the first written beat, the infinite nuances of a rhythmic freedom which, long before his day, was instinctively felt and expressed without having to be written down, by using a notation in which the isochronism as written was merely a simplified approximation.[2] This point of depature gave rise to speculations of a more and more complex and involved nature, aimed essentially at *rationalizing the irrationality of true rhythm*, a very different thing, as we know, from the rhythm that is taught in an elementary way in our schools of music.

In this connection the following anecdote is perhaps significant: one evening at Royaumont a group of musicians were playing and listening to some music by Messiaen. One of them was at the piano, surrounded by others who were following the score. Others, again, were seated round the room, merely listening. At the end of the piece, those who had been reading the score exclaimed: "What complicated rhythms!" The listeners who had not seen the score were astonished by this remark. "What do you mean?" they said; "Nothing could be simpler; it's merely common time, in *rubato*." I heard this from someone who was present at this little scene, which is a striking comment on the illusions produced by complexity on paper.

---

[1]Cf. *Technique de mon langage musical*, 1944. The date of this quotation is of some significance. It may be doubted whether Messiaen would have inscribed it on his *Modes de valeur et d'intensité* or any other of his more recent works conceived with the object of illustrating above all a "system" of rhythmic order.

[2]This may be due to the fact that, as an organist, Messiaen studied with Marcel Dupré, who taught his pupils that, in order to phrase on the organ when playing classical music, they should analyse the length of respiration in definite and very short values, for example, one-fifth of a quaver.

This particular preoccupation, which did not originate in the serial system, had one point of contact with the latter in so far as it opened up the possibility of applying a similar "rationalization" to the only remaining field which the system had left open. The junction was effected as it happened by a former pupil of Messiaen—and later of Schoenberg's leading propagandist in France, Leibowitz—Pierre Boulez, whose mathematical training rendered him particularly fitted for speculations of this kind. By deducing from tables of equivalence extracted from the series the time-values to be employed, and then establishing the formulae which would also make it possible to attach to the series all the other elements involved, such as pitch, dynamics, attack, rests, etc., Boulez became the inventor of what might be called "multi-serial music"—in other words, music pre-fabricated in all its component parts by calculations based on the serial numbers whose translation into notes can then be left to the copyist, who need pay no attention to the resulting sounds.[1] We saw in the previous chapter an example of the mechanical method suggested.

Some supporters of dodecaphony do not accept criteria of this kind. Antoine Goléa, for example, declares that his only standard for judging works of this type is his own sensibility. Furthermore, most serialists are at pains to point out that, though the result of the various possible combinations is settled for them by their basic postulates, they are still free to choose between these different combinations, and can determine the order in which they will be used. Stockhausen has even gone so far as to advocate the intervention of an element of "chance" by writing these combinations on a long roll, without any connection between them, while requesting the interpreter not to decide in advance in what order they should be played until the moment of performance. Boulez, on the other hand, suggests that a formula should be sought for in the series itself to decide in what order the pieces should be played; at the same time, he has announced that it is a matter of indifference to him in what order the interpreter chooses to play the five movements of his *Third Piano Sonata* provided No. 3 remains in the middle. This intervention of "chance" in what has come to be known as "aleatory", or "indeterminate" composition, became a fashionable gimmick during the 1960-61 series of concerts given under the auspices of the *Domaine Musical* in Paris.

---

[1]This is not meant to be a joke. As I write, one of my students is engaged, in order to earn his living, in "setting to music" the "work" of a serial "composer" who has supplied him with the series and a list of the desired combinations. Obviously this method is not one in everyday use. In the United States, at present, electronic machines are being used for serial composition. In the winter of 1961 the Bull Machine Co. invited musicians to listen to the results of experiments in electronic composition in various fields. Those in a classical, and especially contrapuntal style, were disastrous. Two styles only proved to be equal in "quality" to music produced by the human brain: popular dance tunes of specially low quality, and twelve-note compositions.

What can one, in all honesty, think of this orientation, having no connection with any movement before it, imposed upon an important section of contemporary music, which considers itself in the front rank of modernism and claims to be the only real *avant-garde*?

This is a very difficult question to answer. Posterity, so often and so thoughtlessly invoked, has not yet confided in any of us, whether we happen to be supporters or adversaries of the system. Amongst the former are many most estimable musicians whose merits and sincerity are above suspicion. But there are others, at least equally meritorious and no less numerous, and by no means confined to the older generation of "diehards", who take an exactly opposite view. And the dodecaphonists and their friends have no reason at all to doubt either their competence or their good faith.

Let us try, then, to balance up the arguments on both sides. More often than not they boil down on both sides to a few *clichés* endlessly repeated which provoke in their turn equally stereotyped counter-clichés. The dialogue can be roughly summarized as follows:

—I don't understand this music at all, says Bouvard.

—So what?, says Pécuchet.[1] You are the past: we are the future. Your fathers booed *Pelléas* and the *Rite of Spring* which today you yourselves applaud. They treated the *Saint Matthew Passion* with contempt.[2]

---

[1](The allusion, of course, is to Flaubert's famous book *Bouvard et Pécuchet*—Translator's note.) Pécuchet's typical response recalls the celebrated remark made by Vincent d'Indy to a lady who had confessed to him that she did not like some symphony of Beethoven's: "It doesn't really matter, Madame." To find out who scores the first point, we ought first to evaluate the respective weight and numbers of our two interlocutors. Even weight in this context is subject to revision: history records some astonishing opinions expressed by great musicians about other great musicians. As regards numbers, Pécuchet triumphantly points to an impressive bibliography, programmes of festivals and specialized societies (Unesco, Darmstadt, Donaueschingen, Domaine Musical, etc.) and to the ever-increasing vogue for this music among the young composers. Bouvard reminds him that for the last fifty years they have tried in vain to reach a wider audience without the aid of explanatory lectures for the benefit of specialists or of society snobs easily impressed by something they are incapable of understanding.—"But people are talking about it more and more," replies Pécuchet. Whereupon Bouvard quotes the old Arab proverb: "Three chattering women make more noise than a hundred silent men," and points to the disquieting deficits and empty halls that are the only reward of those who, in an effort to leave the beaten track, try from time to time to treat contemporary music as a living reality.

[2]Here Pécuchet travesties history. As we saw above, no hostile clique or conspiracy has ever prevented a work of genius from imposing itself, even if at first it caused some surprise for a short time. There is nothing to compare with the history of twelve-note music, which, far from being a novelty, is nearly half a century old today; two generations had known it and rejected it before it was taken up again by the present generation. The "revenge of posterity" is a romantic notion invented in the nineteenth century. A "discoverer of genius", such as Liszt, lavished the same exaggerated compliments on Marie Jaëll as he did on Wagner or César Franck (cf. J. Chantavoine in the *Revue Internationale de Musique*, No. 12, 1952, p. 31).

—What is dissonance today becomes consonance tomorrow.[1]

—Everything has been said in tonal language; the language has got to be changed to find something new.

—You are condemning yourselves, retorts Bouvard, by confessing your inability to produce any innovations from inside and having to rely on external artifices to conceal it.

—Not at all, replies Pécuchet. You couldn't point to a single important and really new work composed within the last twenty years without having recourse to our methods.

—There are plenty I could mention, cried Bouvard, reeling off a list which merely makes Pécuchet shrug his shoulders, as a matter of principle.

The discussion hangs fire. Bouvard passes to the offensive.

—Your music is mere intellectualism; nothing but mathematics.

—And what about the classical fugue?, interposes Pécuchet.

—That's not at all the same thing, protests Bouvard; I'm talking about language, and you bring up the question of form. Tonal language offers possibilities of contrast and variety which you deny yourselves. You express nothing but tension and confusion.

—Why not? retorts Pécuchet triumphantly; aren't these typical symptoms of the times we live in? —Wars, disasters, cybernetics, surrealism, existentialism. . . .

—Ah! cries Bouvard; then you are just one of those sinister individuals who can only see our young generation in terms of Saint-Germain-des-Prés and certain morbid films. . . .

The discussion becomes heated and runs off the rails again. Pécuchet accuses Bouvard of being an out-of-date bourgeois, while Bouvard swears that Pécuchet's *protégés* are nothing but the snobbish product of a decadent bourgeoisie who can be made to swallow anything. The discussion than takes a Marxist turn, and the terms "dirigism" and "socialist realism" are bandied about. Complete confusion reigns, and now, paradoxically, it is the alleged "bourgeois" who defends the Jdanov decrees,[2] while the

---

[1] This is true. But it doesn't happen automatically, and not at all as the dodecaphonists pretend. I apologize for quoting myself, but after having spent twenty years of my life in studying this phenomenon and, without having solved it in every detail, I have tried to make the process clear in my *Traité Historique* (Leduc, 1950) supplemented by my Sorbonne lectures on *Formation et transformations du langage musical* (already cited).

[2] Official instructions given in February, 1948, by the Central Committee of the Communist Party in the USSR banning the works, among others, of Muradelli, Prokofiev, Shostakovitch, Katchaturian, etc., and calling on composers to conform to "socialist realism", the criterion being accessibility to the popular taste of the masses. Among the foreign musicians stigmatized as the "great representatives of the decline of bourgeois civilization" were Schoenberg, Stravinsky, Hindemith, Messiaen and a number of American composers, including Menotti. Cf. N. Nabokoff, *La Musique en Union soviétique*, in the *Revue Internationale de Musique*, No. 11, 1951, p. 505—an indictment, followed by a plea for the defence by J. Prodromidès.

"avant-gardist" asserts that they only produced rubbish. Pécuchet starts to swear, and Bouvard goes off in a huff, banging the door behind him. . . .

Let us now endeavour to steer clear of polemics and tackle the fundamental issue at stake. "There are no mistakes," said Vauvenargues, "which, if seen clearly enough, do not die a natural death."

What strikes one in a discussion of this kind (and I have heard scores of them) is its negative aspect. At no time does the opponent really study the system, nor does the dodecaphonist attempt to justify his theories. He attacks traditionalism, and pleads the necessity of changing one's direction, without ever proving that the one he has chosen is the right one. After that, he assumes, without any transition, that he has demonstrated the legitimacy of the principle which he arbitrarily describes as "rules" or "laws" If, by any chance, he ventures to evoke the example of the past, his reasoning will be so full of factual errors and far-fetched interpretations that it is impossible to go very far with him in this particular field.[1]

One hears a lot of talk about "musical mathematics" in discussions on this subject. This is what is meant, I suppose, by the terms "purity", "strictness", etc. These mathematics ought, at least, to be correct; but it may be doubted whether they are. Childish and elementary in their application, despite what appear to be the most ingenious developments, they have never established the principle on which they claim to be based, namely *the substitution of an order of succession for a relationship*.[2]

To the best of my knowledge, there has never been *any kind of music*, past or present, *which has ever used such a criterion*, or whose evolution has led to the substitution of such a principle. This is based neither on tradition, even transformed by evolution, nor on an instinctive or intuitive development, and can therefore only claim to be a creation *ex nihilo*, elaborated by pure reason.

But in matters of this kind, everyone can make mistakes in their reasoning—both he who propounds and he who criticizes. One can only judge by results. This brings us to the fundamental question: can this music which is purely a product of speculation

[1]This is not the place to embark on a thorough-going examination of the whole problem. Let us confine ourselves to a few examples, such as the idea of "going beyond tonality", which is based on a confusion between tonality and consonance, or the "extension of chromaticism", based on a tendentious and incorrect analysis of what chromaticism really is. By quoting the opening of *Tristan* in his *Lyrical Suite*, Berg thought he was paying tribute to a precursor, whereas he was actually emphasizing an antinomy.

[2]As we shall see presently, once the qualitative relationship of sounds which, together with rhythm, forms the only basis of all non-Schoenbergian music, is eliminated, what is the point of continuing to use notes which have only been conceived in terms of this relationship? The question has obviously been asked, and it is only logical that dodecaphony leads to "organized noise", like concrete or electronic music.

produce effects equal or superior to those resulting from music having its origin in an instinct which has been evolving for thousands of years? Can it really become, as one twelve-note composer wrote, "the only valid music of our time" and, as such, eliminate as many people would wish, all other modern music which, while developing and re-shaping them, as happens in every generation, is founded on traditional bases?

The answer to this is that we can only judge by results. The twelve-note composers assure us that the series alone is capable of replacing all the old criteria, and can, by its permanence, give a piece of music the necessary coherence and unity. Some very precise experiments, we are told, were carried out for this purpose two years ago. These showed that even professionals, experts in the serial technique, were unable, even in quite simple examples conforming to the principles laid down by the theoreticians in this field, to determine which of two pre-arranged series was the one on which the piece in question was based.[1] There must therefore be, as R. Francès suggests (see above), a transition from a perceptive to a conceptual order.

That the manipulation of this conceptual order, owing to the variety of combinations it makes possible, gives a speculative kind of satisfaction to composers who indulge in it can readily be imagined, and would account for its success with young composers. But the object of music is not the satisfaction that may be experienced by the composer in writing it,[2] but rather the transference of the same satisfaction to the person who hears it. But can this satisfaction, in fact be conveyed when translated into sound?

If we take as a criterion the ability on the part of the hearer to identify and reconstruct mentally the composer's often elaborate treatment of his series, we shall be obliged, in the light of the experiment described above, to answer frankly NO—since it has been shown that the criterion adopted by the composer is no longer perceptible to the ear. It will therefore be necessary to adopt some other criterion. But which? A convinced apologist like Stückenschmidt has warned us that "atonal music. . . has adopted as a rule the revolt against immediate sensibility".[3] Therefore to attempt to apply to this music the criteria of such sensibility is to deny implicitly its efficacy. If it is possible to say, for example, that Le Soleil des eaux by Boulez is "borne on a wave of lyrical

[1]R. Francès, La Perception de la musique, Paris, Vrin, 1958, p. 140. The percentage of error, in any case, seemed largely a matter of chance, and there was no noticeable difference between the answers given by specialists, non-specialists and merely ignorant people.

[2]Of course. The musical novice who tries to compose, and discovers the common chord, is also overcome by the pleasure of covering his music paper with ungrammatical platitudes. Whether serial composition needs study or not is beside the point.

[3]Musique nouvelle, Corréa 1956, p. 153.

fervour worthy of Schumann"[1] then the old criteria are still being invoked. But this surely implies that the writer, forgetting that he has disowned them, is conferring upon these criteria the absolute right to refuse their sanction to anything that does not satisfy them; at the same time, one may well ask, as one serial composer did with reference to some of the more lyrical effusions of Alban Berg: "If this is the result, why have a series?"

And yet the only sensible attitude, whatever differences in appreciation it may give rise to, would seem to be that adopted by Antoine Goléa in this particular case—namely to take into account these pure reactions of affective sensibility. For my part—and I am certain my views are shared by countless musicians, including professionals—I confess that, in all good faith, I have never been able to discover, except through these old reactions of "immediate sensibility", what it is that distinguishes a "valid" piece of serial music from one of the kind which Goléa himself denounces, produced by "those young musicians who imitate and add technical improvements to late Webern, and only succeed in making music as empty of sound as it is of sense."[2]

---

[1] A. Goléa, *Esthétique de la musique contemporaine*, 1954, p. 182.

[2] Perhaps I may be permitted to reproduce here the conclusion of the article I alluded to above (p. 119) written in a journalistic style scarcely suitable for inclusion in a book of this kind, except in a footnote:

"In the absence of a revelation of which, though I would welcome it, I see as yet no sign, my only recourse is to shut my ears to the delirious flood of commentaries liable to be provoked by the slightest croak from some ataxic clarinet, and to open them wide again to listen to real music which needs no commentary. And I would advise you, my readers, to do the same. When the day comes on which, without any previous solicitation or instruction, you will be able, with the same enthusiastic spontaneity with which you would hail a classical work, to exclaim, on hearing a twelve-note composition: 'That was a masterpiece'—assuming, of course, that your enthusiasm was not due to any traditional elements which may have found their way into this dodecaphonic work—then, when that day comes, the gardener will have every justification for praising his plant; the most reasonable objections will no longer hold good. If, on the other hand, in all sincerity, and without allowing yourself to be influenced by a well-conducted publicity, you think that the aforesaid plant has produced nothing but barren and hideous abortions, then I beg you, be honest with yourselves: throw the catalogue into the wastepaper basket, and read again *Les Dupes*, by Jean Dutourd."

19

Concrete and Electronic Music

Dodecaphony was based from the start on a principle entirely opposed to what had always been the essential foundation of music until then: in place of the relationship between one note and another, it substituted an order of succession, paying practically no attention to the nature of this relationship. This could only lead in the end to the question: Why use a C or a G when the relationship between these notes, which used to determine their quality, is no longer of any interest?

At first an attempt was made to find a means of increasing the number of notes to be employed. An English composer, Foulds, as early as 1898 had introduced quarter-tones in a string quartet. In 1906 this idea was adopted by a German-Italian pianist, celebrated for his transcriptions of Bach in the Liszt-Thalberg manner, Ferruccio Busoni, and by a composer-philosopher, a pupil of Humperdinck, himself the author of a thesis on the psychological foundations of Wundt's *Ethics*, named Richard Stein. Stein built quarter-tone clarinets, wrote works for the 'cello in the same idiom, and in 1909 published an analytical thesis on the subject. Later on, in 1914, horrified by the results of his teaching as shown in the works of his disciples, he refused to allow his compositions to be published any more, and forbade the sale of his instruments. In the same year a Czech composer, who was also a theosophist, named Aloys Haba, devoted himself to microtonal composition and also made his own instruments. Quarter-tone pianos were built in Vienna in 1917 by von Möllendorf, and in Paris in 1922 by a Russian *émigré*, Ivan Vishnegradsky. The latter first used a piano with two keyboards, and later two pianos tuned a quarter-tone apart which formed between them a scale of twenty-four tempered quarter-tones. From the subdivision into smaller multiples of existing intervals the next step was the division of the octave into different unities. A Dutch engineer, Fokker, on the basis of the theoretical writings of his eighteenth-century compatriot Huygens, constructed in Harlem a "tricesimoprimal" organ, with thirty-one degrees to an octave; Belgian engineer, Vuylsteke, also constructed a micro-interval organ incorporating a scale of his own invention which he named "our true musical scale". Experiments of this kind are still being carried on today.

But all these experiments were still concerned with relations between intervals, even if they were losing their traditional character sanctioned by centuries of habit. Yet the ideal of this new aesthetic was really something more extreme: it was bound to end in the total abolition of these relations. In other words, it was to lead to a music of noises. Such today, under the name of "concrete" or "electronic" music, is the ultimate goal of what it is fashionable to call "*avant-garde*" music.

But this was not a mid-twentieth century novelty, any more than dodecaphony had been. The idea of organizing noises rhythmically and qualitatively so as to arrive at the equivalent of a musical composition had already been news as early as 1910. It was part of the programme of the Italian "Futurists", under the leadership of Marinetti. In 1911 Pratella published a *Manifesto of Futurist musicians* (reproduced in the journal S.I.M. of December 1913) which contained, among other things, this categorical statement: "It gives us far more pleasure to combine ideally the noises of tramways, motor-cars, vehicles of all kinds and vociferating crowds than it does to listen, for example, to the *Eroica* or the *Pastoral* symphonies."

Continuing in the same strain, the Manifesto went on: "As we walk together through a great modern city, paying more attention with our ears than with our eyes, we shall obtain an added satisfaction of our senses as we distinguish the gurglings of water, air and gas in their metal tubes, the belching and rattling of motor engines whose respiration has an unmistakable animal quality about it, the palpitations of the valves and pistons, the strident screams of mechanical saws, the bumping and banging of the trams on their rails, the cracking of whips and flapping of flags. We shall amuse ourselves by orchestrating ideally the creaking of sliding doors in the shops, the hubbub of crowds, and all the confused noises of railway stations, forges, spinning-mills, printing machines, electric power stations and underground railways. We would like to regulate harmonically and rhythmically all these different noises. . . . *The art of manipulating noises should not be confined to mere imitative reproduction.* Its main source of emotion will be derived from the special acoustic pleasure which the artist's inspiration will conjure up from the combination of various noises. . . ." The Manifesto then proceeded to classify noises into six categories, and announced that the "Futurist orchestra" would soon be able to realize them mechanically.

The result was a concert of "bruiteurs" (noise-makers) organized in Milan on August 11, 1911, by Russolo, the author of an article on "The Art of Noise", in which the following instruments took part: three buzzers, two exploders, one thunderer, three whistlers, two rumblers, two gurglers, one row-maker, one din-machine and one snorter.

The reception was, it must be admitted, ironical rather than enthusiastic. And the

promoters of *musique concrète* today are reluctant to talk about these "forerunners".[1]
And yet it was with the same end in view, only with new means at their disposal, that
the *musique concrète* team, sponsored by the French radio and directed by Pierre Schaeffer,
was set up in 1948.

I knew Pierre Schaeffer in 1931. He was then at the Polytechnic, the leader of a
group of theatrical amateurs, and belonged like myself to a band of rover-scouts.
During the long walks we took together our conversation often turned to music, and
Schaeffer surprised me by a curious lack of proportion between his natural curiosity and
the intelligence of his questions, showing a very genuine taste for music, on the one
hand, and a surprising ignorance of its rudiments and basic principles on the other—all
the more so, since he was the son of two teachers (of violin and singing) at the Nancy
Conservatoire. (He described himself as self-taught.) In 1939—he was then sound-
engineer at the French Radio—he was a pioneer in stereophonic research, and we were
studying together the possibility of introducing a modern pedagogic installation at the
Conservatoire (of which I was then secretary-general) when the war put an end to our
experiments. In 1945 I came across him again when he was at the head of the technicians
who enabled the French Radio to play its part in the Liberation; and it was there that
he created, under the title of the *Club d'Essai*, a research laboratory where all sorts of
new techniques were tried out. He himself relates[2] how in 1948 he had the idea of using
as the elements of a new music, instead of the notes hitherto employed by composers,
noises that would be manipulated and transformed in the studio by the various machines
which were daily becoming more and more proficient. In this way *musique concrète* could
start from any sort of pre-recorded noise—hence its name: a saucepan falling downstairs would serve as raw material just as well as a verse by Racine or a soap advertise-
ment (in any case only disconnected syllables would be used) or even a fragment of
piano or guitar music subjected to the same treatment.

Using this basic material, the tricks of the laboratory could bring about the most unexpected transformations: the sound could be recorded backwards, slowed down or
accelerated, deprived of its "attack" and resonance, or on the contrary surrounded by
its own reverberations, etc., etc. Stereophonic appliances would distribute it throughout
the concert-room, for example, and its volume could be intensified to any degree by
the "potentiometers".

[1]In his book *A la recherche d'une musique concrète*, P. Schaeffer refers only once to Marinetti, and then only
in a very cursory way in a footnote stating briefly that he had merely side-tracked the issue as his noises were
"direct", and not formed through distortion by being recorded; writing in 1952, he also wrongly dated the
Futurist movement, referring to "twenty" years ago instead of forty.

[2]Cf. *Journal d'une découverte*, in his *A la recherche d'une musique concrète*.

After the first empirical experiments, they began to classify the sounds and to write "scores" on measured graph paper. Schaeffer's first collaborator was a young percussion player, a student at the Conservatoire, named Pierre Henry. Later the team was joined by "real" composers, including, but only for a brief period, Olivier Messiaen and later Henri Sauguet. When Pierre Boulez appeared on the scene in 1951, the latent connection with the twelve-note system was soon revealed, and the calculating tables which he devised served as a basis for all sorts of combinations, obviously imperceptible to the ear, but of great value for instructional purposes and for the personal satisfaction of the composer.

A spirit of rivalry soon animated our neighbours across the Rhine, and in their hands *musique concrète* soon became *"electronische Musik"*, very similar in results, but different in its method of presentation, in so far as the initial sonorous material, instead of being taken from existing sounds, was produced by elaborate machines built according to specifications recalling those employed by Russolo. A studio of electronic music was thus built at great cost at Cologne, and others soon followed.

As for the aesthetic value of the results of so great an expenditure of time and money, it would no doubt be premature to estimate it in the light of the "works" produced so far. These experiments have been going on for nearly fifteen years. Too long, say some; not long enough, say others. Which of them is right? The writer would prefer not to express an opinion.

One of my girl students who was working in the *musique concrete* studio arrived one day in a great state of excitement. "Something very amusing has happened," she explained. "Imagine, in the course of our manipulations, a very strange thing happened, quite by chance: an extraordinary sound which intrigued us all very much. We studied it carefully to find out what it was, and then we saw that it was a perfect fifth! It made us all laugh."

We can perhaps derive some comfort from this story. Let us suppose that, by some extraordinary turn of events, "concrete music" one day succeeded in eliminating altogether every other kind of music. Some "concrete" musician of genius would then no doubt, in the twenty-first or twenty-second century, discover the virtues of the octave, then of the fifth or fourth, in accordance with the process that has been going on, we may suppose, since pre-historic times when "plain" music was still in its embryonic stage. A few centuries later the interval of the third would perhaps be discovered. And—who knows?—the history of music might then begin all over again.

20

"Canned Music"

Of all the transformations throughout the ages which have affected the social significance of music, there is certainly none which has had such far-reaching and profound repercussions, or has come about so suddenly, as the one which we are now experiencing. When I was a child, the radio—we used to call it "the wireless" in those days—was a pastime for inveterate amateurs of gadgets, and the gramophone a rather disagreeable curiosity whose nasal tones, mingled with those of the mechanical piano-player, provided a background of noise in suburban cafés. If anyone had predicted that these machines would, in twenty or thirty years' time, become one of the pivots of our musical life today, he would have merely been laughed at.

It is not perhaps generally known that the first notion of a machine for reproducing sounds was probably due to Cyrano de Bergerac. Not Rostand's hero with the stalactite nose, but the authentic author of the *Pédant Joué* and *La Mort d'Agrippine*. This forerunner of Jules Verne in describing his adventures in 1654 during an imaginary voyage in his book *Estats et Empires de la Lune*, tells of the wonderful things he is supposed to have seen. Among these was an extraordinary box, which he describes as follows: "On opening the box I found inside some kind of metal object, rather like a clock, full of machinery and what seemed like little coiled springs. It was really a Book, but a miraculous Book with no pages nor writing in it: it was, in short, a book from which you could learn nothing with your eyes, but only with your ears. So that if anyone wants to read what is in it, he winds all sorts of little wires round this machine, and then turns a needle to the chapter he wants to hear, and then, as if issuing from the mouth of a man or from a musical instrument, all sorts of different sounds come out, which is the way in which the Lunar men converse with one another. When I reflected later on this miraculous invention to take the place of books, I was no longer astonished to see that the young men in that country are more learned at sixteen or eighteen years of age than our own grey-beards; for, since they learn to read as soon as they can talk, they need never be without reading matter; whether abroad or in their homes, on journeys or in town, they may carry in their pockets, or suspended from their belts, as many as thirty such Books, of which they need only wind up one spring to hear a single chapter, or even more if they desire to listen to a whole Book; in this way you are perpetually surrounded by all the great men, living or dead, who speak to you with their living voices."

This, of course, belongs to the world of fantasy. But very real efforts were made as early as the eighteenth century to reproduce mechanically musical tunes in a fixed and permanent form. The first apparatus of this kind was modestly designed for the musical education of canaries and other song-birds.[1] To avoid the monotony of having to play over and over again on the flageolet the tune they were supposed to learn, someone invented a kind of miniature organ, with a bellows worked by hand which turned a cylinder similar to those used in a barrel organ or pianola. Some of these "serinettes", as they were called, are still in existence, and thanks to them we can hear exactly the same tunes which they recorded two hundred years ago.

Mechanical devices of this kind had been in use for a long time. About 1830 they even used perforated discs which were placed on a turn-table very similar to that of the modern gramophone. These were, it is true, only toys, whose modern equivalent would be something like the musical cigar-boxes (or even toilet paper distributors) which are to be met with today. The same might be said of the perforated rolls used in barrel organs and pianolas, had not the principle, which was perfected about 1900, made it possible for musicians no less distinguished than Gustav Mahler, Busoni, Granados, Saint-Saëns or Debussy to record, as early as 1905, interpretations which, thanks to modern techniques, it has been possible to issue as records which have recently been put on the market.[2] Stravinsky himself was sufficiently interested in the new invention to write some pieces directly for the *Pleyela*.

All these inventions, however, were designed to reconstitute rather than reproduce the original sounds as actually played or sung. The original invention, which was to lead to the reproduction of such sounds, was due to a simple, self-taught French typesetter, Edouard-Léon Scott, of Martinville. On January 26, 1857, Scott delivered to the Academy of Sciences in Paris a sealed envelope containing a description of his *phonautographe*. This consisted of an acoustic horn, a membrane with a needle that inscribed on a cylinder imbued with lamp-black the sinuosities of a curve corresponding to a

---

[1]Automatic singing birds belong to a different category. A description of one of these by Philo of Byzantium, circa. 200 B.C., is extant today.

[2]In the series *Musikalische Dokumente*, issued by Telefunken. It should be noted, however, that though these records reproduce faithfully, with the full tone of the modern concert piano, the pedalling effects and time-values, neither the nuances of expression, the original sonority, nor even, perhaps, the correct *tempi* (due to faulty synchronization) can be considered altogether reliable.

voice speaking or singing into the horn. This was the first apparatus to "record" the human voice. The recording, however, was as yet only visual. It did not reproduce the sound, but enabled it to be studied and analysed in the laboratory. To reproduce the sound, it was necessary to find a means of reversing the recording. On April 16, 1877, the poet and scholar Charles Cros dated and signed a *mémoire* showing how this could be done, and describing not only the engraved cylinder with which he replaced Scott's lamp-black cylinder, but the spiral disc which later on was to take the place of the cylinder.

Charles Cros's *mémoire*, sent to the Academy in a sealed envelope two days later, was registered and accepted on April 30th and read at a public sitting of the Academy on December 3rd of the same year, 1877. In the meantime, on October 10th an article in *La Semaine du Clergé*, signed by the Abbé Lenoir, announced the discovery, and for the first time gave the apparatus, which its inventor had called a *"paléophone"*, its final name of "phonographe".

Scarcely a month after the reading of Charles Cros's communication to the Academy, an application for a patent was received both in France and in the U.S.A. from an American savant, Thomas Alva Edison, which was concerned with the "improvement of instruments to control by sound the transmission of electric currents as well as the reproduction of sounds". The formula was still obscure. But on January 15, 1878, Edison took out a supplement to his original patent, which contained a description of a method for ensuring the practical realization of what, following the Abbé Lenoir, he himself now called a "phonograph". On February 19th, Edison obtained his American patent, and on March 11th his representative in Paris presented to the Academy of Science a fine, well-constructed apparatus—a gramophone complete with cylinder and tinfoil. The story is told—which may be apocryphal—that one of the "Immortals" was asked to say a few words into the machine, but on hearing his own voice come back to him disguised with a nasal twang, he wanted the person presenting it to be examined to make sure that he was not a ventriloquist!

Edison naturally declared that he knew nothing about Charles Cros's work, and this is perhaps true. It obviously must have been equally true so far as Cros was concerned, for the latter had made his communication to the Academy in April, while it was not until the following July that Edison formulated the preliminary sketch of what he considered to be his own invention.

This idea came to him, he said, like other discoveries, by chance in the course of an experiment. He was working at that time on a scheme for increasing the speed of the Morse telegraph, and was using for this purpose a needle fixed to a diaphragm which inscribed dots and dashes on a ribbon imbued with paraffin. While trying to ascertain the maximum speed at which the ribbon could be rotated, he noticed that when the needle was moving very fast it made a slight sound which had a musical and rhythmical quality which he thought was "rather like a human voice heard indistinctly". Now Edison was engaged at the same time in perfecting the Bell telephone, and there seemed to him to be some connection between the two experiments. He therefore attached a needle to the membrane of the telephone and noticed that if he placed the needle on his finger and spoke into the machine, the vibration set up in the needle was also perceptible to the touch. He then conceived the idea of engraving it on to a rapidly moving paper treated with paraffin, and repeating his Morse experiment using this material. He wrote down his conclusions on July 18th as follows: "The vibrations of speech can be clearly recorded, and there is no doubt that I shall be able one day to transform them into sound again and reproduce automatically and to perfection the human voice." We have no record of the subsequent stages of his work until one day he approached the machine he had had built and recited into the horn the nursery rhyme, "Mary had a little lamb"; then, with a beating heart, he put the needle into the groove and listened. Miraculously something resembling the words came back to him . . . .

The date of this memorable occasion is obviously of great importance in deciding the question of priority as between Cros and Edison. Officially it is supposed to have taken place on August 12th, 1877, but this date was only fixed some years later when it was desired to celebrate its anniversary. Roland Gelatt[1] who goes into the question very thoroughly, points out its improbability, and thinks that the apparatus can hardly have been constructed before the end of November or the beginning of December of that year. Yet the Abbé Lenoir's article on Charles Cros's invention had appeared on October 10th. Gelatt also draws attention to some other improbabilities in the official version, which was no doubt designed to eliminate any suspicion of influence on the part of the French inventor. The only historically certain fact is that Edison obtained his patent on February 19th, 1878, eleven weeks after the reading of Cros's communication to the Academy, so that the generally accepted conclusion is now the one propounded by Gelatt, namely that the Frenchman was the first to "conceive" the phonograph, and the American the first to "realize" it.

On Edison's phonograph recording and reproduction were done on the same machine, still in a rudimentary stage. After one or two auditions the groove was worn out and the poor acoustic quality ruled out the possibility of using it for any artistic purpose.

[1] *The Fabulous Phonograph*, Philadelphia, 1955, p. 22.

Improvements, however, were soon introduced, at a surprisingly early date, which the commercial market was sometimes very slow in adopting. On June 27th, 1885, Graham Bell and Charles Traiter took out a patent to replace the sheet of tinfoil by a film of wax; this enabled the groove to be deeper, and instead of using the original again in performance, which caused it to wear out very quickly, it was replaced by an electroplated surface which helped to preserve the matrix. The cylinder, which Edison alone had

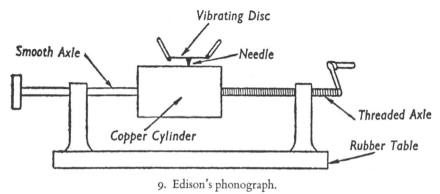

9. Edison's phonograph.

perfected, was the only one that remained in use until the beginning of the twentieth century—an object of curiosity for collectors which also has a documentary value; we shall see, for example, in the next volume, the part played by cylinders in the early stages of ethnomusicology. And yet Charles Cros, in his communication to the Academy, already advocated the disc in preference to the cylinder, and as early as 1887 an amateur German acoustician, Emile Berliner, reverting to Cros's "disc", invented the principle on which the modern micro-groove is founded, i.e., lateral engraving instead of the deep groove.

And yet the latter survived for quite a time—for example in those machines with the enormous horn depicted in the famous trade-mark *His Master's Voice*.

The catalogues vaunted the durability of those big sapphires pressed into the groove by the weight of the diaphragm, but failed to point out that though the needle might not wear out, the surface which bore this weight would inevitably be affected. The fine steel needle, which had to be frequently changed, did not completely relace the sapphire until around 1920.

Pope Leo XIII was the oldest person whose voice had been preserved, for in 1903, at the age of 93, he had recorded on two cylinders, for the Italian engineer Enrico Bettini, an *Ave Maria* and a *Benedictus*. A few records on cylinders or discs were made by some famous operatic singers, including Caruso, who at the age of twenty made three cylinder recordings around 1900, and also by music-hall artists; but their interest is clearly documentary rather than artistic. Then as the needle replaced the sapphire, all kinds of artists began to make recordings. One of the first orchestral records, made in France around 1925, was Honegger's *Pacific* 231, played by the Pasdeloup Orchestra and conducted by the composer. On March 21st, 1925, Alfred Cortot made for the Victor Gramophone Co., in Camden, New Jersey, the first classical recording to employ a new technique, thanks to which the gramophone was to play an important part in musical life: electric recording. It was nearly thirty years before the companies decided to use this process which the French physicist, François Dussaud, had presented to the Academy of Science on December 29th, 1896, under the name of "microphonograph", and it was not until 1919 that it was tested for the first time in England and the United States.

Up to the 1939 war there had been improvements in points of detail, but the general principles remained much the same. A recording session was an exhausting ordeal. Although with the advent of the microphone it was no longer necessary for the singer to plunge his head into an acoustic horn while the pianist on a high platform thumped away in the hope of letting one or two notes make their way through the wall, everyone dreaded the fatal four-minute-twenty-second period. If the piece was at all long it had to be cut into sections of the required length, each of which had to be tested and rehearsed—a laborious process, often repeated many times before the "take" to enable the engineer to adjust his apparatus and warm up his wax.

When it was time for the actual recording, the artist, who was already tired out, could not afford to make a mistake, because it was impossible to make corrections and the wax was expensive. If the final cadence lasted half a second too long, the whole thing would have to be scrapped and done again. Checking for quality was also impossible, since playing over the wax would have destroyed it; it was not until 1938 that the practice of making a double recording was adopted—the authentic one which was left untouched, and a copy on some pliable material on which a final decision had to be taken before the recording was passed for publication.

After the 1939 war strange rumours began to circulate; it was whispered that there had been some extraordinary inventions, but that they were being kept secret and would not be put on the market for many years owing to fierce opposition from the gramophone companies which feared the competition and the scrapping of their existing stocks. There were rumours of a new system which would make it possible to listen for hours on end without interruption—to rub out and make corrections; surface noises would disappear, and sounds could be recorded with the same accuracy of perception as the human ear. And presently, and almost clandestinely, the first "magnetophones" made their appearance.

Now the magnetophone was almost as old as the phonograph[1] but nobody had thought of establishing a connection between the two appliances.

The history of the newcomer is curiously similar to that of the phonograph: it was a French invention "realized", after a patent had been applied for, by a foreign savant.

In 1887 Professor Paul Janet presented to the Academy of Science a communication on "the transversal magnetization of metal conductors", which was followed in 1890 by a report on "the extension of the theory relating to the conservation of the flow of energy in conductors". This was the principle of magnetic recording.

Janet, however, did not go so far as Charles Cros, who described an apparatus that would work; he only propounded a theory. It was the Dane, Valdemar Poulsen, who enabled it to be put to practical use.

In 1900 Poulsen showed at the Paris Exhibition his "telegraphone", patented in America as No. 661,619, which earned for him the *Grand Prix* of the Exhibition. It was a cylinder "around which was wound spirally a steel tape in contact with a small electro-magnet which could be connected with a microphone, a head-phone or an electric current. This bobbin could thus be used for either recording, reproduction or erasing".

However, the American company, founded by Poulsen in 1903, went bankrupt, and nothing more was heard of his project. In 1929 the business was resuscitated by a German called Stille who, after making some improvements, founded the "Telephon Patent Syndikat". The following year the patent was sold to a certain Blattner, who had the idea of using it for the synchronization of films in the cinema.[2] The "Blattnerphone" was then sold to the British Marconi Co., which invented the process known as "Marconi-Stille", and after that to Bauer, who made the so-called "Dailygraph" dictaphones; in 1932 Bauer sold his apparatus to the I.T.T., who resold it to the C. Lorenz Co. The latter rechristened it "Textophon", and created a steel-band recording apparatus which, incidentally, was used to record Hitler's speeches.

The recording companies began to be alarmed at the prospect of possible competition, especially on account of the length of the pieces which could now be recorded without

---

[1] Cf. F. Schuh and N. Mikhnewitch, *L'enregistrement magnétique*, Paris, 1952.

[2] Note the date: 1930; this was about the time the hitherto silent film became "100 per cent talking and singing". It is perhaps not generally known, incidentally, that the pioneer of film music was none other than Saint-Saëns! He was the first to write, in 1908, a score specially intended for the screen: the film was *L'Assassinat du duc de Guise*, by Henri Lavedan, played by Albert Lambert.

cutting. In 1931 the Victor Gramophone Co. was already experimenting with reduced speed records—33⅓ revolutions per minute:[1] a demonstration was arranged on September 17th at the Savoy-Plaza Hotel in New York, but the substance of which the discs were made—shellac, mixed with carbon particles—could not stand up to such a slow speed. Beethoven's *Fifth Symphony*, conducted by Stokowski, seemed to the critics invited to hear it to be so "woolly" that the experiment, interesting as it was, seemed doomed to failure.

In the meantime magnetic recording was making steady progress. In 1927 Pfleumer had taken out a patent for replacing the steel tape by a strip of paper, or plastic material, imbued with a magnetic paste. In 1931 the same inventor was working on a dictating machine called a "magnetophone" which, after the addition of some improvements, was soon to be used on the radio. Further improvements, mainly American or German, reduced surface noise and, among other things, strengthened the lower register which, until then, had been very unsatisfactory. Nevertheless, when war broke out in 1939, the magnetophone was much inferior in quality to the best standard recordings. During the tragic year 1940, experts in the Anglo-American Intelligence Service, whose business it was to study the German broadcasts, noticed some surprising improvements in sound-fidelity. Soon the pre-recorded emissions which they picked up seemed to have attained an unprecedented degree of perfection; surface noise was practically non-existent, timbre undistorted, and there were no breaks in the continuity. It was not until September 11th, 1944, when the Allies took possession of the Radio Luxembourg studios, that the key to the mystery was discovered: it was a magnetophone of an entirely new design with a plastic tape treated with oxide of iron moving at thirty inches per second and capable of recording without the slightest distortion up to 10,000 cycles for half an hour without a break. But the apparatus was too heavy and too cumbersome for domestic use. The Americans then began to study how it could best be adapted. The St. Paul Laboratories were soon manufacturing a so-called "Scotch" tape, imbued with oxide of iron which was better than the German one and capable of recording 15,000 cycles at a speed of 7½ inches per second. In 1947 the Minnesota Mining and Manufacturing Company launched this apparatus on a nation-wide scale. Its musical quality was confirmed by some jazz recordings made by Bing Crosby, and the old-fashioned disc seemed definitely outclassed.

The magnetophone began to make its way in Europe. Musicians, both amateur and

---

[1]This is now the standard speed of L.P. records, but these also enjoy other advantages which at that time were unforeseeable.

professional, were delighted with this marvellous toy, so valuable for work or teaching purposes. And, although it had managed to stave off the danger of commercial magnetic recordings, the gramophone industry felt itself increasingly threatened.

It avoided the danger by forming an astute alliance with its adversary. Thanks to the invention of a new supporting material, a thermoplastic resin free from the surface noise inseparable from the old shellac, and also lighter and unbreakable, it was possible to resuscitate without its old drawbacks, the 33⅓ L.P. record that had been tried and discarded in 1931. Lateral engraving and very fine grooves made it possible to dispense with heavy arms and unpractical needles, while the combination of the two processes prolonged the playing time of a twelve-inch record from four minutes twenty seconds to nearly half-an-hour. Furthermore, with a lighter arm, a quartz crystal, cut under a microscope, would last, with no apparent signs of wearing out, for some sixty hours of listening (from force of habit it was referred to again as a "sapphire"). By using the magnetophone for all studio operations, including "collage" and all the other devices, and reserving for the laboratory the actual recording from the magnetophone on to the disc, the latter could now be put on the market with all the advantages inherent in tape; the micro-groove was born.

Manufactured in New York for Columbia by the Hungarian engineer Peter Gold-mark, the first new-style record made its appearance on June 21, 1948. Six months later, 1,200,000 were in circulation.

It was two or three years before the revolutionary model reached Europe. In 1951 the standard record was the old 78. Less than two years later the microgroove had supplanted it.

On December 10, 1957, on the initiative of the *Académie du Disque français*, and in the presence of the President of the National Assembly, a box containing the prize-winning records of the year was buried under a paving-stone in the peristyle of the *Théâtre Français*. This was the modern record's response to a similar ceremony that had taken place fifty years previously, when on December 31, 1907, and again on June 13, 1912, some records were buried in the basement of the Paris Opéra, not to be heard again until the year 2012. When on that date the two boxes are dug up, a comparison between them will no doubt constitute one of the most astonishing proofs of technical progress in the twentieth century.

But we have no idea what technical progress may have been achieved by 2012, and perhaps our microgroove "high fidelity" records, of which we are so proud, will be laughed at by future generations. Already stereophonic recording, which is slowly but surely gaining ground and making audible the "three dimensions" of sound as it really is, is gradually relegating to the past what is already being called "monaural" sound. The extraordinary fidelity of a good stereophonic recording has been convincingly demonstrated in various tests.[1]

The fantastic success of the L.P. record, which has found its way into every home, is perhaps the most important single event in the history of twentieth-century music. Combined with the no less spectacular diffusion of radio and television, it has resulted in "canned music" having become the essential musical nourishment of our generation. The two forms complement one another perfectly, one ensuring a continuous renovation, and the other a personal element in the sphere of selection and serious study. Both are a vehicle for the best and the worst, abolishing time and space, removing obstacles, and restoring to music that quality of familiarity which it was losing, but which is so necessary to it, by bringing the greatest artists in the world within the reach of the humblest housewife as she goes about her daily chores.

Thanks to "canned music" we hear infinitely more music than ever before and, if we desire it, of infinitely better quality. But do we listen to it as well as we used to? The best tinned products can never take the place of a sauce carefully prepared and left to simmer slowly over the fire. Is not the loss of that human contact which the concert hall ensures an exorbitant price to pay for this extraordinary all-round enrichment? The effort which a young girl had to make to learn her "piece" to play on Granny's birthday, though possibly not appreciated as an artistic pleasure by members of her family, may well have been *for her* of greater lasting value than that of extracting from its envelope a gramophone record. The concert-goer, who had to buy his ticket, dress and go out to hear the artist of his choice obtained, in return for his pains, a pleasure which he both desired and deserved. There is nothing comparable to be got from merely turning a knob. It is true that the concert has survived in the face of this formidable competition. The latter, though of inestimable benefit as a complement and as a stimulant to the desire to hear "live" music may, if it tends to supplant the latter, have a disastrously stifling effect. But fortunately there is still the student who saves up to buy a record of a Bach Concerto to reassure us and remind us that, even in an age of "canned music", music can still hold its own.

[1]An experiment was carried out in Paris in 1958 for the firm of *Erato* which consisted of playing a stereo record made by the pianist Gyorgi Sebök while he was sitting at the piano, apparently playing. The record was then stopped, and he continued from where it left off until the record took over again. Not one person in the audience, which consisted mainly of professional musicians and experienced critics, was able to say which passages were played live and which were recorded.

PART IV

IN SEARCH OF "STARS"

21

Madame Melba's Peaches, or The Singers

In this rapid race towards individualism which has characterized the history of music since the beginning, it is not so much the composer as the interpreter, and more especially the singer, who seems to have taken the lead.

We have seen how kings and princes, by their usurpation of divine attributes, first opened the door, unwittingly, to a new conception of music. It was they again who, still without knowing it, helped to create the image of the artist as a definite type.

In all ancient societies, the social rank of the individual was determined by his birth. Later, as society evolved, the barriers became less rigid, but it was not until the drama of 1789 that they were definitely broken down, however weakened they may have been by centuries of repeated assaults.

At a time when these barriers were more impregnable than ever, it was probably the artist who first succeeded in breaking them down, thanks to the protection and favours he enjoyed in high quarters.

The behaviour of the Sardinian singer Tigellius at the Courts of Cleopatra and Augustus was sufficiently objectionable for Horace to make it the subject of his third Satire. Caligula made the singer Apelles his favourite, until the day when the latter was foolish enough to hesitate before replying "You, of course", to the Emperor's question: "Which do you think is the greater, Jupiter or I?" The history of Imperial Rome is full of stories of this kind.

Christianity—where at first music and singing were synonymous, since music had no other purpose than to accompany words in praise of the Deity—hesitated a long time before considering the singer to be a minister or, more precisely, before transforming the Christian community into a hierarchy of singers.[1] As early as the fourth century the question as to whether it was desirable or pernicious to praise God in song gave rise to violent controversy—which perhaps has not entirely died down in our own times. By a curious coincidence it was always on the side of those who defended the cause of

---

[1]It is interesting to note that the highest dignitary in a cathedral, after the Bishop, was the *Precentor*, i.e., literally, "the one who sings first". The Bishop himself was often called the *Praesul*, which meant originally "the one who dances first".

sacred music that the future saints were to be found: St. Augustine, St. Ambrosius, St. Athanasius, St. John Chrysostomos.

But even for those who defended it, the rôle of music was clearly defined in principle. A Christian sang to express his feelings, but not to be heard. If he sometimes had an audience, this was because he was acting as a delegate and interpreter of the sentiment of the collectivity, and not inviting admiration for his art.

In other words, the soloist was now the intermediary between his audience and the Deity; the former was, as it were, a collective source of inspiration to the singer, but it was *for* them, and not *to* them that he was singing.

And yet, as might have been expected, singers were not content for long with this anonymous rôle. Towards the eleventh century they began to pose as artists and demanded attention. This shocked the ecclesiastical authorities. The English Cistercian, Aelred de Rievault, in his *Mirror of Charity* (circa. 1150) fulminated against the new fashion: "You can sometimes see a man, with his mouth wide open, stop making a sound, as if to imitate silence; at other times he simulates the agony of a dying man or the delirium of the sick; his whole body is agitated; his shoulders shake, his lips are contorted—and these ridiculous antics are what they call religion! These lascivious gestures and harlot's tones are more suited to the theatre than to the Church. . . ."[1]

Such complaints were soon to become a commonplace: we find them a century later copied word for word in a sermon by Guibert de Tournai.

At about the same time Guido d'Arezzo castigated in vigorous terms the singer—and through him every kind of executant—reminding him of the subordinate part he played, but from an entirely different point of view:

> Musicorum et cantorum magna est distantia
> Isti dicunt, illi sciunt quae componit musica
> Nam qui facit quod non sapit diffinitur bestia.[2]

The singers, for their part, certainly did not agree that the same criteria could be applied to them. At the beginning of the seventeenth century opera was for them a kind of serum which, by creating the professional singer, gave them a new function to perform; and no sooner had this new social category come into being than its mem-

---

[1] *Speculum caritatis*, ii, XXIII.
[2] "Between musicians and singers the distance is great. The former know how music is made, the latter reproduce it. For only animals do things they do not understand." Two centuries later "facit" was altered to "canit", making the last line more malicious than before: "For he who sings what he does not understand is no better than an animal."

bers began to claim for themselves the right to revise, at their own discretion, the works entrusted to them by composers.

Needless to say, this "collaboration", of which we saw an example on p. 110, was not always approved of by the composers who inclined to be highly critical of Guido d'Arezzo. Lully, Gluck, and Berlioz in turn favoured a certain strictness, which did not, however, necessarily mean a slavish adherence to the written text. No one before the twentieth century would have dreamed of denying that Boyé in 1779 was merely stating the obvious when he declared that a good actor playing a musical rôle could not fail to see that "if he confined himself to singing only what was written down, his audience was not likely to be satisfied with such a puerile performance."[1]

Gluck in 1783 advised his visitor Reichardt "to go to Paris to hear his works before it was too late and the tradition had been lost."[2] As for Berlioz, he wrote an enthusiastic preface to an edition of Gluck's *Orfeo* containing the astonishing "cadenza" of her own invention which Pauline Viardot in 1859 added to the final aria in the first Act (Plate XXV). Far from being scandalized, Berlioz was full of admiration: "To describe what Mme. Viardot did with this *bravura* air," he wrote in *A travers chants*, "is almost impossible. When you listen to it, you do not think of the style of the piece, but are carried away by this torrent of elaborate vocalizations arising out of the situation."

Grand Opera did not only leave it to the discretion of the singers to decide how they would deal with what they were given to sing, but made them the idols of a public which had at first been drawn from the highest-ranking Court circles, but in the nineteenth century represented almost every class in bourgeois society. It was thus that a famous French *chef* in a London restaurant, Escoffier, on learning one day that Nelly Melba was among his customers, asked her to do him the favour of giving her name to his culinary masterpiece: the famous ice-cream with peaches which keeps alive among us today the memory of the great *prima donna*.

Popularity of this kind naturally encouraged capricious and sometimes tyrannical behaviour. Hortense Schneider refused to sing *La Grande Duchesse de Gérolstein* unless she could wear the "grand cordon" of some Order or another. The counter-tenor Crescentini, when singing in 1794 at the Tuileries theatre *Gli Orazi e Curiazi*, an opera which Climarosa had composed for him and La Grassini, noticed that the costume to be worn by the tenor Brizzi was more dashing than his own; it was white, whereas

---

[1] Eugène Borrel, *L'interprétation de la musique française de Lully à la Révolution*, 1934, p. 14.
[2] J. G. Prodhomme, *Gluck*, 1948, p. 353. This meant, in plain language: "When my music will only be sung as it is written, all that remains will be a caricature."

his was merely a dull green. He refused to go on until he had seen the tailors and designers and asked for an explanation. He was told that they had only followed the rules of the Comédie-Française, and had paid more attention to the correctness of the costumes than to the singer's rank. This produced a furious outburst which ended in Crescentini forcing Brizzi to exchange costumes, so that in the subsequent acts the public could see a tall Curiace with a Roman jacket much too small for him, and a small Horace with an immense Alban tunic trailing on the floor.

Though these stories do not show the protagonists in a very sympathetic light, they are none the less a symptom of the vitality of a form of art; and, after all, the fact that the lyric stage is tending to be monopolized by film stars rather than opera singers is perhaps an equally disquieting sign of the times. Fortunately, a few picturesque specimens still remain with us. The fantasies of Madame Callas may still provide journalists with sensational and ironical "copy": nevertheless, they preserve for us, and for the good reputation of the lyric theatre, one of the most persistent of the traditions which have always been amongst its greatest attractions.[1]

*   *   *

So long as vocal music was essentially monodic, it would seem that no particular importance was attached to differentiating between one kind of voice and another. Today in monastery choirs the monks still sing together the same music, regardless of whether they are tenors or basses. It is the same with the children in choirs who sing Gregorian plainsong, and it must not be forgotten that women's voices were forbidden in churches until the nineteenth century.

It was a long time, too before any rational attention was paid in polyphonic music to the various vocal *tessituras*.[2]

Until the fifteenth century men's and children's voices do not seem to have been mixed in sacred music, nor even men's and women's voices in secular music. The

---

[1]Cf. Horace, Sat. 1, 3:

> Omnibus hoc vitium est cantoribus, inter amicos
> Ut nunquam inducant animum cantare rogati,
> Injussi nunquam desistant.

(The trouble with singers is that when their friends ask them to sing they never will, but when they are not asked to, nothing can stop them!)

[2]The old terminology of Tenor, Counter-tenor, Triplum, Motetus, etc., refers to the style of composition and not to the *tessitura* of the singer's voices. It was in the sixteenth century that the terms: *bassus, altus, superius* were first introduced. The word *tenor*, derived from the Italian (in old French it was called *teneur*), then simply changed its meaning. The modern Italian *soprano, contralto*, etc., came into use with the advent of opera. It is noteworthy that the word *altus* (our *alto*) means high; consequently it applies, as we shall see, to a high male voice, and not, as commonly used today, to a low woman's or boy's voice.

organum was sung in the choir by cantors wearing a cope, one for each voice.[1] The *conductus* was also performed by soloists, one for each voice. In Machaut's time it was the same, and, it is probable that the famous *Messe Notre-Dame* was scored for four cantors and some unspecified instruments. There were already children's choirs in the fourteenth century, but it seems unlikely that they sang any polyphonic music before the middle of the fifteenth century.

Until the eighteenth century at least, children's voices in these choirs were not divided; they sang only the treble part, all the others being divided among the men's voices. From this it will be seen that polyphonic vocal music in the sixteenth century did not sound at all like it does today. The alto part, for example, was, as its name suggests (see footnote p. 154) a high male voice and not a low woman's or boy's voice. This division of voices in choirs also applies to solo voices, notably in opera where for a long time the female contralto was unknown.[2]

10. Polyphonic singing, 13th century.

The latter were employed for the first time, it seems, by Rossini. Nevertheless there were "contraltists" before his time, but they belonged to a very special category of singers who for two hundred years made the Sistine Chapel famous and dominated the world of opera. It is difficult to say with any exactitude when the vogue of the *castrati*, nearly all Italians, began. It is probable that, at first, advantage was taken of accidental cases. The first *castrato* mentioned at the Sistine was a certain Hieronymus Rossinus in 1562. But about 1570 there were already six in the choir in Bavaria where Roland de Lassus was *maître de chapelle*. Later their voices came to be admired, and by the end of the seventeenth century met with such success that their numbers increased in a way that owed nothing to accident. They were operated on between the ages of ten and fourteen, after which they had to study for eight or ten years before appearing in public. They played both female and male parts—"sopranists" or "contraltists": it

---

[1] At any rate in the vocalized, so-called *organal* parts. How, then, was the "teneur" performed in notes of long duration? The word *organum* and the length of the notes suggests an organ (probably a *positive*), but this is only a hypothesis, and there are no texts to prove it.

[2] Cf. J.-J. Rousseau, *Dictionnaire de musique* 1767, art. *Voix:* "All the different diapasons arranged in order together have a range of nearly three octaves, usually divided into four parts, three of which, known as *Haute-contre, taille* and *basse* belong to the lower voices, the fourth only, called the *dessus*, being assigned to high-pitched voices." He defines "low" voices as being those of adult men, and high voices, those of women, eunuchs and children, as well as the male *falsetto* which he calls "the most disagreeable of all the timbres of the human voice."

was for the *castrato-contraltist* Guadagni that Gluck wrote the first version of *Orfeo* in Vienna. But in France the *castrati* were not liked.[1] When in 1774, Gluck revised for Paris his original 1762 version of *Orfeo*, he had to adapt the part for a normal tenor (Legros). It was in 1859 that Carvalho, the Director of the *Théâtre Lyrique* conceived the bizarre idea of entrusting the contralto version of the *castrato* part to a famous female singer, Pauline Viardot, thus making the part of Orpheus a *travesti*. Mme. Viardot's success in this rôle was no doubt partly responsible for the extension of this bizarre and irritating custom[2] which became widespread towards the end of the nineteenth century, so that not only Verdi, Chabrier and Richard Strauss adopted it, but even Debussy at one time was seriously considering entrusting the rôle of *Pelléas* to a woman![3]

A fair revenge for the Mysteries of the Middle Ages from which women were excluded, with the result that at the Mons *Passion* in 1501 the part of Mary Magdalene singing at her toilet was played by . . . . a priest!

The *castrati* disappeared about 1830. The last of them, Velluti, died in 1861 at the age of eighty long after he had retired (in 1829 the English, although they had granted him a generous pension three years before, showed their disapproval even at a time when his voice was becoming deeper).

The end of the epoch of the *castrati* coincided more or less with the establishment of the present standards in the technique of singing. And it should not be forgotten that these are not only recent in time, but still only apply to Western concert and operatic music. A popular audience today will still often prefer the "natural" voice of the music-hall artist to that of the highly trained operatic singer. To Eastern ears this careful "placing" of the voice, with its full volume and vibrato, is not only unfamiliar but actually displeasing. Their idea of good singing is singing with a flat, rather guttural voice: their style of voice production may not always be the same, but it never resembles

---

[1]Cf. J.-J. Rousseau, *Dictionnaire de Musique*, art. *Castrato:* "These men, who sing so well but without warmth or expression are, in the theatre, the most disagreeable actors in the world. They lose their voice at an early age, and become disgustingly fat. They speak and pronounce worse than ordinary men, and there are some letters, such as R, which they are quite unable to pronounce."

[2]The *travesti* was used in the eighteenth century for boys' parts for purely vocal reasons. Cherubino, in Mozart's *Figaro*, was created by Mme. Bussani, Bartolo's own wife . . . On the other hand, Yniold, in *Pelléas*, was first played by a boy. It is true that in Gluck's *Les Noces d'Hercule et Hébé* in 1747 Hercules and one of the Titans were sung by women, and Jupiter by a *castrato*! (See Prodhomme, *Gluck*, p. 53.)

[3]Vallas, *Claude Debussy et son temps*, 2nd Ed., p. 254. Debussy even auditioned for the part a woman singer, Mme. Raunay, who sang the part of Pelléas for him "with the voice of an old man with a hoarse voice, but full of passion", as he described it to Messager. It should be added that in the 1898 production of Maeterlinck's play, in London, for which Fauré had written incidental music, the part of Pelléas was actually played by Sarah Bernhardt! (Cf. *Mary Garden's Story*, p. 76.)

in any way our conception of what a "trained" voice should sound like. As for vibrato, they do not consider this, as we do, to be exclusively a way of imparting colour to the timbre of the voice; if they use it at all, it is only on certain specified notes, for purposes of ornamentation associated with a given style or repertory.[1]

We do not know much about the style of classical singing in the ancient world; but we are discovering every day enough points of similarity between the Oriental and the classical Greek conception of music to make it seem reasonably certain that their ideas about singing were also very similar. Greek singers, like many Orientals, were no doubt taught to stretch out their necks so as to produce a somewhat hoarse and flattened sound, as can clearly be seen from the illustration.

1. A singer of Ancient Greece. An amphora painting from second half of 6th century B.C. attributed to the Berlin Painter.

From the little we know about the Middle Ages, it seems likely that their methods of voice production were very similar. St. Augustine informs us categorically that it was "in the Oriental style" that St. Ambrosius taught the faithful in Milan to sing hymns and psalms after St. Hilarius of Poitiers, on his return from the East, had been the first to attempt an adaptation of this style.

Many Oriental conceptions persisted for a long time in plainsong. In the thirteenth century Jerome of Moravia drew up a catalogue of "harmonic flowers" which, he tells us, "govern all the notes in ecclesiastical chants".[2] He speaks of trills, vibrations and repercussions, and we are told that the French were particularly lavish with ornamentation (is this an anticipation of Couperin's ornamental style for harpsichord?), that words were governed by strict and complicated rules of *rubato*, and that there were three vocal registers—chest, throat and head—ranging from low to high —as had already been observed in some of the old Hindu treatises on the subject.[3] To make his meaning clear Fr. Jerome adds: "We call it a 'chest voice' when the notes are formed in the chest; a 'throat voice' when they

[1]We know that, as in Greek music, much Oriental vocal music is characterized by extremely small intervals for which there can be no place in the *vibrato* style affected by our singers, since they would be obscured and rendered indistinguishable by the "thickness" of the unconscious *vibrato*. We know, too, the importance in Eastern music of ornamentation whose character is completely altered by what we call the "placing" of the voice.

[2]de Coussemaker, *Scriptores*, I, 91.

[3]Cf. Vishou-Dharmottara, III, 18, cited by Daniélou and Bhatt, *Textes des Purana sur la théorie musicale*, 1959, I, p. 115.

are formed in the throat; and a 'head voice' when they are formed in the head." This is an example of the limpidity with which explanations are so often given in musical text-books, and this tradition is too strong to be dropped even in our own modern treatises.

To these Oriental "refinements" the West seems to have added long ago a certain element of coarseness. Pambon, in the fourth century, in anathematizing the monkish style of singing, involuntarily describes it for us. He calls for "an attitude of great contrition and not a piercing voice", pointing out that the former cannot be expressed by "bellowing like an ox". Jean Diacre compares to a chariot rolling downstairs "the booming of the deep and strident voices, like those of a lot of drunken barbarians", of the Franks chanting their liturgies. From which we may assume that, in the famous Gregorian "golden age", our ancestors must have made a lot of noise without caring much about the "delicate adjustments" of the *ictus* demanded by the modern theoretician. . . .

One of the oldest refinements of our solo singers seems to have been the cultivation of the falsetto voice. The moralists lost no opportunity of condemning the *voces femineae* of these church singers, though as yet there was no question of these being due to any physical abnormality. Aelred de Rievault, in his *Speculum caritatis*, inveighs against the effeminacy and affectations of these singers. His description throws some valuable light on the style of Romanesque singing, which makes it clear that the cult of vocal virtuosity was not, as is sometimes thought, exclusively a product of the late Italian Renaissance.

Nevertheless, it was then that it really started. From the preface to Caccini's *Nuove Musiche* it is clear that Italian singers of the great humanist epoch already had a considerable repertory of *passaggi, trilli, gruppi, giri*, etc. And we have seen in a previous chapter (see p. 110) how a phrase of Monteverdi's which we admired, on paper, for its noble simplicity would have sounded (and we have the composer's word for it) in actual performance. Towards the end of the eighteenth century two opposing, yet complementary conceptions of the art of singing made their appearance; one, Italian, gave priority to the beauty of the voice, the other, French, was mainly concerned with correct diction.

The Italian *bel canto* was already a reality by the middle of the seventeenth century. And yet this was a paradox, for Italian supremacy, which began around the year 1600, was due to the invention of a style of musical declamation which, as Riemann points out, "consciously avoided any melodic distortion" in order the better to "represent" the movement of the words—hence the term *stile rappresentativo*. Opera, one of Italy's glories, can be defined, in its early stages, as the junction between this style (originally associated with the reform of the madrigal) and the various stage spectacles derived from the interludes, pastorales and ballets of the Franco-Italian Court.

The text-books invariably state as an accepted fact that opera owes its origin to the learned deliberations of a sort of Florentine musical Academy, the *Camerata* of Count Bardi, which gave birth simultaneously in 1600 to the first two operas in history, the two *Euridices* of Peri and Caccini, which illustrated the theories propounded in the *Camerata* by Vincenzo Galilei, father of the illustrious astronomer.

This version, however, contains so many improbabilities that in 1953 a Roman musicologist, Nino Pirrotta, decided to investigate the sources of this legend on the spot, and study the original text of Vincenzo Galilei's famous memorandum. By so doing he was able to discover one of the most monumental frauds ever recorded in the history of music—and, as we all know, there have been quite a number of these.[1]

The story is worth telling in some detail. The origin of music drama is undoubtedly one of the numerous episodes in the quarrel between the Ancients and the Moderns which has loomed largest in three centuries of literary and artistic history. In considering this affair, the first thing to note, is that Bardi, so far from being an ardent reformer was, on the contrary, a traditionalist, an anti-modernist and a staunch supporter of the ancients, while the *Camerata* was not a musical institution or even a regular assembly, but merely the occasional meeting place in a private house of a few enlightened humanists who discussed every subject under the sun including, but only incidentally, music.

In 1581 the chief musical member of this circle, Vincenzo Galilei, published the work to which everyone refers, but without having read it, the *Dialogo della musica antica e moderna*. This consisted mainly of philological discussions on the interpretation of ancient authors, and mathematical and acoustical demonstrations of the various scales. Incidentally, however, the author discusses the madrigal, which he considers to be the essential form of music. He does not wish to abolish it, but to renovate it, and for that purpose he advocates the monodic form, without, however, claiming to have invented it, but accepting it as an idea already put forward by the celebrated Swiss theoretician Glarean, and vouched for by the Ancients. He makes no reference to music drama, confining himself to this one subject. Monody, it should be noted, already existed and had been practised for a long time, both in France and in Italy where it was customary

---

[1] *Temperamenti e tendenze nella Camerata fiorentina*, in "Le manifestazioni culturali dell' Accademia Nazionale di Santa Cecilia", Atena-Roma, 1953. See also: *Tragédie et comédie dans la Camerata fiorentina*, in *Musique et poésie au XVIe. siècle*, Paris, C.N.R.S., 1954. The present writer published in *L'Education Musicale*, June 1955, under the title of *La Camerata florentine et la naissance de l'Opéra* an analytical summary of Pirrotta's paper, extracts from which have been included in this chapter.

to sing *villanelles, villottas, canzonettas* or other derivatives of the *frottola*, accompanied by one or more instruments, generally the lute.

Shortly afterwards Galilei, abandoning theory for practice, published two monodic songs (which have been lost) accompanied by viols: *Il conte Ugolino*, and some extracts from the *Lamentations of Jeremiah*. Then, in 1587, he returned to the traditional polyphonic madrigal, and published his second book of madrigals in this usual form. Bardi himself did not believe the madrigal could be reformed, and in his *Address to Caccini* he speaks of this as a Utopia which could only be attained very gradually in a distant future. He was not far wrong: the true spiritual offspring of Galilei are the last three books of Monteverdi's madrigals, which appeared some thirty-five years later.

The activities of Bardi's *Camerata* ended here. They seem, moreover, to have been confined to a period between 1577 and 1582. When they ceased in that year, there had never been any discussion of the theatre or of music drama. And yet in 1581, in France, Balthasar de Beaujoyeux had already staged a performance of *Le Ballet Comique de la Reine* which, except for recitative, contained all the elements of the opera of the future.

In 1587 a new prince came to power in Florence. The new ruler was a political adversary of Bardi, who then ceased to have any influence, faded from the scene and was finally, in 1592, exiled to Rome. In the meantime, however, his former secretary, the singer Caccini, who until then was practically unknown, revealed himself as a composer and, like Galilei, wrote in 1589 some monodic madrigals which attracted no attention. We shall return to him later.

The "affaire Bardi" was now over: end of the first act.

The second act transports us around 1590 from the camp of the Ancients to that of the Moderns. The latter, unlike the former, were not interested in the madrigal, but in the theatre. Their aim was not to re-discover the style of the Ancients, but to "follow the fashion"—and the greatest novelties at that time were the musical *divertissement* and the French Court Ballet. Like their predecessors, they used to meet as a group in the house of another nobleman, Jacopo Corsi. Corsi enjoyed the favours of the Prince which were now denied to Bardi. The two *grand seigneurs* detested one another, and their entourage followed suit. Nothing therefore, could be further from the truth than to pretend that the Corsi *salon* was merely a resuscitation of the Bardi *Camerata*. Furthermore, its members were not the same. Now they included Cavalieri and Peri, with incidental visits of others such as Monteverdi and Tasso.

The first to join was Cavalieri. He was a man of action, impresario and choreographer —not a singer, like Caccini. As a good courtier he was in 1588 appointed overseer to the Grand Duke. He took as his model the ballets at the Court of France, and on that model organized for Corsi in 1590-91 a performance of Tasso's *L'Aminta* with musical interludes; later, he wrote two pastorales (now lost) *Il Satiro* and *La Disperazione di Filena*. In 1594 another, younger musician, Peri, followed his example with a pastorale *Dafne* with words by Rinuccini.

But Peri, who was a singer, was one of Caccini's first disciples. This he didn't forget, and when in 1600 he was commissioned by Corsi and Rinuccini to write the music for *Euridice* to be performed at the Pitti Palace, and Cavalieri was at the same time preparing his *Rappresentazione di Anima e di Corpo* for the Oratory of St. Filippo Neri, the two muscians must have profited from their knowledge of the madrigals of Caccini, sole survivor of the rival coterie. These two works of Cavalieri and Peri are like twins, conceived in the same spirit, in the same atmosphere and under the same auspices. Caccini, still faithful to the now dethroned Bardi, was cold-shouldered. And so almost simultaneously, the first oratorio and the first opera came into being—eighteen years after the dissolution of Bardi's *Camerata*!

End of act two. And now for the third and last act. We have to go back, if not to Bardi, at least to his faithful Caccini, who had been deeply hurt by the success of Peri's *Euridice*. He considered himself to be the inventor of the *stile rappresentativo* and, although he had made no contribution to the theatre, he felt that he had been robbed. To assert his rights, he returned to Rinuccini's *Euridice*, which had served Peri for his libretto, and in his turn set it once again to music. He then lost no time in revising his 1589 monodic madrigals, to which he added some new ones, publishing the whole collection under the challenging title of *Nuove Musiche*. Assisted by Bardi's son, he then went about telling everybody that the new form of opera, which was having such success everywhere, had its origin in Bardi's salon—and to such good purpose that this has always been believed to be true up to the present day.

Some thirty years after the invention of the *stile rappresentativo*, Monteverdi perfected, in his turn, a new style of recitative which he called *stilo concitato* ("agitated style"). This was a kind of free declamation, of an ardent and sustained nature, on a single written note, with no bar lines, one of the finest examples of which is to be found in the celebrated *Lettera amorosa* in the 7th book of madrigals.

And so, for the Italians of the heroic period of opera, in the words of Caccini: "the most important elements in music are language and rhythm, and only after them, sound". The advent of Neapolitan opera, however, of which the founder was Alessandro Scarlatti, completely reversed this valuation. The recitative, sacrificed musically, became simply a link between the arias, and the words merely a pretext for melodies which could be interchangeable; the *passaggi*, which Caccini cultivated, though he disapproved of their abuse, now became of the first importance. Famous teachers wrote carefully calculated exercises to develop the voice and extend its register. It is said that Porpora, having undertaken, in 1719, the vocal training of the celebrated *castrato* Caffarelli (whose real name was Gaetano Majorano) made him study for five years without allowing him to sing anything, except a few exercises all contained on a single sheet of paper. After this, he is reported to have said: "Now you can go, my son; there is nothing more I can teach you; you are the world's finest singer."[1]

The *bel canto* thus became a veritable cult of the voice for its own sake, independently of musical content or any connection between the music and the words. Reynaldo Hahn defined its rules as follows: "*Bel canto* was not concerned with the spiritual interpretation of a work, but with achieving absolute perfection in singing, in which vocal clarity and agility and melodic phrasing were all important, as well as an infinite variety of tone colour and an irreproachable purity of pronunciation; in a word, its aim was to extract from the vocal organ, independently of any emotional factors, the highest possible degree of material satisfaction in terms of sheer beauty of sound. It was thought that the pleasure afforded by a beautiful and well-trained voice was all that was needed in the best interests of music and to arouse emotions in the hearer."

By the middle of the eighteenth century this conception began to be misinterpreted and became an excuse for mere vocal acrobatics. As an example: the famous "F.'s in *alt.*" which Mozart wrote for the part of the Queen of the Night. Soon they became the sole ideal of a whole generation. Berlioz derided the fashion in a chapter of his *A travers chants* under the expressive title of "The little-dog school". (*L'Ecole du petit chien.*) "These high F.'s," he writes, "are about as agreeable as the squeal of a little dog who has had his paw trodden on." Despite these excesses—or perhaps because of them—the Italian style of singing, which had deliberately refrained from identifying itself with music, enjoyed all through the nineteenth century an extraordinary vogue and the names of the great singers of that epoch are still surrounded by the halo of a quasi-mystical legend.[2]

---

[1]Fétis, *Biographie universelle des musiciens*, art. *Majorano*. These famous exercises by Porpora have been preserved, but never published, by several generations of singing teachers. Joseph Noyon, choir-master of Saint-Honoré d'Eylau, showed me a copy which he had only been able to obtain on condition that it would never be published.

[2]It is interesting to speculate on the future prospects of a lyric theatre in which, so far as modern music is concerned, some critics seem to think that anything that resembles singing is a "concession", or an "impurity". We offer for their consideration the following ingenuous sentence written by a pupil, who, after studying the works of critics of this school, summed up what he had learned from them as follows: "In the nineteenth century singing in opera attained a high degree of development. In order to remedy this decadence. . . . etc." The blunder of a pupil is sometimes the best criticism of the stupidity of professionals. . . .

Until the Revolution, at least, the French conception of what singing should be was very different. Singing for the sake of singing was something that the French could not tolerate. What they looked for, above all, was intelligence and an expressive diction. "Real song," wrote Béthisy de Mézières in 1760, "is only the confirmation of the sense of the words." Michel de Pures, in 1668, "would just as soon hear an actor who stutters or see a lame man dance" as listen to a singer "who eats his words, or fails to make what he is singing intelligible". Hence the enormous importance attached to recitative in all French writings about opera. Bérard, in 1755, devoted pages to showing how consonants should be pronounced, doubling them if necessary according to the meaning of the words, sometimes "clearly and gently", sometimes "harshly and roughly . . . wherever there is any suggestion of passion". But until the middle of the eighteenth century, not a word about what is known today as "vocal technique".

It was not until 1741 that a French savant, Ferrein, discovered the vocal chords and explained the nature of phonotation.[1] Yet in 1767 Rousseau in his *Dictionary* repeated the old theory according to which both the singing and the speaking voice, so far as their actual sound is concerned, are produced in the glottis, whereas their undulation is caused by a movement of the whole larynx. In his *Code de Musique pratique* (1760) Rameau was the first, in France at all events, to speak not only of musical declamation, but of actual vocal exercises to increase its flexibility.

The Conservatoire, under Cherubini, naturally taught the Italian style of singing. The last century produced a large number of great singers, both French and Italian; but the difference in their respective styles gradually became less marked, to the detriment of the traditional French respect for the text, which was already frequently ignored in the theatre and seems today—especially in France—to have been transferred to the sphere of the concert-hall.

It is legitimate to suppose that our present system of "placing" the voice did not come into being until the very end of the eighteenth century, and that our ancestors would no doubt have admired the progress made as regards *timbre* and range; but they might also have thought that this was too high a price to pay if the result was to make the text incomprehensible, or at any rate to discourage that meticulous study of the text which was an art common to both opera singers and actors.

One of the most singular examples of this culpable indifference with regard to the text is the doctrine of "vocal compensation", which consists in changing the sound of

[1]His memorandum entitled *De la formation de la voix de l'homme*, published in the *Histoire de l'Académie Royale des Sciences* excited great controversy. The term "vocal chords", moreover, is liable to be misunderstood. Did not a singer complain one day that "*all* her vocal chords were tired?"

certain vowels, not in order to ensure their correct pronunciation, but so as to adapt them to the *tessitura* of the voice and thus guarantee an equality of *timbre* which might be adversely affected by a correct pronunciation. It is scarcely surprising, then, that when this kind of teaching is accepted so many singers, and especially women, are completely unintelligible on the stage. Our ancestors would doubtless have considered this theory quite as monstrous as the practice of singing, instead of "acting" recitative. The tradition here, no longer observed in France, has been preserved in Italy and in Vienna. The French language used at one time to have the equivalent.[1] In Rousseau's *Dictionary* the word *"Chanteur"* appears, not under the letter C, but under A together with *"Acteur"*. This perhaps is the answer to those seeking a cure for the disfavour into which the lyric theatre has fallen today.

[1]It is known that Lully modelled his recitatives on the style of declamation of La Champmeslé (famous actress who excelled in the tragedies of Racine). Since, unfortunately, we have no recordings of La Champmeslé, we can amuse ourselves by reconstituting her declamation from Lully's recitative. The result is very curious, and shows us how each line, in classical diction, was dissected, analysed and freely modulated, though emphasis was not avoided. And this provides us with the key to all the quarrels with regard to recitative in opera that raged throughout the seventeenth and eighteenth centuries—besides showing us the way in which it should be interpreted at the present time. We shall be reverting to this subject later.

22

Paganini's "Horns", or the Virtuoso

—Signor, I am a virtuoso.

—I've nothing for you.

—That's not what I'm asking. But since I go in a bit for music and dancing. . . .

This dialogue in Molière's *Le Sicilien*, so the etymological dictionaries inform us, marks the first appearance in the French language, in the year 1664, of the word "virtuoso". "A man of exceptional merit," they add, the allusion being to Madame de Sévigné and the Italian *virtuoso*. That the term "virtuosity" should now have acquired the meaning, more or less, of being able to play music at record speed, throws a somewhat curious light on the standards of musical taste of our ancestors.[1] Although the word may date only from the seventeenth century, the character of the virtuoso, as portrayed in several celebrated comedies, is as old as that of the singer. . . .

Examples are to be found as far back as the Egypt of the Pharaohs, as we have seen in Chapter 14. Since they were privileged to frequent the company of Kings and to attract their attention, it was inevitable that both flautists and singers, flattered by compliments and applause, should have tended to forget their original status of being sacred "interpreters"—interpreters of the Deity, it should be remembered, not of the composer—and have attributed to themselves qualities only too likely to give them swollen heads. Phaedrus records that a *princeps tibicen*, i.e., a first tibia player,[2] returning to the platform after having been long in retirement, heard the chorus singing: "Rejoice, Rome, thy Prince is safe." Convinced that these words could only apply to him, he bowed and distributed kisses; and when at last he was with difficulty made to realize his mistake, he flew into a rage and, before leaving the platform, hurled his shoes at the jeering crowd.[3]

[1] I am reminded of the story of the pupil who was rebuked by his teacher for playing a piece too fast. "But," he replied in surprise, "since I *can* do it. . . .?"

[2] The equivalent of the Greek *aulos*. It is often translated "flute", which is quite incorrect, as both the *aulos* and the *tibia* were reed instruments.

[3] The same thing happened in Warsaw some years ago to a celebrated pianist who entered the hall at the same time as Queen Elizabeth of the Belgians, and could not for a long time believe that the ovation she heard was not for her.

Nevertheless, between antiquity and the nineteenth century such incidents are rare. This is because, as we have seen, the "concert", with its artificial atmosphere—and above all the "solo" recital designed for the glorification of the executant, did not yet exist. Instrumentalists, when they were not merely humble artisans employed in the theatre or church, were nearly all composers first and foremost, and it was in this capacity that they came before the public. The most celebrated among them performed mainly in private houses, and were often asked by amateurs to submit to all kinds of strange tests to prove their skill, and were generally ready to stake their reputation on the result. Thus we find Handel excelling at the organ, and Scarlatti at the harpsichord. In 1717 a contest of this kind was arranged between J.-S. Bach and Louis Marchand by the Dresden Kapellmeister, Volumier. On the appointed day Bach was there, in the salon of a minister where the encounter was to have taken place. Marchand, however, being not at all anxious to affront the giant, had departed in haste that morning by special coach.

The virtuoso "recital" dates from only a little over a hundred years ago. Liszt, it would seem, was the first artist who dared to give a concert entirely by himself, and this enterprise at first described as a "concerto-solo" or "mono-concert", was considered extravagant by a writer in *La France musicale* of April 21, 1844, who expressed himself as follows: "we do not imagine that there are many pianists who would dispute his invention of the mono-concert. It requires the audacity of a Liszt to attempt such a thing, and the immensity of his talent to ensure its success."

It must be admitted that the way in which concerts were usually conducted seemed to bear out this prophecy. . . . Except for the "academies" devoted to a single composer, concerts were for a long time in the nature of fashionable society gatherings, advertised in a manner suggestive of the circus or of some sort of school entertainment. The style in which Leopold Mozart announced the exhibition in Frankfurt on August 30, 1763, of his two prodigies, seems to us today not only startling, but slightly shocking—and could equally well have served to introduce a performing monkey.[1]

"Today, Tuesday, August 30, the last concert—and this time positively the last—will take place at six o'clock in the evening at the Scharf Concert Hall. At this concert will appear the little girl, who is in her twelfth year, and the little boy who is not yet seven. Not only will they both play concertos on the harpsichord or piano—the little girl will play some of the most difficult pieces by the great masters—but the little boy will, in addition, play a concerto on the violin. He will also accompany symphonies on

---

[1]For the full text of this announcement, see Saint-Foix and Wyzewa, *Mozart*, I, p. 32.

the piano [sic], and play on a piano after the keys have been covered with a cloth as perfectly as if he could see the keys. Not only that, but he will also recognize, without ever making a mistake, and at a distance, any notes played alone or in chords on a piano or any other instrument, including bells, glasses, musical boxes, etc. Finally, he will improvise freely (as long as you wish to hear him and in any key you like to suggest, even the most difficult ones) not only on the piano, but also on the organ, so as to show that he knows also how to play the organ, which is very different from the piano. Tickets, price one thaler, can be obtained at the Inn of the Golden Lion."

Of a similar nature was the announcement in London on June 2, 1824, of a benefit concert for "Master Liszt, aged twelve years, a Native of Hungary". "Mr. Liszt," trumpeted the poster in huge letters, "will execute on the new piano-forte, patented by Sebastien Erard, a Concerto by Hummel, some new Variations by Winkler, and, in addition to the published programme, will improvise on a theme which Mr. Liszt will ask some member of the amiable company to propose to him." After this, the poster, in smaller characters, proceeded to announce the items of the programme.

Seventeen years later, M. Nicolas-Joseph Franck, of Liège, very nearly ruined, according to Leon Vallas, the budding career of his son César Auguste, in his attempt to out-do the "clumsy verbiage of the commercial traveller".

We have already referred to the haphazard, mixed-bag type of programme which was almost universal in the last century, in which several performers took part, both singers and instrumentalists. A typical example is the programme organized at the Salle Pleyel on February 26, 1832, by "M. Frédéric Chopin, de Varsovie" to introduce himself to the Parisian public. After a Beethoven quintet, in which he took no part, and a vocal duet, the young *maestro* then came on to play his Concerto in F minor (no mention in the programme of an orchestra). Mademoiselle Tomeoni then sang an aria, after which Chopin appeared again, this time accompanied by five other pianists, to play Kalkbrenner's *La Grande Polonaise*, with Introduction and March, for six pianos. "There was one very big piano," wrote Chopin a few days later, "which Kalkbrenner played on, and a very small one for me." After this Mademoiselle Isambert sang some songs, followed by an oboe solo; and finally Chopin came back to play his variations on *La ci darem la mano*.

But perhaps of all these astounding concerts the palm should be awarded to the programme reproduced here (see next page), one of a series in which César Franck took part regularly, between 1845 and 1863 at the *Institut Musical* ar Orleans.[1]

---

[1]Cf. René Berthelot, *Une page ignorée de la vie de Franck*, Revue Internationale de Musique, No. 10, 1951. The documents discovered by Berthelot were used by Vallas, without indicating their source, in his *Véritable histoire de César Franck*, 1955.

INSTITUT MUSICAL.

D'ORLÉANS.

VINGT-TROISIÈME ANNÉE.

5ᵉ CONCERT. — LUNDI 30 MARS 1857.

PROGRAMME.

1ʳᵉ PARTIE

1ᵒ Ouverture de **Guillaume Tell.** — ROSSINI

2ᵒ { **L'Insomnie,** chantes par M. *Jules* MERCIER. — NADAUD
{ **Le Clocheteur de nuit,** — CLAPISSON

3ᵒ Fantaisie mélodique sur des motifs de la **Favorite**, exécutée sur le violon et composée par — AMÉDÉE DUBOIS

4ᵒ Duo de l'**Éclair**, chanté par Mˡˡᵉ LEFEBVRE et M. *Jules* MERCIER. — HALÉVY

5ᵒ **Hymne à la Vierge**, trio pour violon, orgue et violoncelle, exécuté par MM. DUBOIS, FRANCK et LASALLE. — LEFÉBURE-VÉLY

6ᵒ Sicilienne des **Vêpres siciliennes**, chantée par Mˡˡᵉ LEFEBVRE. — VERDI

7ᵒ { **Histoire d'un sou,** chansonnettes chantées par M. J. MERCIER. — CLAPISSON
{ **La fille de ma portière,** — E. LHUILLIER

2ᵉ PARTIE

8ᵒ Ouverture de **Maria di Rohan,** — DONIZETTI

9ᵒ Élégie pastorale, exécutée sur le violon par M. DUBOIS. — A. DUBOIS

10ᵒ Air du **Domino noir**, chanté par Mˡˡᵉ LEFEBVRE. — AUBER

11ᵒ **Souvenir d'Auvergne**, grande scène exécutée sur le violon par M. DUBOIS. — A. DUBOIS

12ᵒ { **Le Rouet,** romance, } chantés par Mˡˡᵉ LEFEBVRE — A. NIBELLE
{ **Expliquez-vous,** couplets }
{ du Père-Gaillard, — REBER

13ᵒ { **Paris,** } chansonnettes chantées par M. J. MERCIER. — NADAUD
{ **La Pluie,** }

Le Piano sera tenu par M. César FRANCK.

La Quête au profit des pauvres sera faite entre la 1ʳᵉ et la 2ᵉ partie.

Imp. de Pagnerre.

12. Programme of a concert given by César Franck at Orleans in 1857.
Author's collection.

To judge in their proper perspective these concerts, so different from our own today, two points should be borne in mind.

The first is that most of the instruments we use today have only quite recently acquired the shape and timbre with which we are familiar; and the second is that, even where identical instruments are concerned, technique has advanced so enormously in the last hundred years that Paganini was believed to be inspired by the devil when performing acrobatics which any advanced student today would think nothing of.

Take, for example, the case of the piano. To say that this instrument replaced the harpsichord in the course of the eighteenth century does not mean that there was an abrupt transition from one world of sound to another. No doubt the first pianos with hammers were made by Cristofori in 1711, while the celebrated organ-builder Solbermann was able to introduce J.-S. Bach to his first "piano-fortes"—though the great man regarded them with some suspicion. But the principle of the modern piano's mechanism, known as "double escapement", was not perfected by Sébastien Erard until 1823; Beethoven's Op. 111, the "Hammerklavier", was written in 1822. We know that the pianos Mozart used were of the "square piano" type, with a thin, jangly tone, examples of which are still to be found in some forgotten attics. But it is difficult to realize that it was at the keyboard of one of these old-fashioned instruments that Liszt was portrayed in a print as late as 1824 during a triumphal series of concerts he gave in London (Plate XXVI); that Prince Radziwill's piano, at which Chopin composed his F minor Concerto, was still fitted with knee-, instead of foot-pedals; or that at the time of the French Revolution Grétry, like the young Beethoven, used to compose his operas at the minute keyboard of a portable clavichord.

The fact is that "ancient instruments" were often still in use long after the appearance of their successors. Bach was still writing for the lute and the *viola da gamba* even in such important works as the *Passions*. The violin family did not, historically speaking, represent an improved form of viol, but was rather an alien rival which existed for nearly two centuries side by side with the viol family, endeavouring to supplant it, but only succeeding in doing so after a long and bitter struggle: in France, especially, the violin, an instrument for dancing, was as much looked down upon by musicians as the accordion today. It was, moreover, a former dancer, Jean-Marie Leclair (who was assassinated in his own garden in 1765) who was the first, at any rate the first soloist, to ensure a place for his instrument in the literature of French music.

In 1740, four years after the death of Stradivarius, the viol family still had its ardent supporters, so much so that an amateur of these instruments, Hubert Le Blanc, a Doctor of Law, was able to write and publish in Amsterdam a violent pamphlet entitled:

Défense de la basse de viole contre les entreprises du violon et les prétentions du violoncel.[1] Fétis, who delighted in racy stories, even though they are not always strictly authentic, relates that the author's concern for the preservation of his favourite instrument was so great that when he heard from his publisher that his M.S. was accepted, "he was so transported with delight that he left for Holland in the state in which he was when he received the good news—namely, in his dressing-gown and slippers, with a night-cap on his head."

Wind instruments, too, have only been as we know them today for a comparatively short time. Until the seventeenth century it was only possible to play on the flute, whether straight or *traversière*, the notes corresponding to each hole, one for each finger at the most. To obtain accidentals the player had to employ "forked" fingerings, which was not only awkward but from the point of view of intonation left much to be desired. The invention of keys, which extended the compass beyond the actual reach of the hand, was designed at first to enable the last hole, ("the little finger") to be moved further out. Quantz, the celebrated flautist of Frederick the Great, was the first to introduce a second key, and the discovery that the generalization of these keys would enable the emplacement of the holes to be independent of the position of the fingers was due to Theobald Boehm who died in 1881.

It was not until the eighteenth century that the harp, one of the most ancient instruments, had its range of tones extended so as to be able to play more than one note per string. A modest chromaticism was at first achieved by increasing the number of strings (as in Monteverdi's *Orfeo*). Until the nineteenth century, however, a harpist could only add sharps; it was the application by Erard in 1801 of Cousineau's invention, in 1782, of a double pedal movement that made it possible to play in every key. It is curious to note that Erard's work was based on the old "unequal temperament" scale: he wanted to prove, in order to defend himself against the attacks of his rival Naderman, that with his system a C sharp was not to be confused with a D flat, whereas the whole technique of the instrument, which has since been adapted to the equal temperament, is on the contrary based on the absolute identity of these two notes.

The transformations undergone by "brass" instruments are still more striking. Except for the trombone, the technique now in use as regards all the other instruments, is based on the invention (by the Englishman Clagget in 1790) of the valve, which makes it possible to play any combination of notes. It naturally took half a century for the invention to be developed, and even by the middle of last century it was often

---

[1] "A defence of the bass viol against the encroachments of the violin and the pretensions of the violoncello."

necessary, for each different key, to change the instrument, in the case of the trumpet, or to add a crook to the horn. To make it easier for the player (whose lip movements were the same whatever the key he was playing in) the wind parts were always transposed, so that the fundamental, "natural" sound of the instrument was always called "C". It was illogical, but convenient for the player, although the result was to turn score-reading into something of a puzzle.

It is nevertheless an absurdity that although the valve-system was by now in common use and the "key" of the instruments remained unchanged, no one saw that this convention no longer served any purpose, and it has been piously preserved up to the present time.[1]

Happily the trumpet had the good idea to remain in C major, but as the horn chose the key of F for its normal crook, you have to write middle C in the treble clef if you want it to play the F on the fourth line of the bass clef.

But, quite apart from the notation, before the invention of the valve composers had to choose very carefully what notes to use in any given key, and to refrain from writing rapid passages, which could be dangerous. It is for this reason that Beethoven's trumpets, like the kettle-drums, are generally only used in the tonic or the dominant. A typical example is to be found at the beginning of the Finale of the *Ninth Symphony*, where in order to obtain the shattering effect produced by the brass at the beginning of the *Presto* Beethoven had laboriously to combine two horns in B flat and two trumpets in D [the latter having changed instruments since the *Adagio*] with the result that the brilliantly conceived passage of rushing quavers is strangely interrupted by gaps that do not make sense musically; but when they are combined they coincide, more or less, with what the woodwind are playing at the same time. Most conductors today have the sense to re-establish the complete line, and our trumpet players, well-equipped with "valves" have no difficulty in performing it. I draw the attention of the purists to this little episode: someone is sure to talk about "respecting the original text", and will want the uncouth sounds of the primitive version restored as being "what the composer intended".

The trombone is the only instrument in the modern orchestra that has remained unchanged in all essentials since the Middle Ages. With one not very important exception—the disappearance of a handle that used to be attached to the slide—there is no

[1]The same thing happened in the case of certain wood-wind instruments, e.g., the clarinet and *cor anglais*. As regards the latter, the reason for this still exists since the same instrumentalist often changes from an oboe in C to a cor anglais in F, using the same fingering. In the case of the clarinet uniformly in B flat, the system is as stupid as it is for the horn.

difference between a sackbut dating from the Hundred Years War and a trombone in our modern orchestra.

Without going quite so far back, the violin family, together with the trombone, are the only instruments in the modern orchestra whose construction and design, after going through a brief experimental period, have remained unchanged since the classical era: our soloists today are proud to play on instruments signed by Stradivarius or Guarnerius which, though dating from the beginning of the eighteenth century, are still just as "modern" as a violin made yesterday at Mirecourt or Angers.

And yet what would J.-S. Bach, violinist at the Court of Weimar, have thought if he had been asked to play the Szymanowski *Concerto*? Neither his right hand nor his left would have been able to give even an approximate rendering of the notes. . . .

Let us take the right hand first: the modern bow, with its convex stick and tightly sprung hair, only dates back to François Tourte, who died in 1835. This is why in Bach's violin sonatas there are so many chords of three or four notes which our violinists, however skilful, can only arpeggiate, and that with some difficulty. The old bow, which was concave and flexible, could easily play them across several strings at a time. On the other hand, the "bite" and virtuosity of which the modern bow is capable would have been quite beyond its capacity.

The left hand would have been equally ill at ease. It is true that Corette in 1738 mentions the seventh position, and Locatelli in his *Arte del Violino* (1733) the fourteenth on the E-string exclusively; but those were exceptions, theoretical rather than practical. The fourth was the highest position in common use. The finger-board was shorter, the bridge flatter, the neck narrower, and the chin-rest unknown—for the instrument was held against the chest. *Vibrato* was already practised in the seventeenth century (Mersenne describes it), but only exceptionally, while to attack a note from beneath or to slide with the same finger from one note to another, gypsy fashion, was looked upon in the eighteenth century as an "agrément" which added charm to the performance. Collectors of old gramophone records are surprised to hear more or less strident

13. A seventeenth-century violin and bow from an illustration in John Playford's *Brief Introduction to the skill of musick* (1654).

examples of this style of playing, and I remember as a child being horrified when for the first and only time I heard the Capet Quartet.

The art of violin-playing would, no doubt, not be what it is today had not, in 1799, a young nineteen-year-old Genoese occupied his forced leisure, on his return from a successful concert tour, during a whole year while Masséna was defending the city, by practising on his violin what he described as: "continuous exercises in difficulties of my own invention, all of which I mastered." When the guns ceased firing, Nicolo Paganini had composed his 24 *Capriccios* and was ready to astonish Europe.

This he did so successfully that, aided by his physical appearance (and also a keen sense of publicity), he was soon preceded in his triumphal tours from Parma to Warsaw by the most fantastic legends—which also helped his box-office receipts considerably. Women glanced furtively at his feet in search of a cloven hoof, and Heine was only being half ironical when he described him "in his black evening dress, with black waistcoat and tailcoat of sinister cut such as perhaps was *de rigueur* at the Court of Proserpine".[1]

All this idle gossip achieved its purpose so effectively that when Paganini died at Nice in 1837, and despite the fact that—after forbidding any composer to write a Requiem in his memory—he asked in his Will for a hundred Masses to be said by the Capuchin Order and recommended his soul "to the infinite mercy of Our Creator", the Bishop of Nice, Mgr. Galvano, none the less refused to allow him a religious burial.

It is true that the Bishop could have cited innumerable scandals in Paganini's private life, and that the report which Canon Caffarelli despatched after attending the musician on his death-bed was no doubt scarcely complimentary: according to Teresa Repetto, the old servant in attendance, the worthy prelate, entering the sickroom suddenly, could think of nothing better to say than: "Ah, Ah, Moussu Paganini, *a hura, es plus l'oura de sonna lo zon-zon*" (" ... this is hardly the time to be scraping your fiddle") a remark which had the immediate effect of restoring to the dying man enough strength to show his visitor the door. . . .

The body of the magician of the violin, fortunately embalmed, was thus denied burial for four years, during which it was the subject of innumerable lawsuits, and then wandered about for another thirty-four years until in the end it found, in Parma, a resting-place, which even then was not final, as the cemetery was transferred elsewhere in 1896. . . .

[1] R. de Saussine, *Paganini*, p. 143.

23

"Camargo's Neck", or The Ballerina

We mentioned in Chapter 15 how astonishing it would have seemed to one of our distant ancestors to go and buy a ticket in order to sit in a hall to listen to music. To do the same thing for the purpose of watching dancers going through their steps would certainly have appeared to him no less monstrous and insulting to the prestige of what was in his eyes the sacred art of the dance; and this view would certainly have been shared, so far as concerts were concerned, by any one for whom music, too, was a sacred art.

We saw (in Chapter 9) how the dance was originally inseparable from religious ritual, whether it was slow and solemn, like certain Cambodian dances, or frenzied, like the majority of African dances. The steps were regulated in accordance with a strict tradition, for to change the steps of a dance would have led the gods to unleash the same catastrophes which would have been provoked in ancient Greece had anyone dared to alter a "mode".

There were, it is true, spectators at these sacred dances, but not everyone was admitted, for the sacred dancers formed a veritable caste, and the coveted honour of being a spectator was reserved for a privileged few. In Rome the *salientes* belonged to a priestly category, as do in Islam the whirling dervishes. In Java dancers, even today, are selected and trained in special colleges, and form a most exclusive aristocracy.

The spectators at these dances were not just spectators: they were taking part in a ceremony. The dance was not for their amusement, but on their behalf. Everything that we have already said about the social aspects of religious music is true also of dancing.

The dance is often associated with the theatre; but the theatre, too, has a religious function to perform, by delegation. Whether it be Greek tragedy, Japanese *No*, or African *Glaou*, it all stems from the same conception. The dance is only incidentally an art; above all it is a cult.

And so, as with music, dancing was primarily addressed to the gods, then to the Kings, and finally to the dancer himself.

The idea of taking as an individual partner a "person of the opposite sex" is a very recent notion; the introduction of an erotic element was probably due to other reasons—

perhaps to flatter the ruler's baser instincts (cf. Herod and Salome). It may also have originated in the degradation of primitive dances in connection with fertility rites.

Though we hear a lot about the legendary "purity" of Greek classical art, we are apt to forget such things as the so-called "cordax" dance in which the dancers carried an enormous phallus made of cloth or similar material, and the "wasp" dance in which the dancing girl, pretending to look for an insect in her clothes, performed a regular "strip-tease" in the process. No doubt such excesses would account to some extent for the hostility towards dancing displayed by the Church from the earliest days of Christianity. The religious dances of the Middle Ages, on the other hand, to which we have already referred, were nearly always popular dances in which the people took part, and not a spectacle for them to look at. The dance of the Precentor of Sens, however, forms a curious exception.[1] There is no direct connection between the sacred dances of antiquity, still surviving in the East, and the modern "Ballet".

It would be equally difficult to say when dancing began to assume the character of a social pastime which it is today. "Ballroom" dancing was unknown in ancient Greek or Roman society. Only the country people, at weddings, or on public holidays such as the "Saturnalia" festivities, took part in communal dancing (cf. our carnival) which was partly an amusement and partly a religious or magic rite. Our own country dances are the direct descendants of these ancient and immemorial customs. The "art" dance, which we call "ballet", did not begin to make its appearance until, by a process of social evolution of which there were no signs until around the thirteenth century, the aristo-cracy, in its turn, began to want its own kind of dances.

Thus in 1285 (*circa*) Jacques Bretel describes how on festive occasions, at tournaments and public holidays, lords and ladies met in the great ball room to perform:

> Une carole[2] si très noble
> Que jusques en Constantinople
> Ni deça jusqu'à Compostelle
> Ne crois-je qu'on en vit plus belle

("A 'Carol' so noble that 'twixt Constantinople and Compostella, I doubt that any ever saw a finer.")

---

[1] See Chapter 9.

[2] The origin of the word *carole* has been the subject of long study. According to Lacroix-Novaro (*Revue de musicologie*, Feb. 1935) it was a term with magical connotations: the *caragolus* is a Celtic sorcerer. The circular ambulatory in churches was for a long time called a *carole*, as were many round dances. In English the word "carol" has many meanings and is even applied to Christian legends connected with the Christianization of the old *saturnalia*.

He has left us a detailed account of the "tournament at Chauvency" at which the festivities lasted from Monday to Friday, and describes how the ladies, holding hands, danced together while the "bachelors" looked on admiringly. Then one of the ladies would start to sing a refrain, but the dance was interrupted by a call to arms. It was resumed in the evening after the meal that followed the last joust. This time it was quite an elaborate ballet with a scenario, improvised on the spot by the ladies and their squires, interspersed with popular songs—*rondeaux* or "rondets de carole"—and enlivened by the "*jeu de chapelet*" (or crown of flowers) or the "*tour du pied*" and other games. One of the ladies in the company—"Madame de Lucembour"—was the ringleader and played the principal part in the proceedings (a precursor already of the future *danseuse étoile*) while the gentlemen competed for her favours in a succession of varied episodes. Having finally chosen one of the suitors she gave him her hand and led him away singing happily: "chantant l'emmène à grande joie". This was perhaps the first modern "ballet", sung and danced by the guests themselves, without any separation between spectators and participants.

From now on the dance entered into the life of "high society", accompanied either by singing or instrumental music. Some of the earliest ballet "*divertissements*" were given at the Court of Burgundy in the fifteenth century, often during a banquet—hence the term *entremets* originally applied to the dances presented on these occasions. One of the most famous *divertissements* of this kind no doubt was the banquet of the "Pheasant" offered in Lille in 1454 by Philippe le Bon soon after the capture of Constantinople by the Turks. On this occasion a woman dressed in white satin and riding on an elephant, representing the Church, sang a lament, and was followed by an effigy in the form of a gigantic pie containing twenty-eight musicians; at the end of the repast, a pheasant, with all its feathers on, was brought in over which all the knights present swore a solemn oath to accomplish some specified feat of arms, after which the festivities ended in a ball.

At the banquet of the Pheasant, the music was more important than the dance. Three years later, however, music was to play an important part in the "Peacock's Festival" in Tours, to which the Hungarian ambassadors were invited by Count Gaston IV de Foix. One of the attractions was a "mock tiger" breathing fire from its nostrils and bearing on its back six dancers from the Béarn. The third *entremets* was in the form of a mountain from which fountains gushed and on which children, dressed like savages, danced the "Mauresque", which was a very popular feature in fifteenth-century entertainment. Soon dancing was introduced into the theatre, by way of an interlude: e.g., in *La Passion* by Jean Michel at Angers in 1486, in another Passion, known as the

Semur in 1488, in the *Mystère du Vieil Testament* and the *Mystère de la Santa Margherita*. In all of them we find the *Mauresque*.

Nevertheless, before it was established definitely in the theatre, ballet had first of all to make its way via the banqueting hall and the ballroom in which the Court ballets were held.

We saw in Chapter 16 how in 1573 Catherine de Medicis provided in honour of the Polish Ambassadors an entertainment in which for the first time dancing was the main attraction. A contemporary engraving (see Plate XV) shows that the dancers performed in the middle of the hall, and not on the stage, or platform which was reserved for the guests of honour for whose benefit the ballet was being performed. We do not know the exact nature of the entertainment, but it seems clear that it was principally an exhibition of pure dancing. An important step forward was taken in 1581, when Henry III, on the occasion of the marriage of his favourite, the Duc de Joyeuse, engaged an Italian impresario Baltasarini, known as Baltazar de Beaujoyeulx, to produce a new form of entertainment. Baltazar enlisted the services of several musicians and conceived a special kind of scenario, known as *à tiroirs* (a play within a play), which enabled the story of Ulysses and his companions being bewitched by Circe to be presented, with all kinds of elaborate scenic devices, to the accompaniment of spoken recitative, songs and dances, which formed the backbone of the entertainment. This was the first "Court Ballet", the celebrated *Ballet comique de la Reine* (see Plate XVI). But this famous ballet was still only a Court entertainment devised for the benefit of some special guests of honour. As in the "ballet" of 1573 referred to above, the stage was reserved for the king and his suite. The other invited guests stood at the sides, while the action took place in the middle of the hall, with moving scenery mounted on wheels. The musicians and choir were hidden by the scenery; at a later date they took part in the action, as can be seen from the frequent stage directions, even in Molière's plays, such as "entry of the violinists, dancing" (cf. Plate XVII) or from amusing prints such as those depicting the ballet of the *Douairière de Billebahaut* in which the extraordinary fantasy of the decorators and costume designers is strikingly revealed. At first, the stage was merely a prolongation of the hall, as can be seen in the engraving by Jacques Callot representing *La Liberazione di Tirreno*, danced in Florence in 1616 (Plate XXVII), and it was not until the middle of the seventeenth century that the orchestra "pit", which at first merely served to separate the hall from the stage, came into use with the first real operas.

Opera, which is often believed to have been created out of nothing by the Florentine humanists (see Chapter 21) was in reality nothing but a transformation of the Franco-Italian Court Ballet. That is why ballet, from the first, has always had a prominent place in opera. Dancing was not just an extra *hors d'oeuvre* as it were, but the basis and whole *raison d'être* of the entertainment. It was not by chance that Lully, the renovator of French opera, was an ex-baladin, i.e., dancer. In addition to pure dancing, there was also the pantomime. In his "new-style" madrigals Monteverdi interpolates an episode on the deliverance of Jerusalem—*Il combattimento di Tancredi e Clorinda*—in which the narration is in the form of a musical recitative, while the protagonists, mime at length the action described, singing only occasionally the short passages of dialogue occurring in Tasso's text. Interludes of dancing between the scenes or acts of plays, and even operas, became more and more common; it may even be wondered whether Molière interpolated interludes of singing or dancing in his comedies, or whether some of them were not intended to be no more than a brilliant "linking" text to justify the sort of spectacle the object of which, in accordance with the taste of the day (and of the king), was primarily to give pleasure to the eyes and ears of the spectators.

It is noteworthy that until the end of the seventeenth century there was no such thing as a female "star" dancer, or *prima ballerina*. Whereas the glorification of the latter was a cardinal feature of nineteenth century ballet, so much so that the main function of the male dancers seemed to be restricted to carrying her about or providing a background for her, it was originally the male dancer who reigned supreme. Feminine rôles used to be played by men disguised and masked; later they were assumed by the great ladies of the Court, or even the Queen herself; thus, in 1664, the rôle of Proserpine in *Les amours déguisés* was played by the Queen surrounded by her companions which included on this occasion—O irony of Fate!—Mademoiselle de Lavallière and Madame de Montespan. The King, moreover, did the same; it is well known that he acquired his nickname *Le Roi Soleil* from having danced in this rôle. The first professional ballerinas did not make their appearance until 1680, in Lully's *Le Triomphe de l'Amour*. There were, indeed, some famous ballerinas in the eighteenth century, such as Marie Sallé or her rival Anne Camargo, celebrated by Verlaine.

> Ce vieux vin de Chypre est exquis;
> Moins, Camargo, que votre nuque.[1]

Equally famous, however, were the male dancers Vestris and Gardel, whereas in the nineteenth century all the famous dancers known to posterity were women.

In the Court Ballet the rôle of the composer was still a secondary one: he was more or less anonymous, and often, as in the music-hall today, there was a different composer

---

[1]A literal translation would be: "This old wine of Cyprus may be exquisite, but not so exquisite, Camargo, as the nape of your neck." Quotation from Verlaine's *Fêtes galantes*. (Translator's note.)

for each scene or tableau. Nevertheless, as early as the beginning of the seventeenth century musicians were no longer content with being mere accessories. Monteverdi took as much trouble over his sung ballets as over his madrigals; Peri, in adapting the "new-style" recitative to the dramatic Pastorale, emphasizes the purely musical aspect of the tragedy; while the humanists, both in Italy and in France, were dreaming, long before *Euridice*, of a "total" scenic spectacle embodying their quasi-mythical ideas about antiquity. Baïf, for instance, when he writes to the King in 1571 to explain the work of his Academy, says that he is reviving the dances of the Ancients as well as their songs and poetry.

Gradually music, at first treated as a mere pretext, came to acquire, by the sheer merit of the masterpieces it produced, a very different status. Towards the middle of the eighteenth century opera ceased to be a ballet interspersed with arias and recitatives, and became a purely musical entertainment. Mozart asserted the pre-eminence of the music over the other ingredients of the spectacle, while Gluck, on the other hand, gave priority to the action which, he said, should take precedence over both music and the dance. The latter, nevertheless, was still an essential element in music-drama. It no more aspired to break away from opera than opera was prepared to do without ballet. It was then that Noverre appeared upon the scene.

Born in Paris in 1727 of a Protestant family, Jean-Georges Noverre started at the age of eighteen as an obscure member of the corps de ballet in a troupe organized by Frederick II to introduce an Italian *danseuse* who had taken the King's fancy. On his return to France two years later, he was engaged at the Théâtre de la Foire Saint-Laurent, where he put on a Chinese ballet which had considerable success, with all sorts of theatrical effects, pantomimes, changes of scene, etc.: this marked the beginning of the story ballet ["*ballet d'action*"].

It was at these "Fair" theatres that the pantomime was first introduced, since the Opera jealously forbade any singing at such theatres. They therefore had the idea of making the actors mime the action, to the accompaniment of well-known tunes, the words of which explained the action. Noverre transported this form of pantomime into the realm of the dance. His first "*ballets-pantomimes*" paid little attention to the music, which generally consisted of a succession of airs borrowed from already existing operas, symphonies or vaudevilles. (Diaghilev was to adopt this system in, for example, *Les Sylphides*.) Gluck was probably the first to write music for a completely independent ballet: *Don Juan ou le Festin de Pierre*, produced in Vienna in 1761 on a theme inspired by Tirso de Molina and Molière; it was in three acts, with thirty separate numbers held together by a certain degree of tonal and even thematic unity. The *ballet d'action* had hitherto been based on a series of different pieces, artificially juxtaposed, and it was customary to divide it into separate "numbers" corresponding to individual pieces of music—a custom which lasted until the beginning of the twentieth century—which of course gave great satisfaction to the *danseuse étoile*, and accounts for the vogue of the solo "variation".

Until the middle of the nineteenth century dancers were encumbered by their heavy costumes. In Lully's days, the men were often in short petticoat-breeches, with ribbons and feathers in their hats, the women in long, full skirts (Plate XXVIII). La Camargo was the first to appear in a short skirt which revealed the calf of the leg, which created something of a scandal (Plate XXIX), but it enabled her to undertake feats of "elevation", involving leaps and *entrechats* which had hitherto only been performed by men. Others naturally followed her example, but a rather comic incident threatened to put an end to this fashion when one day a short-skirted dancer caught her skirt in a piece of projecting scenery and tore it. The police intervened, and the upshot of it all was a solemn regulation forbidding women dancers to appear on the stage without a "precautionary" undergarment.[1]

It was not until 1841 that the "tutu", a creation of the Romantic movement, definitely came to its own in the second act of *Giselle*. At first it was long and straight, as worn by Taglioni in *La Sylphide* in 1832 (Plate XXX), but gradually became shorter and shorter until it was (as we know it today) little more than a frill round the hips, thus giving complete freedom to the legs and creating a new criterion by which to judge a dancer's technique.

In the meantime steps and positions were classified in great detail according to the theories of Carlo Blasis, a pupil of Gardel, based on the guiding principles laid down by Noverre in his *Lettres sur la danse*. In 1832 Marie Taglioni revolutionized feminine dancing technique by appearing one day in a ballet on her "points". Like so many discoveries, this was more or less due to chance: La Taglioni used to practise steps in this way in private, and never thought the method could have any artistic merit until one day a friend encouraged her to try it in public on the stage. Somewhat apprehensively she agreed to do this "as an experiment", without ever suspecting that the innovation would be so enthusiastically received.

Romantic ballet did not as yet, though composers were now writing for it, call for music of very high quality. All that was required was a straightforward rhythm in

---

[1]The name "precaution" was for a long time after applied to this garment. It was said that Camargo, when asked if she wore one, replied that "without this precaution she would never dare appear in public"—and so it got its name.

regular sections of from eight to sixteen bars such as we find in Adolphe Adam's *Giselle* or, with a little more liveliness and fantasy, in Léo Delibes's *Sylvia* or *Coppélia*. When in 1882 Edouard Lalo wrote for *Namouna* music of a symphonic nature in separate movements hitherto unknown in the sphere of ballet music, it surprised nobody that this turned out to be one of the most sensational failures in choreographic history.

In the meantime operatic ballet had been undergoing other vicissitudes. When Gluck in his day had insisted that dramatic action should take precedence over music and the dance, he certainly had no more intention of minimizing the former than of abandoning the latter; nevertheless his theories, once they had been generally adopted, soon had the opposite result to what he had intended. He wanted to make dancing a more integral part of the action, and consequently to do away with ballets which had no logical connection with the drama on the stage. But by neglecting the first of these conditions and concentrating on the second, the result was that dancing ceased to be introduced at every moment to supplement the action, so that in the end it was practically dispensed with altogether. But since the public regretted the disappearance of ballet, which it looked upon as its "own", the latter was brought back again, but, as it were, as an "adjunct" to the action to which it was linked by the simplest artifices. Thus Mephistopheles takes Faust to see the Walpurgis night ceremonies with the sole object of placing virtually a whole act at the disposal of the choreographer. Again, in order to seduce Manon, for whom Des Grieux had refused to engage the Opera Ballet to perform at his house, another suitor offers her a seat on the stage at Cours-la-Reine where the public forgets all about her, while the ballet is going through its evolutions without paying any more attention to her than the spectator. In short, all this was exactly the opposite of what Gluck had advocated. With the advent of Wagner all this changed; the remedy in his eyes was simple: no more ballet in opera. Only once did he make a concession to the contemporary fashion—in the Venusberg music in the revised version of *Tannhäuser* produced at the Paris Opera, and to meet the expressed wishes of the Emperor Napoleon III. He agreed, then, to have a ballet to start with, before the drama proper began, but obstinately refused to place it in the middle of the second act for the benefit of the members of the Jockey Club who only went to the Opera for the sake of the ballet and never arrived on time. We know the price he had to pay for this decision. . . .

So great was Wagner's influence that, after him, the divorce between opera and ballet seemed irrevocable. Neither Albert Roussel's sumptuous "opera-ballet" *Padmâvati* nor Arthur Honegger's *Jeanne au bûcher*, in which the spoken word, song and dance were ingeniously mingled, had any lasting influence: from now on opera ceased to be an "Academy of music and dancing", and became just an "academy", in which music and dancing alternate.

But at least the dance was now once again allied with music. No one did more to bring this about than Serge Diaghilev. By one of those paradoxes in which history abounds, the *Russian Ballet* (largely centred on Paris), was about to renovate the decadent French ballet which, half a century earlier, had created the Russian ballet.

For it was a choreographer from Marseilles, prophetically named Marius Petipa, who was summoned to St. Petersburg in 1847 and there had organized and developed the Imperial ballet which, thanks to him, became one of the foremost in Europe. As for Diaghilev, he was not, as was sometimes thought, a musician,[1] and his interest in the dance developed comparatively late in life. Belonging to an old and semi-noble family, having failed to realize his musical ambitions, it was in the sphere of painting that he gave evidence of his rare gifts as an "*animateur*"; organizing exhibitions and founding a review, *The World of Art*, which was in existence from 1898 to 1904, and played an important part in Russian artistic life. He was for a time attached to the administrative staff of the Imperial theatres, but had to relinquish his post after failing in his efforts to persuade the management to entrust the *décors* of the ballet *Sylvia* to real artists instead of to specialized artisans.

The incident is significant. In *The World of Art*, which though mainly concerned with the plastic arts yet from time to time contained articles on music or the theatre, the ballet had never been discussed, certainly not before 1902. It was in revenge for the *Sylvia* incident that Diaghilev first began to show any interest in it.

In 1906 he made his first contacts with Western Europe, organizing exhibitions and a "Russian season", first at the *Salon d'Automne* in Paris, and later in Berlin. It was in Paris that he was encouraged to extend his activities from painting to music, and in 1907 he organized a series of concerts at the Grand Palais,[2] introducing an hitherto unknown Russian singer, Feodor Chaliapin, who had a great success in extracts from *Prince Igor* and *Boris Godunov*. This led Diaghilev to his decision to produce Russian operas in Paris. He then returned to St. Petersburg to prepare the production of *Boris* at the Paris Opera for 1908. After the first night, Mussorgsky was as famous as Chaliapin. And Diaghilev, always on the look-out for some new formula, began to wonder, after a

[1]He did, however, have a few lessons from Sokolov and Rimsky-Korsakov, who did not give him much encouragement, and in 1894 he wrote the music for a scene from *Boris Godunov* which had such a frigid reception that he never tried his hand at composition again. (Lifar, *Serge Diaghilev*, pp. 13-14.)

[2]Russian music was not as unknown in Paris in 1907 as is sometimes believed; see on this point the well-documented article by André Schaeffner, *Debussy et la musique russe* in Pierre Souvtchinsky's *Musique russe*.

season of painting, a season of concerts and a season of opera, what his fourth season would consist of. Only then did he think of ballet.

There was no "Russian Ballet" in Russia; there were, as Diaghilev himself said, Russian dancers trained in the French style who danced traditional ballets. But he could not help "noticing among the younger members of the St. Petersburg *corps de ballet* a sort of reaction against the classical tradition so jealously preserved by Petipa". And so the plan appealed to him, because he saw in it a way of making his dream come true, which was to establish "a closer union than ever before between the three principal factors—music, scenic design and dancing".

With his *flair* for talent, which had caused in to "find" Chaliapin for the opera, Diaghilev succeeded in forming, in record time, a marvellous team, including Pavlova and Karsavina, Fokine and Nijinsky, with brilliant and colourful scenery by Alexandre Benois, N. Roerich and Golovine.

He had no time to think about composers. The 1909 season consisted mainly of extracts from operas or musical arrangements including, under the title *Les Sylphides*, a re-hash of arrangements of Chopin by Glazounov formerly known as *Chopiniana*. To undertake this revision, Diaghilev had approached, among others, a new young composer named Igor Stravinsky who had greatly impressed him. And for the following season he commissioned from this young man the music for a new ballet. This was *The Fire Bird*. "Take a good look at this young man," Diaghilev remarked during a rehearsal, "he's going to be famous." He was right. From now on the Russian Ballet had found its true vocation. This is not the place to retrace its history, which has already been done most thoroughly by Serge Lifar (who was both a spectator and an active participant), nor that of contemporary ballet which has never ceased to prove its vitality. The lines on which it is now developing are perhaps directly due to the influence of Diaghilev, who not only taught it to rediscover colour and movement, but also re-minded composers that music for the ballet ought to be music in its own right.

Naturally collaboration between artists of the calibre of those assembled by Diaghilev did not always proceed smoothly—far from it. Stravinsky has recorded his impressions of Nijinsky as a choreographer in his *Chronicle of my life*, and Serge Lifar, in his *Serge Diaghilev*, tells us what the dancers thought about Stravinsky's music. Both opinions are equally unflattering. The important thing is that Diaghilev, by surrounding himself with a team of choreographers, dancers, painters and musicians of equal distinction had realized his great ambition, which was to bring about a union of all the arts which go to make up a ballet, assigning to each one an equally important rôle, thus ensuring an ideal unity of purpose and design. It is not surprising that, after Diaghilev, each of these separate elements attempted to break away and to achieve independence at the expense of one or other of its neighbours.

This happened, as regards music, when some of the best-known scores began to take their place in the concert-hall on their own merits, independently of the ballet. The hullabaloo which was caused by *The Rite of Spring* prevented proper notice being taken that same year (1913) of a more austere work which nevertheless represented, in the history of ballet music, a revolution in depth of equal importance: *La Péri*, by Paul Dukas. Constructed symphonically, in one continuous movement, it effected for the first time a junction between ballet-music and another *genre* which hitherto had been confined to the concert hall: the symphonic poem. And when Ravel presented Diaghilev with his masterpiece *Daphnis et Chloé*, it was clear that a divorce was in the air, and that the triumph of this music in the concert hall would be matched by an equally complete failure on the stage.

A reaction was inevitable: Serge Lifar launched a violent campaign in favour of the supremacy of the choreographer, and devised, as a demonstration, his *Icarus* in which the rôle of music was reduced to a purely rhythmical accompaniment on percussion instruments. Jean Babillé, and Jean Cocteau, in *Le jeune homme et la Mort* attempted a still bolder experiment, which consisted in mounting a ballet to the accompaniment of jazz records to begin with, to be replaced later by music of an entirely different character —a *Passacaglia* by Bach.

How will this guerrilla warfare end? It is probable that, as usually happens, the issue will not be decided by theories, but on the merits of the conflicting parties. The Russian Ballet was a living force because it combined great choreographers, great dancers, great painters and great musicians. It reminds one of the famous recipe for jugged hare: "Take a hare. . . ."

24

Edouard Colonne's Bow, or The Conductor

Of all the visitors to the concert platform, the most spectacular today is the orchestral conductor. Readers of *Monsieur Croche Anti-Dilettante* will remember how Debussy poked gentle fun at Nikisch conducting the Berlin Philharmonic Orchestra in Paris, remarking how easy it was to arouse an audience to enthusiasm by merely striking an attitude or allowing a lock of hair to droop romantically across the forehead. . . .

Many people might be surprised to learn that this exalted "profession" was only an invention of the late nineteenth century, and that the "time-beater", as he used to be called, was for a long time a mere hack with a specific function to perform, to whose gesticulations no one in the audience paid the slightest attention. The conductor's name was sometimes not even listed on announcements of opera performances in the nineteenth century.

It is possible that conductors, but of a very special kind, were not unknown in ancient

14. Egyptian cheironomy. A fragment from the tomb of Nekauhor and Sekhem-Hathor (Fifth Dynasty, 2563-2423 B.C.).

times. In Egyptian bas-reliefs depicting musical scenes there is often a strange personage seated in front of the performers in a peculiar attitude, who often seems to be signalling to them with his hand, with his forefinger bent back. According to the famous Egypto-musicologist H. Hickmann, he was actually a kind of musical "prompter" whose gesticulations indicated, by means of an agreed sign-language, what notes were to be played. According to a method employed in the last century by some teachers of the tonic *sol-fa* the children sang *do* or *fa* or *sol* when the teacher put his hand to his forehead, or his chin or his chest; and it is probable that this method, or something very like it, was employed by music teachers in the Middle Ages. The "musical hands" so often to be seen in manuscripts up to the sixteenth century, the invention of which is attributed to Guido d'Arezzo in the eleventh century, could only have been used for this purpose.

15. Guido d'Arezzo's "Harmonic Hand".

Pupils were taught that the first joint of the thumb represented the "gamma"—the first note of the scale (*gamme*)—and so on through all the fingers, so that by pointing in turn to the different parts of the hand it was possible to "dictate" to the pupil the tune he was to learn. But this was a pedagogic process, not really conducting. It seems that the liturgical chant, in the choir, did not call for any conducting.

With the introduction of polyphony, it was necessary to have someone in control to regulate the ensemble. The earliest polyphonic music was for soloists only, and to ensure a proper ensemble, it was necessary for them to stand close together, just as folk singers in some countries do today when singing polyphonically, so that they can see one another at the beginning and in the course of the piece. Should this not suffice, they follow the examples of the Ancients, and beat time with their feet.

This explains why we still speak of "feet" in connection with the metre and rhythm of verse. The Greek *cithara* player is generally represented barefooted; but his Roman opposite number is often depicted wearing a shoe with a kind of hinged double sole which enabled him to beat time audibly. This was called the *scabellum*, and the noise it made filled the naïve Quintilian (cf. *De musica*, I, 12) with admiration: "See," he exclaimed, "this admirable artist: not only does he sing and play at the same time, but even manipulates with his feet while doing so a third, supplementary instrument!"

The first description of a "conductor", or at any rate of a vocal ensemble, occurs in a treatise on music by a French priest, Elie Salomon, *circa* 1275, and shows us four *cantors* singing what was probably a four-part *organum* or *conductus*. They are standing close together, clad in silken copes, at the same lectern, with the *tenorista* (that is to say the singer entrusted with the principal part, or *tenor*) in the middle conducting the ensemble. By simply moving his fingers he indicates changes in time. (This is the *flexus digitalis* to which Aelred referred in his *Mirror of Charity*, see pp. 152, 158.) He also controls the balance of the voices, and from time to time instructs the singers, telling them when they are singing too loud or not loud enough.

According to this ancient system of beating time, each "beat" was indicated individually and not in groups of 2, 3, or 4 as in our classical music divided into "bars". Thus one would count, for example, 1, 1, 1, 1, and not 1, 2, 3, 1. . . . This would often be done by tapping the desk with the hand (see Plates XXXI, XXXII).

This procedure was known as the "*tactus*", and was the only method used in old music for beating time until the eighteenth century. We shall see presently that traces of it still persist today.

In the Middle Ages instrumental ensembles were never "conducted"; the players kept an eye on one another, or rather on one of their number who led the rest.[1]

---

[1] The miniature in Plate XXXII is believed to represent Ockeghem "conducting" the choir at Saint-Martin de Tours. But if so, which of the personages depicted is Ockeghem? The one who is touching the lectern with his hands appears to be only a young cleric of no particular distinction. Behind him stands another, rather older, with his hand on the younger man's shoulder ready to correct any mistakes. In the background we see a third who also has his hand on the lectern. But the most important looking personage, a much older man wearing spectacles and a cape, is standing a little behind the others and seems merely to be supervising them. If this is really Ockeghem, it looks as if the picture shows a "lesson in conducting" by *tactus* and not a performance conducted by the composer.

A fifteenth century miniature, from the Diurnal of René II of Lorraine, is significant in this respect. David is seen with a bell in each hand, in company with two other musicians, one of whom is playing a psaltery and the other a viol. Despite the royal crown on his head, David, like the violinist, is keeping his eyes fixed on the tympanist who, seated at his instrument, is "conducting" the ensemble while he plays (Plate XXXI). On the other side we see the singers grouped round the lectern. One of them stands a little apart, and touches with his hand the lower rim of the lectern, which he is probably tapping to mark the *tactus*.

This is one explanation of the origin of the conductor's *bâton*. When seventeenth-century opera began to call for enormous masses of instrumentalists and singers, both soloists and chorists who, owing to the size of the stage, had to be controlled from a distance, the problem arose as to the best method of communicating to them the repeated strokes of the *tactus* (which by that time was only just beginning to be superseded by more modern methods of indicating the time).

The very prosaic reason, then, for the adoption of the *bâton*, both in the theatre and in churches, was to enable the "conductor" to make more noise in striking the desk so that the singers could hear better from the back of the stage. If the *bâton* was not strong enough, then a stout stick would be used to strike the floor with. It was with such an instrument that Lully, while conducting his *Te Deum* on January 8, 1687, struck his foot with such force that gangrene set in, and brought about his death a few weeks later.

The only drawback to this system was that the "beat" was audible not only to the singers, but to the public as well. J.-J. Rousseau in 1767 complained bitterly of the noise made by the conductor at the opera, and compared it to the sound of a woodman chopping wood!

The system, however, was in use for a long time. The Museum of the Paris Conservatoire possesses the *bâton* used by Offenbach at the *Bouffes-Parisiens*. The wood, which is very hard, is covered with dents, showing how vigorously the maestro must have struck the edge of his music-stand. . . .

Among the alternative and more discreet methods of marking time which had been tried out, the method most commonly adopted was a roll of paper, held firmly in the middle and moved from left to right and fron right to left to describe a half-circle with a movement similar to that of a window-cleaner (Plate XXXIII). Later, a heavy cylindrical *bâton* took the place of the roll of paper, sometimes made of ebony, boxwood, or even marble, and ornamented in the middle and at either end with copper or silver plating.

The modern fashion of "beating time" in accordance with a conventional and standardized code of movements, in which the first beat is always a down-beat, was at first used only in teaching *sol-fa;* the regular beat, as we have seen, was always lateral, unless it was a succession of strokes tapped out.

The practice of beating time according to bar-divisions, indeed, only became possible when the notion of the "bar" itself, indicated by actual bar-lines, was generally adopted in the seventeenth century. Rousseau in his *Dictionary of Music* informs us that "French musicians do not beat time like the Italians. The latter, when beating "four-time", strike the two first beats with a down-beat, and the others with an up-beat. They also do the same when beating triple time. The French always strike the first beat only, and mark the others with different movements of the hand, to the left and right." Brossard specifies that in triple time, which he calls *tripola,* the first beat is executed by a downward movement of the hand, the second by turning it slightly, and the third by raising it—which is still the way we do it today. In any case, whether a stick, a roll of paper or a *bâton* was used, it was by no means a regular custom for the choir master[1] to beat time.

Very often the method adopted was for the conductor to signal to the players by a nod of his head from his place at the harpsichord. There is a well-known picture (Plate XXXIV) representing a scene from Haydn's *opéra comique L'Incontro Improviso,* being performed at the Esterhazy château. One can see clearly in detail, not only the stage, but the players seated in what appears to be a miniature orchestra pit; and this was in 1775.[2] The fifteen musicians are seated in a row (apart from the double-bass and harpsichord) some with their backs to the stage, the others facing them. In this way, they can all see the harpsichord-and-bass group at the side. Haydn is at the harpsichord, from where he can direct the players with a movement of the head. Behind him, reading from the same score, are one 'cellist and two double-bass players, who are thus in a position to supply both the *continuo* of the recitatives, and the bass parts in the *tutti.*

This is explained by the fact that in every style of opera until the nineteenth century, only the airs and choruses were performed in strict time. Nothing in the nature of a recitative can logically be conducted in strict time, since the music as written is only an approximation, and in performance the decisive factor is the musical reconstitution of

---

[1] It will be recalled that this term, which today is used only in churches, was in common use in the eighteenth century to designate the director of any musical institute, sacred or profane. In Germany the word *Kapellmeister* is still used in a general sense, and the leader of an orchestra is known as a *Konzertmeister.* We shall see why presently.

[2] The original belongs to Mr. V. E. Pollak in Vienna. It was first reproduced by H. Wirth in his analysis of Haydn's recently re-discovered *Orfeo ed Euridice* (Haydn Society, Boston) and in France by the review *La vie musicale,* No. 8, July-August, 1951, p. 5.

the spoken words in their scenic context with all the rhythmic freedom this implies.[1]

Gradually, in the second half of the eighteenth century, the harpsichord disappeared from the orchestra.[2] The bass *continuo* was now only a memory. At the same time the direction of the orchestra passed from the keyboard to the conductor's desk.[3] It was then that the function of an orchestral conductor became the highest to which an instrumentalist could aspire. It was thus that Kreutzer (to whom the famous Sonata was dedicated) was promoted at the Opéra in 1816 from the rank of violin solo to that of second, and subsequently, first conductor of the orchestra.[4]

His place was then filled by Habeneck, who, in his turn, became conductor of the Société des Concerts du Conservatoire. Until the end of the nineteenth century the most distinguished conductors were all drawn from the ranks of orchestral players, and had no special training apart from their experience as executants—unless they were composers, like Beethoven or Berlioz, who occasionally mounted the rostrum to conduct their own works, but who likewise had had no special training in conducting. A very curious print which, so far as I am aware, has never been published (now in the Berlioz museum at La Côte-Saint-André) is dated 1887 and shows Edouard Colonne conducting, not with a *bâton*, but with a violin bow. (Plate XXXVI).

The conductor's *bâton* by this time was in pretty general use, and sometimes assumed the strangest forms. Berlioz, in one of those theatrical gestures in which he delighted, once exchanged *bâtons* with Mendelssohn, and celebrated the event in a letter in the

---

[1]There are plenty of flagrant examples today of ignorant conductors who try to "conduct" recitative in strict time, of singers who learn it note by note without making any distinction of style between the recitative and the aria, and of teachers who, in France at least, have allowed the tradition to die out, although in Italy and Vienna it has fortunately been kept alive.

[2]Its death warrant was signed at the Paris Opera on Jan. 26, 1770, during a revival of Rameau's *Zoroastre* to mark the inauguration of the second hall at the Palais Royal. Its place was then taken by the double basses. (Cf. Grimm, *Correspondance Littéraire*, Feb. and June 1770, and *Mémoires Secrets* of Jan. 26, 1770).

[3]It is noticeable, however, that Gluck, who was one of the first to orchestrate all his recitatives, was careful to avoid allowing a vocal phrase in the recitative to coincide with a passage in the orchestra in strict time, so that the conductor could always *wait for the singer*, leaving him to speak his words freely.

[4]It should be remembered that in the theatre the conductor was often placed not, as is customary today, between the audience and the orchestra, but facing the stage in front of the orchestra which enabled him to follow the singers better without bothering too much about details in the orchestra which, from behind his back, followed him as best they could (Plate XXXV). An illustration of this disposition is given in Riemann's Dictionary (French revision 1930) under the chapter *orchestra*, without any comment on the archaism. Until 1901 at the Paris Opéra the conductor sat in the middle of the orchestra and gave indications to the players seated behind him with his elbows. It was Paul Vidal who was responsible for putting an end to this awkward arrangement: he asked for a swivel chair so that he could turn round when necessary, but Messager, instead of agreeing to his request, decided it would be better to place the conductor in the position he now occupies. The custom of applauding the entrance of the conductor is still more recent; it used, when I was young, to be reserved for really great occasions as a mark of special esteem at the beginning of the last act.

style of Fennimore Cooper:—"Great Chief, receive my tomahawk. . . ." The trophy, now in the possession of the Conservatoire Museum, is in the shape of a sort of marrow-bone, made of hollow cardboard. Saint-Saëns was once presented, at Algiers, with a *bâton d'honneur* nearly two feet long. Others, some of which are still in use, had a thick cork handle to be grasped in the palm of the hand: these objects weighed on an average between three and twelve pounds, whereas some modern conductor's sticks weigh no more than fifteen ounces.

It was probably in Germany, with the advent of a generation of Wagnerian conductors, Richter, Mottl, Nikisch, etc., that the professional conductor made his first appearance, having been specially trained for that profession and for no other. At the Paris Conservatoire there was no conducting class before 1914, and the professor in charge was not a professional conductor but a composer, Vincent d'Indy. Until 1943 this class was considered to be for the exclusive benefit of composition students.

The enormous popularity of the gramophone, and especially of the L.P. records, has given a fresh stimulus to the cult of the orchestral conductor. People no longer speak of Beethoven's, but of Karajan's or Furtwängler's *Fifth Symphony*.

One can only guess what the composer would have thought of this. Everyone knows the fantastic late-nineteenth-century print showing a distracted and dishevelled Beethoven on the rostrum standing between two candles and waving his arms wildly. In contrast, the author possesses an amusing contemporary print (Plate XXXVII), after Dantan representing Habeneck, who was universally admired—notably by Wagner—for his conducting of Beethoven's symphonies. He is shown from the back, with his handkerchief hanging from his tail-coat, apparently beating time with his feet, while his right hand is firmly grasping a cone-shaped baguette, which he is brandishing with the gesture of a policeman wielding a truncheon.[1]

The popular conception of the conductor is summed up in the following satirical, but only very slightly caricatural, description which I came across in an obscure little musical magazine: "The belief that a conductor is a gentleman who gives the players the signal to start and then merely beats time with a stick is one that dies hard. Another extreme view is that the conductor is a kind of variety artist, whose turn consists in waving his

---

[1] The famous story, told in Berlioz's *Mémoires*, of how when Habeneck was conducting the Berlioz *Requiem* at the Invalides and put down his *bâton* at the crucial entry of the brass at the *Tuba mirum*, Berlioz bounded on to the platform and snatched his *bâton* from him to give the brass their cue, is obviously apocryphal as Boschot has demonstrated. There is no reference in the press to such a scandalous incident having taken place, and Berlioz sent Habeneck the next day a letter warmly congratulating him on the performance which, of course, contained no mention of anything of the kind.

arms and disarranging his hair, dancing about at the same time and shaking his fists, while the orchestra accompanies him by making appropriate noises. The truth does not lie somewhere between these two extremes, but elsewhere."

The conclusion is, of course, quite right. But does not the modern "conductor", when all is said and done, deserve a little more prestige than the old, anonymous "time-beater"?

25

Beethoven's Hat, or The Composer

If you look up the word "composer" in an old dictionary, you will probably find it has a very different meaning from the one we attach to it today such as, for example, "one who composes a dispute". If it has no musical connotation, it is for the very good reason that no such concept existed. At the risk of appearing paradoxical, one might even say that such a concept was an invention of the Romantic movement.

It is, of course, quite true that ever since music existed someone must have conceived it; we meet with composers' names throughout our history from the earliest time—for example, the Cretan Mesomedes who is credited with several pieces which have come down to us from ancient Greece. But it must be admitted that no one was really interested in them; and they were soon forgotten.

We live today under the tyrannical domination of the "written note" which distorts our ideas about the days when music paper, or whatever preceded it, was totally unknown or at best served only as an *aide-mémoire* or, later, as a more or less rudimentary canvas, having only acquired its present exaggerated prestige in the early years of the present century.

Throughout the whole period of monody and even the early polyphonic era, the *written note*, so far as the composer was concerned, did not exist. A "composition" was merely an improvisation which, if it were particularly successful, was learned by heart and retained in the memory. Sometimes, if considered worthy, it was taught to others, but only by ear.[1] It then became a "traditional tune". On repeating it, other musicians, consciously or unconsciously, would not hesitate occasionally to alter it. This, we know, is the origin of "popular", or "folk" music. It was the same with serious, or "learned" music. Ritualistic or religious airs were practically the only ones which remained more or less unchanged on account of their liturgical or magical character. If they were ever written down, it was only later, after they had been transmitted orally.

---

[1]Aeschylus used to teach the members of the choir the music he wanted for his choruses by singing it to them; on one occasion, according to Plutarch, he was annoyed because one of them laughed at him for singing in the Mixolydian mode. Cf. H. -I. Marrou, *Melographia*.

It is almost certain that no music was committed to paper by the composer before or during the act of composition until about the twelfth century. Composer and interpreter were one; and it was in the latter capacity that he was chiefly honoured. There is no reason why we should be surprised at this, since the situation today, at any rate in the world of jazz and "variety", is very much the same. Who but a very few specialists could name the authors of some of the best known tunes? On the other hand, everybody knows the stars who sing them, and could name the famous "jazz-men" who adapt and "arrange" them for their own purposes.

We saw (in Chapter 17) how the composition of a work was often synonymous with its first performance. Occasionally—especially in ancient Greece—the name of the composer-interpreter was handed down to posterity. But never in the early Middle Ages. In the Gregorian repertory, for example, the authors' names are sometimes preserved, but, as we saw in Chapter 3, these were invariably only the authors of the words. While the famous veil of anonymity surrounding the cathedral builders has occasionally been pierced, that of the innumerable composers of the treasures of Gregorian Plainsong never has been.

It was almost by chance that the first great polyphonists proved an exception to this rule. Their works—*organa*, *conductus*, *motets*, etc.—at least until the end of the thirteenth century, were strictly anonymous—with one important exception which we shall mention presently. We might never have heard the names of Leoninus and Perotinus had not, *circa* 1240, an expert on notation, Jean de Garlande and, a little later, an anonymous English theoretician included in one of their treatises a brief eulogistic note mentioning a few titles which enabled the manuscripts containing the works described, though unsigned, to be identified. Here, again, it is noteworthy that neither Leoninus nor Perotinus are referred to as "composers", but as "organists"—i.e., singers of *organum*.

Except for a few archetypal copies, in the Middle Ages there were rarely two identical manuscripts of the same work. This was because the interpreter very rarely read from an author's MS; he was a creative artist himself, who inherited a tradition and adapted it as he pleased. He transformed what he had been taught by improvising, and paid little attention to the author. It was not until it had been consecrated by tradition that any music was written down.

As we have pointed out, this is exactly what our jazz bands do today. Similarly, Lully revolutionized the Court of Louis XIV by insisting that the violins in his "band" should play exactly what was written; and one of the chief elements in the reforms initiated by Wagner was that recitative should be incorporated in the symphonic development, and performed in strict time as written. We must always remember this fact when we interpret the ancient recitative.

In the fatal decline from the notion of music as a cult to that of its being an art, with all its accompanying pitfalls, personal vanities, etc., it was not the composer who led the way, but the performer. We have seen examples of this in the Egypt of the Pharaohs. The first composers who consciously abandoned their anonymity were those for whom music, important though it was, was not their only interest: the troubadours and poet-musicians of the twelfth and thirteenth centuries.

The first troubadours were no exception to the general rule. They composed, not for the general public—this was the concern of the *jongleurs*—but for the princes and nobility from whom alone they received payment. If they were noblemen themselves, they wrote for their peers as an act of brotherly homage. See for instance the dedication of Guillaume de Poitiers to his friend Estève in his Chanson 7.

But while composers continued proudly to inscribe their names on their *cansos*, *pastourelles* and *sirventès*, the "*déchanteurs*", both sacred and profane, who wrote motets or embroidered polyphonically tunes composed by others or by themselves, continued the tradition of the anonymous artisan. Some five hundred polyphonic motets have been preserved for us in MSS., now famous, discovered in Florence, Bamberg or Montpellier. But none of them bear their author's name, nor can they be identified by cross-references.

There is, however, one exception—and that is because he was not a professional *discantor*, but a *trouvère*, and the only one who was at the same time not only a singer, but a polyphonic composer: Adam de la Halle. His motets, too, were mixed up with a lot of other anonymous works, and the only reason it has been possible to identify them is because another MS. was found mentioning him by name as a *trouvère* and containing some of his *rondeaux* and motets and other works.

Adam de la Halle, moreover, was not just an ordinary musician, but had an official position as poet to the French Court at Naples. A similar honour no doubt enhanced the admiration aroused by the contrapuntal compositions of Guillaume de Machaut, the most illustrious musician of the fourteenth century.

For Guillaume de Machaut, too, was not merely a composer, but a poet, as well as being an important personage in the diplomatic world where, as secretary to John of Luxembourg, King of Bohemia, he was the recipient of various ecclesiastical privileges and benefits bestowed upon him by Pope John XXII, despite the fact that the latter had in 1324 condemned *ex cathedra* the tendencies manifested in the church music of the *Ars Nova* school for which Machaut was chiefly responsible. And so, after Adam de la

Halle, and for the same reasons, Guillaume de Machaut was the first authentic "composer" to be honoured as such, and his manuscripts are proudly adorned with his name.

This was the turning-point: from now on anonymous works, which up to now had been the immense majority, especially in the field of polyphonic music, became increasingly rare. In the course of the fifteenth and especially the sixteenth centuries, the social status of composers became more clearly defined, and their life histories showed a curious similarity. As a child, a composer usually started his career as a chorister in one of the schools attached to the neighbouring cathedral. There he received a classical education, including Latin, sang in the choir and learned one or more instruments. On attaining adolescence, he would then be sent to study abroad, generally in Italy. If he was lucky enough, after his voice had broken, to be able still to sing, he would then join one of the big cathedral choirs in the peninsula, or even—supreme honour—the Papal Chapel which had been reorganized by a Frenchman, Elzéar Genêt, of Carpentras in 1518. He would then proceed by gradual promotion to become a *maître de chapelle*, perhaps in one of the innumerable neighbouring churches. His first motets or masses would be sung by the group to which he belonged, and then, as his reputation grew, in other choirs. As circumstances dictated, he would write songs or madrigals, either in Italian or in his native language. Copies would then be put into circulation, or else, from the sixteenth century onwards would be published along with others, by Petrucci in Venice, Attaignant in Paris, or Susato in Antwerp. But he would still be considered only a novice, and the publisher would not think it necessary to mention his name. Later, on becoming famous, his signature would appear in the printed collection. Soon he might have a whole volume to himself, without commentaries: if he were a priest, he would merely be described as "Maitre X". Towards the end of his life he would be described on the title page as "one of the best authors of our time", or by some such eulogistic phrase, and his friends would compose in his honour quatrains, epigrams or punning inscriptions which would adorn the first pages of the volume, while a preface, often addressed to some dignitary of the Church or State, would praise the generosity of the dedicatee, thus affording our musician an opportunity of alluding, with an appropriate false modesty, to his own merits, or of relating some biographical incident for the benefit of future historians.

Our author is now a celebrity. He leaves the Papal Chapel and starts on a tour of the big cathedral choirs. If he is a priest, he returns to his own country, invested with some high ecclesiastical dignity, and ends his days as choir-master in his own cathedral or neighbouring church while continuing to compose and have his works performed as soon as they are finished. If he is a layman, he offers his services to some nobleman, writing a new work every time he solicits an appointment. If he is accepted, he becomes a Court musician, earning a regular salary and providing a new work whenever called upon to do so. For until the nineteenth century composers were not worried by the problem of how to get their works performed, for everything they wrote was for a specific occasion.

With the advent of opera, a new type of composer came into existence who wrote expressly for the theatre. He was not a product of the cathedral schools, but worked for whomever he pleased, and his hunting-ground was not in the churches, but in the drawing-rooms of influential society ladies or theatrical impresarios. He would have to seek out his singers in London, Vienna, Prague or Paris, noting their particular vocal qualities; and in this profession it was advisable to be Italian, or at any rate to become Italianised as J. C. Bach did in Milan or Handel in Naples. During his travels he might get a job as violinist or oboist at some royal Court where he might even be appointed director of music. Like his colleagues of the Church, he, too, of course would never write music unless commissioned: when Mozart learned that the company which was going to produce his opera-bouffe *Zaida* would be unable to do so owing to a Court mourning, he abandoned the work unfinished, and started on another. To compose for posterity was another invention of the Romantics.

We have mentioned Mozart; beginning with him the rôle of the composer was destined to change: first as regards his training and formation, but especially in the matter of the change in his social status. Haydn thought it quite normal to wear the uniform of the Count Esterhazy; Mozart was furious in 1781 when at Archbishop Colloredo's table he was placed between the valets and the cooks. "An indignation we all share," wrote A. Einstein; "but the rank conferred upon Mozart by his functions as Court organist was exactly that of a *valet de chambre*, and eighteenth century etiquette was not aware that geniuses were entitled to privileged treatment; and so the placing of the guests at table was perfectly in accordance with this etiquette."

The mixture of joy and rage with which Mozart, on that May 12, 1781, informed his father, who was terrified by this news, of his intention to leave the Archbishop and regain his freedom, marked the beginning of a new era in the history of composers. It meant that they would lose their security and regular bread-and-butter irrevocably, but their pride and honour would be safeguarded from now on.

With the German Romantics this pride became enormous. Did not Fichte proclaim, in his enthusiasm for the revolutionary ideas emanating from France, the dignity of the citizen and the supremacy of the German Fatherland for the happiness of humanity;

while Schlegel declared that art was the highest expression of the life of a nation and the symbol of its soul? And so the German artist felt himself to be in the forefront of humanity, and Beethoven was able to write to one of his princely pupils (Prince Lichnovsky): "There have been, and will be, princes by the thousand, but there is only one Beethoven."

The following anecdote is well known, but will bear repetition in this context: Beethoven and Goethe were walking arm in arm at Toeplitz one day in 1812 when they saw advancing towards them the Empress with the Grand Dukes and all the Court officials. "Don't let go my arm," said the musician to the poet, "it's for them to make way, not us." Goethe nevertheless disengaged himself and stood aside, hat in hand, "while Beethoven, with folded arms, walked through the middle of the royal party scarcely raising his hat."[1] He then waited for Goethe and admonished him, saying: "I waited for you because I honour and respect you as you deserve, but you showed them too much respect."

Thirty years earlier Count d'Arco had kicked Mozart out of the room. In 1812 the Grand Dukes were amused by Beethoven's originality, but nevertheless obstructed his path in the Toeplitz Avenue while giving him a friendly smile. *Bettler werden Fürstenbrüder*.[2]

And so, at the dawn of the Romantic era, there came into being the romantic notion of the composer as a kind of demi-god, a sort of phenomenon or abnormal human type: Beethoven was the son of an alcoholic, Chopin a victim of tuberculosis, Schumann died mad—there was no lack of material, and the temptation to generalize was scarcely resisted. Soon the history of the great composers had no resemblance to biography, but rather to the most exaggerated form of hagiography. Some idea of the lengths to which these distortions were pushed can be obtained from the cruel and pitiless study by R. and E. Sterba entitled: *Beethoven and his Family* (1955), even though in the opinion of some serious historians, the authors have gone too far in the opposite direction.

---

[1]The story is told by Bettina von Arnim in a letter written some twenty years later; and another more insolent version is contained in a pseudo-letter from Beethoven to this same Bettina, and copied by her: "I clapped my hat on my head, buttoned up my overcoat and, with my arms behind my back, went right through the whole pack of them." But this letter contains mistakes in names and dates which render it suspect, and no one has seen the original. In any case it is difficult to admire the behaviour of the hero of the story, which would appear to be simply that of a boor—which Beethoven frequently was.

[2]"Beggars become the brothers of Princes." Such is the original text (1785) in Schiller's *Ode to Joy* which had aroused Beethoven's enthusiasm, but which in the final edition was replaced by the words: *Alle Menschen werden Brüder*, "which Beethoven was obliged to accept in 1824 under the terrorist police régime of Metternich". (Massin, p. 249.) But Massin adds: "But for the Beethoven of Toeplitz 1812 there was no question of fraternity: princes became beggars, and that was final. Echoes of the Carmagnole were ringing through the forests of Bohemia."

The deification of the composer brought with it, though much later—certainly not before the twentieth century—the deification of the text as written and the sterilizing notion of the robot-interpreter; we have already (see p. 129) quoted the views of Stockhausen on this subject to which we shall be returning later.[1]

We know what Couperin said on this point: "We do not play music as we write it." We also saw how, with the composer's consent, a singer familiar with tradition, was supposed to interpret an air by Monteverdi (p. 110) and how the Sistine Chapel "arranged" Palestrina's music. Mozart did not play his concertos as he wrote them. Liszt, it is said, was incapable of playing a piece by Chopin without adding something of his own, while when I was a child, nobody played *St. Francis Walking on the Waves* without adding two bars of coda, according, so it appears, to the Leschetiszky tradition. In the following chapter we shall see what Beethoven thought about fidelity to the notes as written.

In the world of the theatre in the nineteenth century the composer had become the "maestro", and his professional training and education was completely transformed. The cathedral choir-schools had lost their vitality: in France they had been dissolved by the Revolution, and when they were resuscitated they were no longer adequate to ensure proper training and opportunities for their students. Instead of growing up in the milieu for which he would be writing music later on, the young composer went to the Conservatoire, where he mixed, not with his future patrons, but with his rivals. Gradually he became accustomed to compose for the sake of composing, as it were, and then seek an opportunity to get his work performed; and he found consolation for his set-backs in the romantic myth that posterity would recognize his genius. He had read the golden legends of his predecessors, and took his own infallibility for granted; moreover, the radio, films and records accustomed him to never even seeing his unknown audience. In the old days he would have worked for a noble patron, and more recently for an audience of a few hundred souls who, so at least he hoped, would listen attentively, and share in his thoughts and emotions. In theory, he works today for the benefit of thousands, but in a closed milieu; he doesn't know them, and perhaps will never see them. In reality, most musicians work for a producer—who may on occasion be the Director of some specialized Festival—or for a few no less specialized critics whose

[1]In apparent reaction to this mechanisation of the interpreter, some dodecaphonists, including Stockhausen himself (cf. *Pièce XI*), have had the idea, not indeed of restoring to him his rôle "from inside", but of "associating him with the act of creation" by such artifices as, for example, presenting him with "combinations" for him to play in any order he pleases, or any other similar device so as to ensure "the intrusion of chance".

opinion is worth more to them than the chance of an increasingly hypothetical success in the concert halls, which tend to be half empty unless the "medicine" of contemporary music is sweetened by a sufficient dose of good old hackneyed symphonies.

In order to understand this strange evolution, in which progress does not seem to be the decisive factor, the historian may find it useful to turn his attention to those who exercise upon the composer the necessary function of a catalyzing agent: i.e., the critics, publishers and, above all, the public.

26

Mr. Choudens' Fur-lined Coat, or The Publisher

When composers first began to write down their music—probably not before the twelfth century, and then only in exceptional cases—Gutenberg had not yet appeared on the scene. Consequently the extent to which a composer's work was disseminated by means of copies depended much more on the initiative of his interpreters than on himself. A work was copied when someone wanted to play or sing it, and this was more likely to happen as a result, not of reading it, but of hearing it performed; we saw in Chapter 17 how unimportant the written "score" was in the early days of music.

Printing was a revolution for music no less than for literature. But again, owing to the fact that the individual "parts" were more important than the score, its effects were not quite the same. Indeed, it was not until centuries later that the "reading" of music began to take the place of listening to it as a means of making it more widely known—and perhaps it never has succeeded in doing so completely. Even today, a record is at least as important as a printing for the diffusion of a musical work.

Music publishing came in with the Renaissance: the first printing presses were probably those set up in 1501 by Petrucci in Venice for the production of a collection of part-songs with instrumental accompaniment called the *Odhecaton*, a copy of which is preserved in the Library of the Paris Conservatoire.

The type-characters were movable; fragments of the stave with the notes attached were juxtaposed, which was the usual procedure in those days. It was intended to be played from, and could not be read as a whole (rather like our modern editions of music for four hands printed on opposite pages); but this method made it easier for a group of musicians to get to know new music and enlarge their repertoire, and it remained in use until the adoption of the bass *continuo*.

Music publishers were very active throughout the sixteenth century, especially in Italy where, in a single year (1587), no less than seventy works appeared in Venice, Rome and Milan. The number of copies printed varied from two hundred (Victoria, 1600) to fifteen hundred (Morlaye's Lute Tablature in 1552). France came second, and Germany third. Competition provided a useful stimulus, but was not always altogether honest. There are many stories to illustrate this of which the following is typical: Beethoven had sold to Breitkopf his *Quintet*, Op. 29, but Breitkopf's rival, Artaria, had managed to have it copied in a single night while it was in the hands of Count von Fries, to whom Beethoven had lent the MS., and published it in great haste, without the composer's consent—thus forestalling its rightful publisher. This clandestine edition, produced with such haste, was naturally full of faults. Beethoven extricated himself from

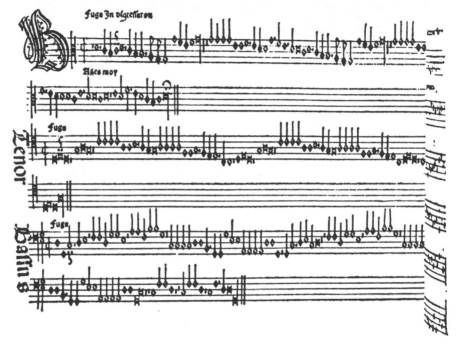

16. The first collection of printed music: the Odhecaton of Petrucci, Venice 1501.

this situation with considerable ingenuity, if not with complete honesty: he requested Artaria to hand the fifty engraved copies to Fries for correction, and at the same time asked the latter to correct them in ink so clumsily that they would be unsaleable. In this way, without any personal affront to one of his publishers, whom he considered a complete rascal (*Erzschurke*) but with whom it was expedient for him to remain on good terms, he succeeded in safeguarding the legal rights of the other.

An attempt was made to safeguard author's rights by a system of privileges, but this proved ineffectual: works were sometimes plagiarized as soon as they appeared!

With the growth of music publishing it became possible to follow, almost year by year, the evolution of public taste; for the publisher was not the composer's representative, but an independent tradesman, who selected his authors among those whose works were most in demand. And so to be published meant that a composer had been officially consecrated.

In the seventeenth century the situation was very different. In Italy production gradually slackened until about 1650, and remained at a low level until the end of the eighteenth century. France then took the lead and retained it until the Revolution despite the fact that an exclusive privilege had been granted to a printer, Pierre Ballard, who had a monopoly.

The part played by the publisher thus underwent a considerable transformation; he was now no longer a potentate making reputations on the basis of consumer-demand, but had become an artisan working to the order of the composer. In 1782 there were in Paris "44 music-publishers, as well as 53 composers who published their own works themselves, in addition to 31 engravers, 19 copyists, 17 printers and 11 who worked in copperplate . . ." "It often happened that a composer was his own publisher; he employed an engraver, and a printer corrected his proofs and sold from his own house copies which he signed as a guarantee of their authenticity. Sometimes the engraver or publisher was a member of his own family. If, however, a composer preferred not to publish his own works himself, he had at his disposal not only a large number of professional publishers, but in addition all those composers and artists who were engaged in the publishing business. . . . some of whom were his friends, or at any rate his colleagues, and used to sit near him in the orchestra."[1]

The privileged position of the music-publisher in Paris was the consequence of the intense activity of the musical life in the capital. Making music at home had become one of the essential pastimes of the upper classes. In 1759, according to Michel Brenet (*Le Concert en France sous l'Ancien Régime*), there were at least a score of musical "*salons*" where concerts took place regularly—and the list is by no means exhaustive. As a result of so great a demand for music, in the course of the eighteenth century Paris became the capital of the world so far as music-publishing was concerned. "It is probable," says Barry S. Brook (*op. cit.*) "that between 1750 and 1770 more music was published in Paris than in the whole of the rest of Europe."

In the other countries, however, music continued to be copied by hand, as a general rule, until about 1775-1780. We know, for example, that although the whole of Bach's vast output (more than half of which has been lost) today takes up forty-five fat volumes of the Bach Gesellschaft, the list of works published during his lifetime takes up

---

[1]Barry S. Brook, *La symphonie française dans le deuxième moitié du XVIIIe. siècle*, 1959.

no more than six lines. Bach wrote for his noble patrons or for the Church, and once a work had been performed, it was put away in a cupboard, and another one was started for the next concert or church service. When, six years after the death of the Cantor, Mattheson published his *Art of Fugue*, the edition was limited to thirty copies!

It was not until the decade 1780-1790 that engraved music, outside France, began to take the place of MS. copies, whereas in France it had been a common practice for some time already. The innovation had some curious consequences. A composer who was writing for a specific occasion was responsible for the performance. He knew how, and by whom his work was to be performed, and was therefore able to foresee all the details of the interpretation which he naturally was careful to note down, except those for which he himself would be responsible, or which, by tradition, could be improvised at sight, and under his supervision, by an artist whom he knew and could trust: e.g., the realization of a figured bass, traditional ornamentation, or cadenzas which the composer would either play himself or entrust to his interpreter. This is why Bach's orchestral scores, for example, really are full scores, with as many staves as there are players, and with all the parts fully written out.

But with the printed score this was no longer the case. The composer did not know who was going to play from it, or how many instruments he would have at his disposal, or what the standard of performance was likely to be.

All the more reason—so a twentieth-century musician might argue—for noting every detail of the interpretation!

But the seventeenth-century musician's reaction was exactly the opposite. He, on the contrary, put down on paper as few details as possible so as not to hamper his unknown interpreter, but leave him free to adapt himself to circumstances which the composer could not possibly foresee. It is precisely because it had been published that a score by Rameau, unlike those of his contemporary Bach, was only an *aide-mémoire*, reduced to the strictest minimum, so that it could be adapted to circumstances at each performance. We know, for example, that clarinets made their first appearance at the Paris Opéra in 1749, in *Zoroastre*,[1] and that it was in this same *Zoroastre*, when it was revived in January 1770, that an audience first heard an orchestra without either harpsichord or *continuo*. It was of no importance that Rameau had not, in fact, scored for clarinets, but had, on the other hand, written a part for bass *continuo*.

[1] Lionel de la Laurencie, *Rameau et les clarinettes*, S.I.M., Feb. 15, 1913. The first composer to write for the clarinet was perhaps Vivaldi in 1720-1740; cf. W. Koldener, in *Die Musikforschung*, 1951, 2-3, and 1955, p. 209; see also Pincherle, *Vivaldi et la musique instrumentale*, p. 102, and R. B. Chatun, *Handel and the clarinet*, Galpin Society Journal, March, 1950.

One of the results of all this was the almost complete disappearance of the autograph MS. The cult of the autograph is, indeed, a purely modern phenomenon. For example, the Boisgelou catalogue in the *Bibliothèque Nationale* mentions that it contains two MS. symphonies by Gossec, but "only until printed copies can be obtained". From which it may be concluded that autograph MSS. were looked upon as rough sketches to be discarded as soon as the works were printed.

It was only, indeed, after 1789 that performers were expected to observe strictly what was written, at any rate so far as orchestration was concerned. Perhaps this was because it was only recently that composers had begun to "orchestrate" in the proper sense of the word; for, in the days of the *continuo*, there was no real orchestration, only "instrumentation"; i.e., a composer chose at the beginning what instruments he required, and these remained unchanged until the end.[1]

Again, this "respect"—to use a neologism now fashionable—for the original text is also comparatively recent. Thus, although the nineteenth century gave up writing *ad libitum*, it went in for transcriptions in a big way. We know what Liszt produced in this domain; while Beethoven did not hesitate to transform his *Violin Concerto* into a Piano Concerto, correcting the printed score with his own hand and rewriting whole passages[2] just as Bach had done when he rewrote in D minor (for his harpsichord concerto) the G minor fugue for the first Sonata for solo violin, with all the transformations suggested by the nature of the instrument, and even a few more. The Knights of the Order of Original Purity are a very recent creation whose statutes do not seem to indicate a very profound knowledge of the history of music. . . .

Beethoven once made his own views on this subject very clear: they were the same as those of all musicians prior to the "purist" creed of the twentieth century.

His Quintet Op. 104 in C minor, in spite of its opus number, and vintage year—1817 — is only a rewrite of an early work, the Piano Trio No. 3 of Op. 1, dating from 1795. The arrangement in the first place had been done by someone else—it is not known by whom. The arranger had scrupulously respected the original text; but was Beethoven pleased? The following note was scribbled by him in a fit of irritation on a copy of the arrangement: "Trio arranged for quintet in three parts by Mr. Good-Will (Herrn Gutwillen) and restored from a version purporting to be in five parts to one with five

---

[1]e.g., a Cantata by Bach: on that particular Sunday he had available oboes and trumpets; accordingly he used his trumpets in the final chorus, but it would never have occurred to him to use them to emphasize some detail in the text or supply a touch of colour in the aria in which the oboe accompanies a contralto.

[2]This transcription, still unpublished but absolutely authentic, was recorded in 1959 by *Harmonia Mundi*, H.M.S. 30, 103, under the unexpected title of *Piano Concerto No. 6*.

real parts, thus being redeemed from abject misery and made presentable, by Mr. Correct-Will (Herrn Wohlwillen) on August 14, 1817.—N.B. The original of the quintet in three parts has been sacrificed in a solemn holocaust to the gods of Hades."

Better still: in a note published on October 20, 1802, in the *Wiener Zeitung*, Beethoven protested against the publication in the form of a string quintet of his *Septet* and *First Symphony*. But it was not the principle of transcription of which he complained, but merely the fact that the edition did not make it clear that it was a transcription, nor that he had not transcribed it himself. "In a work of this kind," he wrote, "not only whole passages have to be omitted altogether or rewritten, but certain additions have to be made. . . . That is why the arranger ought to be, either the composer himself, or *at least someone who thinks in the same way and has the same powers of invention*." Just the opposite, in fact, to the ideal of the champions of "purity". For Beethoven, as for Bach and all the others, a good transcription is not one which slavishly respects the letter, but one which knows when to make changes, or even to omit some passages and rewrite others, so as to create, out of the same elements, an entirely new work, no matter whether this is the same as the original: the criterion is not fidelity, but quality.

There is one point where the twentieth century champions of "purity" reveal their ignorance of ancient usage. The superstitition of the "written note" leads them to think that the ideal would be a "press-button" performance by a robot following, with a metronome, the printed score, neglecting nothing and interpreting nothing. The first composers to advocate this kind of approach—naturally in the case of their own works —were perhaps Ravel and Stravinsky at the beginning of the twentieth century; and with this end in view they made a point of writing everything down most meticulously, so that there was no detail, no shade of expression or *rubato* that had not been calculated and noted in advance. What is stupid, of course, is to apply this doctrine, not to the works for which it had been specially devised, but retrospectively to all kinds of music which had been conceived in quite a different spirit.

In the course of the nineteenth century there was a new development—the advent of the big and powerfully organized publishing firms, such as, for example, that of Breit-kopf and Härtel in 1795 which became, as it were, the G.H.Q. of musical life in Germany, and soon extended its activities on an international scale. Its example was followed, and by the end of the century music-publishing had become an essential feature of musical life everywhere, and was often largely responsible for building up a composer's reputation. More often than not the publisher bought outright a composer's works which he then proceeded to exploit, organizing publicity for it and taking risks which were sometimes by no means negligible, especially in the case of operatic works.

He might make a fortune, or else ruin himself. There is a story that Gounod one day met his publisher Choudens wearing a sumptuous fur-lined coat. "Ah, ha!" said Gounod, caressing the fur; "I recognize this coat: it's *Faust!*" "Quite right," replied Choudens, who was not without a sense of humour; "and this" (opening his coat to reveal a hole in the lining) "this is *Le Tribut de Zamora.*"[1]

There are many stories in connection with composers and their publishers. Beethoven, absent-mindedly or dishonestly, sold his rights for the same work to several different publishers. Chopin's *Préludes*, commissioned by Pleyel, were sold for Frs. 2000 (about £500); whereas Fauré was only paid on an average Frs. 50 apiece for his songs (without any royalties) by Hamelle who in return obtained the two quartets for nothing. . . .

The preparation of orchestral "material" has become, with the enormous growth of the modern orchestra, an almost inhuman undertaking. Publishers who are willing to take this risk in the case of composers whose reputation is by no means established, are really performing an act of charity. Alternatively, the wretched composer, aided perhaps by his wife or friends, has to sit up all night to do the job himself—with results that are often catastrophic. From the Franck symphony to *Pelléas*—to mention only two instances—there have been innumerable works which nearly failed on account of the orchestral players' irritation at the excessive amount of corrections and mistakes disfiguring the composer's score.

In an attempt to alleviate the sometimes almost unsurmountable difficulties encountered by composers in search of a publisher, some countries have set up mutual corporative music-publishing associations which have proved most useful. The idea came from Holland, where a vast undertaking of this nature is now functioning to the satisfaction of all concerned; it is known as *Donemus*—a punning label denoting both its actual title (Dutch Music Publishing Society—*DOcumentatie voor NEderlandsche MUSiek*), and its disinterested character. The same exists now in Belgium as "*Cebedem*".

The development of the L.P. record during the next ten years is also bound to have a profound effect on the dissemination of music; but as this question scarcely falls within the scope of this historical survey, we do not propose to examine it here.

---

[1] An opera by Gounod, also published by Choudens, which never had any success. Before he published *Faust*, Choudens was only a small shopkeeper who published drawing-room ballads.

27

Scudo's Clarinet, or The Critic

Another Romantic invention. Before the Romantics there was no such thing as a professional critic. We owe our knowledge of how such and such an artist was regarded in the past to a historian's records or, maybe, to a theoretician's digression; but there was no methodical or organized criticism. An artist depended for his reputation on his audience; no one would have thought himself entitled to express his personal opinion in order to influence the opinion of others. Occasionally professionals bestowed a word of praise—or more likely, of censure—on a colleague; but no importance was attached to gossip of that kind. The "*razos*" of the *jongleurs* are perhaps the prototype of this form of criticism between colleagues; but they were never considered to have any oracular value. "Peire de Valeira came from Gascony. He wrote poor poetry, as they did in those days. His songs were never much good; nor was he himself. . . . Guiraut de Borneilh was a better troubadour than any of those, and that is why they called him 'master'." However, this same Guiraut de Borneilh was described by his rival Peire d'Auvergne as "looking like a dried-up goat-skin", while his singing resembled that of "an old woman water-carrier". We know what these "criticisms" were worth; the "*razos*" came at a time when "the poetry of the troubadours . . . was losing its attraction, and efforts were being made to revive interest in it by explaining its origins and telling stories about the lives of its authors. . . ."[1] (Programme notes, in fact, or the equivalent at the time of our gramophone "sleeve" notices.)

Even in the eighteenth century there were no professional critics: the Press only discussed music from a news angle, and recorded the impressions of the audience, and that was all. At most it would perhaps just mention the composer's name; but this did not appear as a matter of course on theatre bills.

Music, however, was sometimes discussed, but not in the newspapers, and was usually confined to important issues, such as the rivalry between the French and Italian schools, or to works considered symptomatic of some definite trend; and people were more interested in this than in the work itself, still less its composer.

As for the latter, they were sometimes tempted to explain to the public the ideas they

[1] A. Jeanroy, *La Poésie lyrique des troubadours*, I, 1934, pp. 103-104.

had in mind, and in the sixteenth century this generally took the form of prefaces or dedications, often of a rather apologetic nature. The object still was to justify their work to their audience; the latter, or the person to whom the work was dedicated, whoever he might be, was still considered to be the sovereign judge. Presently composers began to state the case, not so much for any particular work, but for the general aesthetic principles by which they had been guided, and for other composers who shared their views. As a natural corollary, this sometimes led them to attack those who represented or defended a conflicting theory. Teachers and theoreticians often acted in the same way. For example, a Canon of Bologna, Artusi, was the author of a treatise on counterpoint, published in 1586. It did not please him to witness the success of composers who paid no heed whatsoever to his rules. It was thus that he became more famous than he would have wished by publishing in 1600 the celebrated pamphlet attacking the harmonic innovations of Monteverdi and Gesualdo, which caused its author's name to become the synonym of pedantic and reactionary criticism, just as Scheibe, a hundred and forty years later, became, through his attacks on J. S. Bach, the symbol of the *avant-garde* critic who despises everything that is not the very latest fashion.[1] Then there were the philosophers who, judging by eighteenth century standards, would have thought they had failed in their mission had they neglected to make known their views about music, as they did about every other subject under the sun. When a philosopher was also a composer—and a soured one at that—the result was a Jean-Jacques Rousseau.

There was, moreover, strictly speaking, no musical Press. The first attempts, dating from the eighteenth century, were either periodical publications of more or less well-known pieces (such as the *Journal du clavecin*, 1782), or else serial publications like the *Critica Musica* of Mattheson (1722) or the *Kritischer Musikus* of Scheibe (1737). But musical criticism as we understand it was a creation of the Romantic movement.

Above all, it was, for the composers themselves, a means of defending their ideas and those who shared them, with the additional object of discrediting their adversaries. The pioneer in this field was Schumann with his *Neue Zeitschrift für Musik* (1834). His brief and expressive notice of Meyerbeer's *Le Prophète* is well known:

1849
Le Prophète

[1]There was also a personal reason for this attitude: for Scheibe as a young man in 1729 had competed unsuccessfully for the post of organist at Saint Thomas in Leipzig . . . and Bach was a member of the jury. . . .

It also helped the publishers to exploit their productions. Even before Schumann's journal, as early as 1798 the firm of Breitkopf and Härtel had founded the *Allgemeine Musikalische Zeitung*, appointing as editor a man of letters, Rochlitz. During the nineteenth century musical reviews sprang up everywhere, and the big newspapers opened their columns to musical criticism. Here, again, and for the same reasons, this was usually entrusted to composers, of whom Berlioz, following his appointment in 1828 to the *Correspondant*, was the most striking example. Sometimes the critic was a literary man, or even a simple amateur with no particular qualifications for such work.

This is how it happened that for many years musical opinion in Paris was shaped in the columns of the *Revue des Deux Mondes* by a certain Paul Scudo born, according to some, in Vienna, according to Fétis, in Venice, who had had no musical education except for a brief period at the age of nineteen when he attended the Ecole Choron. The latter used to call him "his clown", and apart from the fact that he had once played second clarinet in his regimental band at Nantes, he had no other professional qualification. As for his compositions, they were limited to a few "romances" in which, according to Fétis, "he had accumulated every possible fault in harmony and phrasing".

Books on music were the next step, and learned treatises on the Beautiful in the abstract took the place of polite discussions in the *salons* of a bygone age. A typical example of this kind of literature was Hanslick's *Vom Musikalisch-Schönen* written in 1854 and translated into French, Italian, English and Russian. This became the Bible of all those who, unable to understand the reforms proposed by Wagner, were determined to oppose them by every means. It is in this work that appeared for the first time the argument, contradicted by centuries of experience but enthusiastically and firmly defended by the twentieth century as a result of Stravinsky's *Poetics of Music*, to the effect that music is unfitted to "represent" anything.[1]

A new conception had thus come into being. We have seen how in the past the rôle of supreme arbiter had passed from the gods of antiquity to the prince to whom music was offered as a tribute, and later to an anonymous and spontaneous audience. Now it was the professional critic who ruled supreme. His triple origin explains the diversity of his reactions. The composer turned critic defended his own ideals, if necessary

---

[1] In justice to Hanslick it should be noted that the pendulum had swung too far in the opposite direction, with exaggeratedly sentimental and descriptive accounts of music being freely indulged in. Haydn was delighted with the titles his publishers invented for his symphonies, while Beethoven himself gave titles to some of his sonatas or symphonies, notably the *Pastoral*. But the practice infuriated Chopin, and Fauré, though often requested, would never consent to anything of the kind. Yet "representation" is an important and undeniable element in music, though not the only one, for it is lacking in many masterpieces. To deny it is as puerile as to make random generalizations.

in opposition to the reactions of the public. The journalist, on the other hand, also turned critic, recorded these reactions of which he was merely the interpreter. In the latent duel between composer and public, the two parties thus found an advocate. Soon the aesthetician in his turn became a critic, hoping to set himself up as supreme arbiter. Musical criticism today can be orientated, broadly speaking, in one or other of these directions. But whereas in the nineteenth century it tended to be conservative, thereby reflecting popular opinion, it has now gone to the other extreme, taking upon itself the rôle of "educating" the public and in consequence defending on principle, and as a matter of policy, anything "new" just because it is new.[1] The consequences of this attitude will be examined in the last chapter of this book.

[1]Very important in this field is what has been called "the Camille Bellaigue complex". This famous critic of the nineteenth century had written mere insanities about Debussy's *Pelléas*, which he did not understand at all. This has been so often quoted as an example of the danger of not praising new works that the critics have now become more cautious, thinking that it is less dangerous to praise an unintelligible work than to condemn it.

28

Boubouroche, or The Public[1]

For centuries no one ever gave it a thought. Then one day its existence was recognized, its favours solicited and its tastes consulted. But it did not become really important until concerts had to be paid for, so that it was essential that concert halls did not remain empty.

For a long time, as we have seen, the public only paid for opera. Not until the nineteenth century do we hear much about its reactions in other spheres. Until then, all we have to go on are general indications, such as the number of copies sold of certain works during a given period, which makes it possible to assess the relative popularity of different composers; or, again (from the end of the eighteenth century), concert programmes, which are also a useful guide. Box-office returns at opera houses are also a source of information, which up to now has been insufficiently explored. From time to time echoes of the public's reactions appear in ephemeral chronicles or correspondence; but the opinions of the critics are often very deceptive. A work may be warmly applauded when performed, and denounced as worthless in the Press; while others may be praised in exaggerated terms by a handful of "specialists" who in no way reflect the views of the generality. Thus, at a recent conference at UNESCO, a Japanese musician expressed his astonishment, after three months travelling in the West, that twelve-note music in reality occupied so small a place in ordinary every day concert programmes. Judging from what he had read in the specialized reviews and in manifestos and the programmes of certain "festivals", he had imagined that from Gibraltar to Copenhagen, and from morning till night, musical Europe lived entirely on "series" and their inversions.

Now it is in this confused panorama of the public's reactions that the real history of music is to be found; and this history has hardly yet been attempted. Lionel de La Laurencie has written a history of musical taste, *Goût musical en France au XVIIIe. siècle*, of which the title alone opens up new perspectives in musicology which we are only

---

[1]The allusion is to a sketch by Courteline in which a simple man, deceived by his wife—and finding her in *flagrant délit*—not only cannot utter one word of reproach, but actually apologizes to her for his own shortcomings [Translator's note[

just beginning to explore. It is only in this way that we shall ever rid ourselves of the age-old habit which leads everyone to think that his personal opinion is a final judgment, valid everywhere and in all circumstances. "I do not say that such and such a work is bad just because I think so," said a well-known critic the other day, "but because it *is* so." But from an "absolute" point of view, this may not be true. Groups and individuals form their own criteria according to the times they live in, their tastes and training, and judge a work accordingly. But the continuous evolution of such criteria is an essential element in the history of our art; and it is useless to study the past if the standards applied are those of today. A history of "the public" has still to be written, for the public has become the only real judge, now that there are no more "princes", in either the literal or figurative sense, to speak for it and encourage music to live by assuming the rôle of arbiter.

Never before has this public seemed so varied and heterogeneous as it does today. In a primitive society, where the idea of a "concert" was unknown, it was, and still is, relatively homogeneous. Even in ancient times, and ever since, it seems that the advent of culture has had the effect of cutting it in two. The passage of time will leave the so-called "uncultured" bloc relatively united, faithful to traditions which evolve but slowly, and most of which, in the twentieth century alone, will perish one by one. Rather than adapt themselves to this new situation, we shall see those who until now lived with these traditions abandoning their personality and descending to a lower level to join the other group which, beginning with the nineteenth century *café-concert*, will supply it with its "entertainment" usually of very questionable value.

Until the end of the Middle Ages, and perhaps a little earlier, an almost impassable barrier separated the aristocracy of the towns from the country dwellers. Until the last century the latter preserved their musical habits which have scarcely varied over the centuries; what we call musical "folklore" was for a very long time just music, transmitted orally from one generation to another, and consisting of an anonymous and traditional *corpus* of melodies on which the interpreter could draw at will, improvising or elaborating as he pleased. It was not until the middle of the nineteenth century that the riches of national folk-lore began to be noted down—just when they were beginning to lose their vitality. What remains of these popular musical customs and tunes today is just enough to give us some idea of what the relations between artists and public in the musical civilization of a bygone age must have been.

The label "popular" itself, which could provide a point of junction between the two "blocs", the "cultivated" and the non-cultivated, has not the same meaning in both camps. This music, exclusively oral on one side, on the other is the work of specialists—

artists who were often amateurs in the sense in which the word is understood by professional musicians. Generally written down, it is for that very reason more ephemeral, continually renewing itself when it ceases to be up to date. It is this music that is the basis of the "pop" songs of today, and the public which it satisfies rarely feels attracted to "real" or "serious" music.

The discrimination, however, has not always been as clear-cut as it is today. The popular song played an important part in the polyphonic music of the Renaissance; in the seventeenth century Lully's operas were continually being turned into vaudevilles; Mozart was delighted to hear the waiters in the cafés of Prague whistling airs from *Figaro;* and pianists in Viennese restaurants today often use Schubert's *Lieder* as a basis for their improvisations. It is only during the last half-century that our purists have put "serious" music into a straitjacket and depicted it, behind a notice saying "Please do not touch", in the stilted pose of an old spinster defending her virtue.

Not so very long ago it was possible in Paris, for example to listen to classical music while sipping a glass of beer or lemonade (the *Concerts Rouge*); and while the fact that we no longer treat music quite so casually and with such familiarity is no doubt conducive to higher standards in actual performance, it is possible that it has lost in warmth and communicability what it has gained in prestige theoretically, with the result that a public hitherto well-disposed towards music in general may have been driven to take refuge in music of inferior quality.

Until the nineteenth century the public was eager and responsive, but not "respectful". The fifteenth century "Mysteries" were full of passages, known as *silete* (be silent), whilst some were even sung to such words as *Silete, silete, silentium habete.* The Overture in early opera had no other *raison d'être* than to get the audience to keep quiet (it is the same today in the music-halls); and this explains why in Monteverdi it is usually a kind of noisy fanfare, and in Lully a stereotyped form of solemn introduction in dotted rhythm. It had to wait for Gluck and Mozart before it began to assume a dramatic significance which did not become generalized until Wagner. Berlioz in his *Mémoires* relates with satisfaction how he used to interrupt from his place in the theatre performances of Gluck's operas, if the conductor or singers departed from the notes as written in the score; but if that were to happen today, one can imagine what a scandal it would cause. Yet at the time it seemed quite normal, and there are many stories told of humorous interventions on the part of the public, especially in provincial opera-houses; while it was not uncommon for the artists themselves to engage in conversation with members of the audience.

No doubt the disappearance of these free-and-easy manners is not to be regretted, except from the point of view of picturesqueness; but at the same time one may wonder whether the reaction against them had not gone a little too far in the opposite direction: for example, the icy silence in which an audience is expected to sit for hours on end while listening to some interminable solo suite for an unaccompanied instrument and watching the soloist wiping his nose between the movements with the same "respect" as if he were performing a sublime adagio.[1]

While the public was learning to behave more decorously, it would appear that artists were being encouraged (bizarre though it may seem) to believe that their value was in inverse ratio to their popularity with the public. Performers were taught to restrain their emotions, and to consider that the ideal to aim at was to render the music strictly in accordance with the written notes, like an exercise in *sol-fa*. Composers were advised to look upon spontaneity as suspect, and as a compromising concession to public taste. To achieve "absolute purity" is the highest praise of all, the outward sign of which, according to one of the leading exponents of this creed, H. Stückenschmidt, is "a revolt against immediate sensibility". One of the representatives of the younger school has even gone so far as to declare that "no composer of any value will write a harmony that is pleasing to the ear". The public's right to form its own judgments has been sacrificed in the interests of specialized *cliques* whose competence is not always above suspicion, and who arrogate to themselves the exclusive right of signing certificates of genius which more open-minded audiences are not necessarily prepared to endorse.

What, then, is to be the attitude of this public whose opinions are thus systematically ignored? Is it, as was suggested once at a public discussion in Cologne, to spend a number of years attempting to discover the hidden intentions which Mr. X. or Mr. Y. have concealed in two gurgles from a clarinet? Life today is too short and too busy for this to be possible: the public believes that it has more useful and more urgent tasks to perform. And once again we shall have witnessed the *"trahison des clercs"*.

[1] In France before the Second World War every movement of a piece was separately applauded; since the German occupation it is just the reverse.

EPILOGUE:

An Autopsy for the Twenty-first Century

> "Is it not in music, and in music alone that the secret of music must be sought?"—*Paul Dukas*

If we accept the age attributed by the archaeologists to our fresco representing the first "concert", with a man holding a bow that might be for a musical instrument, this means that what we should call today a "continuous performance" has gone on uninterruptedly for something like forty thousand years. And music is now cheerfully preparing to embark on its third millenary. What aspect will it assume in the course of this new adventure?

In order to find out, we tried to telephone to Posterity, but without success; the line was always engaged. Not having, like some of our colleagues, a private line at our disposal, we therefore had to give up the idea of recording its confidential information. We could at least, however, try to sum up the situation in the light of an evolution whose main stages are now known to us. And on looking back we were filled with pride at what has been accomplished.

At no time in history have our virtuosos attained such technical perfection. An average pupil today at any college or conservatoire would make light of difficulties which a century ago caused people to credit Paganini with being an envoy of the Devil. The standard of sight-reading in our big orchestras is prodigiously high, while our organists are capable of improvising symphonies at a moment's notice which in the old days would have called for months of preparation. The orchestration of any "Prix de Rome" cantata would turn a Berlioz or a Rimsky-Korsakov green with envy. Thanks to the radio, gramophone and television, music penetrates into the humblest homes, and the daily standard of performance is on a level that would have been for an earlier generation a subject of admiration for several years. Concert halls have increased enormously in size and seating capacity, and in most large cities there are three or four concerts on an average every day. Books on music are published by the score almost every month, and musicology has now acquired the status of an authentic science and is being developed in universties all over the world. The composition of new works is encouraged by periodical competitions and commissions from state-run organizations, the radio and the various music festivals. Ballet flourishes, and although opera is going through a crisis, it is hoped that the difficulties will be overcome. And so every prospect is fair, and music is looking forward to a triumphant entry into the year 2000.

At this moment I heard behind me a slightly drawling voice which somehow seemed familiar. It was saying: "Are you so sure of this, my young friend?"—and I recognized the sarcastic tones in which Debussy's "Monsieur Croche, Anti-dilettante", used to speak.

When I saluted him, calling him by his name, he gave me an ambiguous smile.

"What does that mean, anyway," he muttered, "dilettante, or, if you prefer, anti-dilettante? The language of music is indeed strange, since in speaking of it we use a word whose root means 'to love' in a pejorative sense!"

"Let us say 'amateur'," I suggested amiably.

"That's just what I was saying. But the habit doesn't stop there. You speak of a philatelist or a philanthropist, but anyone who loves music is not a 'musicophile', but a 'melomaniac'[1] like a kleptomaniac or an etheromaniac—in fact it has a taint of the madhouse about it. . . ."

I didn't see where this philological discussion was getting us, and said so to Monsieur Croche.

"But my dear Sir," he replied, "this is the heart of the matter. I know you consume quantities of music, and your canned varieties are excellent. A single violinist can serve ten million listeners at the same time: Bravo! you are kindly doing all you can to keep your young Academy prize-winners out of work. But let us leave that to the sociologists and return to our subject. Do you love music, sir?"

Indignantly I protested against the insinuation.

"Let me make myself quite clear: do you love music as it wishes to be loved, not hesitating to surrender yourself to it completely, to cry out with pain if it hurts you, or to walk out of a concert, at the risk of offending someone if you are bored . . . ?"

"Or be roused to fury by the nonsense you may hear talked about it—Yes!" I concluded on a somewhat aggressive note.

But M. Croche only smiled, evidently seeing no allusion to himself in my remark. Perhaps he was thinking that it applied rather to myself. But he made no comment, only shook his head.

"Your twentieth century has forgotten what music is, what its purpose is and for

---

[1]This is impossible to translate into English. In French, the word "melomane", i.e., literally "melomaniac", means simply a music lover.

whose ears it is intended. Nine times out of ten artists and their audience do not even see one another: they are represented on the one side by a microphone, and on the other by a loudspeaker. In the schools you teach it as an 'optional' subject.[1] True enough: music is 'optional' in the education of the average citizen. Do you realize what that implies?"

I was ready to agree with him, but M. Croche did not listen to me and went on:

"Your age has so far forgotten that music is a living thing that those who look upon it as 'optional' think of it only as something belonging to the past. But that's only one way of putting it, for the truth is that the musicians in any age are not those who write music at the time, but those who reflect its tastes."

I thought I had read that somewhere before, but refrained from saying so.

"Your contemporaries," he continued, "are those who strike a note to which you twentieth-century people are responsive: in other words, they are Mozart, Bach and Beethoven. Don't contradict me: I've got here in my pocket all the programmes of the week, and all the names belong to a century which is not our own. *Your twentieth century has no contemporary music.*"

This time he was going too far: I thought of all the great moderns who have become classics, ranging from Debussy to Bartok.

"All dead," he retorted, "including Stravinsky—who has been for the last thirty years at least."

Other names, of musicians not yet dead, came to my rescue. And I could not help noting with some satisfaction that several of my compatriots—from Milhaud to Messiaen, from Dutilleux to Jolivet, and many more besides—were among them.

"I grant you one or two of those," he replied. "And this is your last chance. But you are ashamed of them, and will end by turning them down; already you've begun to do this with some of them. Your so-called 'specialists' will never rest until the notion of 'contemporary music' has been purged of anything that could recall Rameau's definition of music: 'Its aim is to give pleasure and to awake in us various passions'." He laughed scornfully. "To please—they call that 'hedonism', as if it were some shameful disease. And if a tiny suggestion of any human feeling should emerge for a moment in some modern score, they dismiss it as a 'concession' or a 'compromise'. To those who refuse to toe the line they retort: 'You are not contemporary', and boycott them without mercy. The result is that really talented composers—and there are quite a lot—are *afraid*. I'm telling you this because I know it's true. They are afraid of the organized

[1]So is the music paper in the French "baccalaureat".

blackmail, afraid of appearing 'old-fashioned', afraid to express freely, as all their predecessors have done, the music they feel within them and that they *dare not* write."

"But," I said, repeating a well-learned lesson, "Music must renew itself."

"And what do you mean by 'renew'?" exclaimed M. Croche. "To go on producing incessantly the same piece of music which hasn't been new for the last forty years, but which is still referred to as 'the new music' simply because, since nobody wants it, apart from a dozen or so critics and a score of society women, it has never, thank God, succeeded in becoming our daily fare? You accuse the public of being lazy, but if anyone is lazy, it's the people who can't understand that we're tired of empty balloons pretending to be lanterns, and that if we're looking for originality that doesn't merely consist in imitating Webern, it's in music, and not in programme notes, that we expect to find it."

"According to accepted standards, you're nothing but a terrible reactionary."

"Anti-dilettante, shall we say; nothing more. You've known it, ever since I had the honour of confessing it to M. Debussy. And that is why, if there is, as people say, a divorce between modern music and the public, I say it's not the public's fault, but the fault of modern composers. But is there really this division?"

"I'm afraid so—at least more and more people feel there is."

"Then that simply means that your composers have not been able to discover how, on the highest plane (for I'm not interested in any other, you understand), to establish contact with the public of their own day and age: in other words, your famous 'modern music' has failed to carry out its mission. Therefore it's for it to put its house in order, and not the public, which is only there to receive and judge what it receives. I'm well aware that what I'm asking your composers to do is more difficult than to take refuge, as we've actually seen them do, in clowning and performing such idiotic stunts as drawing lots in public to decide what instruments they're going to play, or turning a piano upside-down on a mattress."

"But what about the twelve-note system?"

"What's the good of talking about recipes when I'm only concerned with the actual *raison d'être* of music itself. It's all the same to me whether modern music carries out its mission with or without dodecaphony. If a tool is good, you use it; if it's bad, you throw it away: there's no other criterion. But you don't force people to buy a motor-car which doesn't go just because it's the only one that enables you to use a much advertised tool. And up to now the tool hasn't been worth much."

"As things are today, I doubt whether anyone will understand you."

"In that case, my friend, don't complain of the consequences. I said just now that the real contemporaries of our twentieth century were Bach and Mozart who at least in their day were not doped with talk about making 'compromises'. There's also been the vogue for Vivaldi; and there's still plenty of material in the libraries to provide for another dozen 'resurrections' of the same kind. That will postpone things a little longer. But it's only a postponement. So much the worse for music. It's a pity, for ours was a really fine musical civilization."

He paused, seeming really upset. In order to say something I hazarded a banal: "What then?"

M. Croche spread out his arms despondently.

"What then? Nebuchadnezzar."

At first I didn't understand. Then I remembered that film of René Clair's, *Les Belles de Nuit*, in which an enthusiastic young composer of light music dreams that he's been summoned to an interview with the Director of the Opera. After waiting a long time, an attendant appears and calls out an incomprehensible name. The young man, thinking it's his own, hurries forward. At the same moment, a stout, bearded gentleman, who also thinks he heard his own name, jumps up, and the two of them, stare at one another in none too amiable a fashion. "It's for Nebuchadnezzar," announces the attendant, whereupon the young man shrugs his shoulders, exclaiming: "Do I look as if I could write a Nebuchadnezzar?" "I'm quite sure you couldn't," says the bearded gentleman, and enters the holy of holies alone.

"Have you noticed," observed M. Croche at that moment, "that 'serious' music has only quite recently put up its barriers and become so stand-offish? In the seventeenth century popular songs were based on Lully's operas, and Mozart, as you've already said yourself, was delighted to hear the waiters in the cafés in Prague whistling airs from his *Figaro*. Yet, in a book with which I have good reason to be familiar, M. Debussy comments ironically on the fact that Massenet was honoured in the same way by the midinettes of Paris.

"You are surely not putting *Werther* and *Figaro* on the same plane?"

"That's not the point," retorted M. Croche impatiently. "What I'm pointing out is the opposition between the two attitudes. It way well have something to do with the crisis you deplore."

"And also with the progress of music," I added.

"Progress, progress," grumbled M. Croche: "You're always talking about progress. What does it mean? Do you really think Mozart was more 'advanced' than Bach, or Webern than Perotinus? At a certain level, you get change, but not progress. In the eyes of his contemporaries Meyerbeer seemed more 'advanced' than Beethoven."

"You see," I insinuated, "how wrong public opinion can be."

"Not at all," replied Mr. Anti-dilettante coldly; "Meyerbeer satisfied the taste of his day and offends ours; that's all."

"You must at least admit that between Meyerbeer and Bach or Mozart. . . ."

". . . . The distance from our point of view is immeasurable . . . I grant you that. But note that I was careful to say 'from our point of view'. You remember that saying of Boris Vian: 'Every judgment is a comparison between the whole or part of two systems of reference: that of the judge, and that of the judged.' I was quite fair in citing as an example a musician whom you and I would agree with Wagner in considering as an 'absolute zero'. All the same, who knows whether our descendants will think as highly of Bach and Mozart as we do; and who could swear that there won't one day be a 'return' to someone as despised as Meyerbeer is now?"

"God forbid," I exclaimed.

"I agree; but I'm not so sure. Don't look for logic in the fluctuations of taste. Stravinsky once declared that he preferred *Rigoletto* to *Parsifal*. When I was a child 'serious' musicians put *Rigoletto* in the same basket as "*Les Zuguenots*", as we used to call it for fun. One step further and you'll find jazz and 'pop' songs taking the place of symphonies in all the most respectable text-books."

"Nebuchadnezzar, in other words? . . ."

"Alas! I fear so—so long, at least, as your professionals persist in saying NO when the public says YES, and vice-versa. Can you be surprised, then, that a first performance becomes 'a ceremony at which a composer's most recent work is played for the last time in the presence of a few relatives and friends'!"[1]

"It wasn't you who said that either."

M. Croche turned a deaf ear and continued:

"It's their own fault. There's still time, but only just. Your music is suffering from an attack of dignity, and it's impossible to say whether it will emerge as a great lady or a disagreeable prig. It is so taken up with inventing slogans that are both pretentious and untrue instead of allowing itself to be judged on its own merits, and so increasingly disdainful of the public, that it fails to see that the latter is giving as good as it gets. Believe me, my friend: Pierre Boulez is making Gilbert Bécaud's bed for him."[2]

M. Croche was now recklessly launched on a sea of paradoxes.

"In any case, history will only be repeating itself. Do you not teach your students

[1] B. Gavoty, *La musique adoucit les moeurs*.

[2] i.e., the reaction against the ultra-modernism of composers like Boulez is to the advantage of more "popular" composers such as Gilbert Bécaud [Translator's note].

that the sonata and the symphony are both derived from dance suites? But these dances, my dear Sir, are no longer yours: it's two hundred years since Europe has invented a single dance of her own. A bad sign that. . . . If you go on like that, the only music your children will have will be the offspring of your cabarets and negro dance clubs."

I was thinking of the trouble some of our composers take to write on thirty-two staves what other races would improvise without thinking. And by this time M. Croche had started on a curious parallel between our modern jazz and our music as it was in the old days before it was pinned down and reduced to hieroglyphic signs for robot-interpreters. Nobody then bothered about the composer's name, or the written notes, or the opinion of posterity—everyone knew that what was written today would be out of date in five years; in those days performers and improvisers were the ones who mattered, and they were on familiar, easy-going terms with their audience, who listened or not as they pleased in the confusion and din of surroundings that were identical with the restaurants and dance-halls that were just beginning to encroach upon our theatres.

After another pause, M. Croche began to murmur, as if speaking to himself:

"After all, if our old classical spirit can only be revived by forcing it to make unseemly grimaces; if the genuine 'moderns', who could have preserved the spirit of our music while renewing its means of expression, have to give up trying to make themselves understood, and eventually to express themselves at all; if the two words 'contemporary music' have inevitably to be associated with unpleasant experiences in which people are unwilling to be involved a second time—then who knows but that our bankrupt classicism may not find itself in the end in that camp . . .? A pity: I preferred Mozart."

As he finished speaking I heard through the open window on the neighbour's radio the frantic applause of an audience assembled in the Théâtre des Champs Elysées for a concert devoted to the works of Arthur Honegger. At the same time my eyes fell on a copy of the review *Arts* lying on my table containing an article on the composer of *King David*, hitherto considered as the symbol of modern music independent of any interference from the devotees of the serial school; what I read there seemed in strange contradiction to the sounds of unmistakable enthusiasm which filled the room: "Strange destiny of an artist who in his life-time was considered to be one of the greatest composers of his day and who is now, only five years after his death, an almost forgotten figure. As for biblical operas, the palm after all must be awarded to Schoenberg!"

The sound of the applause was still ringing through the room. A ray of sunlight entered through the curtains. M. Croche got up to go without speaking a word, and for a long time I listened to the echo of his footsteps on the stairs—the footsteps of a tired old man.

Index